The Eighteenth Century

THE CONTEXT OF
ENGLISH LITERATURE

The Eighteenth Century

EDITED BY
PAT ROGERS

HOLMES & MEIER
PUBLISHERS, INC.
NEW YORK

First published in
the United States of America 1978 by
HOLMES & MEIER PUBLISHERS, INC.
30 Irving Place, New York, New York 10003

Copyright © 1978 Pat Rogers, John Vladimir Price, G.S. Rousseau,
W.A. Speck, Peter Willis

Library of Congress Cataloging in Publication Data

Main entry under title:

The Eighteenth Century
  (The Context of English Literature)
   Includes bibliographics and index
    1. English Literature — 18th Century —
History and criticism   2. Great Britain —
Civilization — 18th Century
1. Rogers, Pat.   11. series
PR441.E47   820'.9.   78-15568
ISBN 0-8419-0421-9
ISBN 0-8419-0422-7 Pbk.

Printed in Great Britain

Contents

Illustrations

The illustrations appear between pages 208 and 209

Table of dates

Date	Public events	Literary history	Other arts and foreign literature
1700	Second Partition Treaty	Dryden d. Thomson b. Congreve, *Way of World*	
1701	Act of Settlement General election (Tory success); second election (Whig success) James II d.	Rowe, *Tamerlane* Swift, *Contests and Dissensions*	
1702	William III d. (succ. Anne) War of Spanish Succession begins (to 1713)	Defoe, *Shortest Way with the Dissenters*	
1703	Great Storm	Pepys d. Wesley b. Defoe in the pillory	
1704	Battle of Blenheim	Locke d. Swift, *Tale of a Tub* Defoe, *Review* (to 1713)	
1705	General election	Haymarket theatre opens	
1706	Battle of Ramillies		
1707	Union with Scotland Wreck of the *Association*	Fielding b. Farquhar d.; *Beaux' Stratagem*	

Date	Public events	Literary history	Other arts and foreign literature
1708	General election Battle of Oudenarde		
1709	Battle of Malplaquet	Johnson b. Copyright Act *Tatler* (to 1711)	
1710	Sacheverell trial Fall of Godolphin: Harley ministry General election (Tory gains)	Berkeley, *Principles of Human Knowledge*	Arne b. W. Boyce b.
1711	Occasional Conformity Act	Hume b. *Spectator* (to 1712) Shaftesbury, *Characteristics*	
1712		Swift, *Conduct of Allies* Stamp Act on newspapers Pope, *Rape of Lock* (2 cantos)	Handel settles in England
1713	Treaty of Utrecht General election	Sterne b. Shaftesbury d. Addison, *Cato*	
1714	Queen Anne d. (succ. George I); fall of Harley	Shenstone b. Swift retires to Dublin Mandeville, *Fable of the Bees*	C.P.E. Bach b. Gluck b. Richard Wilson b.
1715	Jacobite Rising General election (Whig success)	Rowe poet laureate Pope, *Iliad* (to 1720) Prior sent to the Tower	Capability Brown b.
1716		Gray b. Wycherley d. Gay, *Trivia*	
1717	Triple Alliance Bangorian controversy	H. Walpole b. Garrick b. Cibber, *Non-Juror*	Handel, *Chandos Anthems* (to 1720)
1718	Quadruple Alliance	Rowe d. Eusden poet laureate	

Date	Public events	Literary history	Other arts and foreign literature
1719	Peerage Bill	Addison d. Defoe, *Robinson Crusoe* Prior, *Poems*	Royal Academy of Music promotes opera
1720	South Sea Bubble	Gay, *Poems* Defoe, *Captain Singleton*	
1721	Walpole comes to fore	Prior d. Collins b. Smollett b.	Bach, *Branden-burg Concertos* Watteau d.
1722	General election Atterbury plot Marlborough d.	Smart b. Defoe, *Moll Flanders*	
1723		Adam Smith b. Reynolds b.	Wren d. Kneller d.
1724	Wood's Halfpence	Swift, *Drapier's Letters* Defoe, *Tour* (to 1726)	Stubbs b.
1725	Peter the Great d. Jonathan Wild executed	Pope, *Odyssey* (to 1726)	Vico, *Scienza Nuova*
1726		Vanbrugh d. Swift, *Gulliver's Travels* Thomson, *Seasons* (to 1730)	
1727	George I d. (succ. George II) General election	Newton d.; English version *Principia*.	Gainsborough b.
1728		Pope, *Dunciad* Gay, *Beggar's Opera*	R. Adam b.
1729	Methodist Society formed	Congreve d. Steele d. Burke b. Swift, *Modest Proposal*	Bach, *St Matthew Passion*
1730	Walpole-Townshend split	Cibber poet laureate Fielding, *Tom Thumb*	
1731		Defoe d. Cowper b. Churchill b. Lillo, *London Merchant*	Prévost, *Manon Lescaut*

Date	Public events	Literary history	Others arts and foreign literature
1732		Gay d. Berkeley, *Alciphron*	Thornhill d. Haydn b.
1733	Excise Crisis Kay's flying shuttle	Mandeville d. Pope, *Essay on Man*	Couperin d.
1734	General election		Romney b.
1735		Arbuthnot d. Thomson, *Liberty* (to 1736)	Hogarth, *Rake's Progress* J.C. Bach b.
1736	Gin Act Porteous Riots	Fielding, *Pasquin*	Hawksmoor d.
1737	Queen Caroline d.	Theatrical Licensing Act Gibbon b.	
1738	Herculaneum excavated	Johnson, *London*	Bridgman d.
1739	War of Jenkins's Ear begins Execution of Dick Turpin	Lillo d. Hume, *Treatise* (to 1740)	
1740		Boswell b. Richardson, *Pamela* (to 1742) Cibber, *Apology*	
1741	General election	Fielding, *Shamela* Hume, *Essays*	
1742	Fall of Walpole	Fielding, *Joseph Andrews* Young, *Night Thoughts*	Handel, *Messiah*
1743	Pelham ministry Battle of Dettingen	Pope, *Dunciad in Four Books* Fielding, *Miscellanies*	Vivaldi d. Dahl d.
1744	Britain drawn further into War of Austrian Succession	Pope d. Johnson, *Life of Savage*	
1745	Battle of Fontenoy Jacobite Rising	Swift d.	Hogarth, *Marriage à la Mode*
1746	Battle of Culloden	Collins, *Odes*	
1747	General election		

Date	Public events	Literary history	Others arts and foreign literature
1748	Peace of Aix-la-Chapelle	Thomson d. Smollett, *Roderick Random* Richardson, *Clarissa*	Kent d. Montesquieu, *L'Esprit des lois*
1749		Fielding, *Tom Jones* Johnson, *Vanity of Human Wishes* Cleland, *Memoirs of Woman of Pleasure* [Fanny Hill]	Handel, *Solomon*
1750		Johnson, *Rambler* (to 1752)	J.S. Bach d.
1751	Prince of Wales d.	Bolingbroke d. Sheridan b. Gray, *Elegy* Smollett, *Peregrine Pickle*	Diderot, *Encyclopédie,* Vol. I Sheraton b.
1752	Britain adopts new calendar	Chatterton b. F. Burney b. Fielding, *Amelia*	
1753		Berkeley d. Richardson, *Grandison* (to 1754)	
1754	Pelham d. General election	Crabbe b. Fielding d.	Gibbs d. Chippendale, *Gentleman and Cabinet-Maker's Director*
1755		Johnson, *Dictionary*	
1756	Seven Years War opens Black Hole of Calcutta	Burke, *Sublime and Beautiful*	Mozart b.
1757	Pitt-Newcastle ministry Admiral Byng shot Battle of Plassey	Cibber d. William Whitehead poet laureate Gray, *Odes* Blake b.	D. Scarlatti d.
1758		Johnson, *Idler* (to 1760)	

Date	Public events	Literary history	Other arts and foreign literature
1759	British Museum opens Battle of Quebec Battle of Minden	Collins d. Burns b. Johnson, *Rasselas*	Handel d. Voltaire, *Candide*
1760	George II d. (succ. George III)	Sterne, *Tristram Shandy* (to 1767)	
1761	Pitt resigns Bridgewater canal opens General election	Richardson d.	Rousseau, *La Nouvelle Héloïse*
1762	Bute ministry		Rousseau, *Émile* and *Social Contract* Gluck, *Orfeo*
1763	Grenville ministry Peace of Paris Wilkes arrested	Shenstone d. Johnson and Boswell meet Smart, *Song to David*	
1764	Hargreaves's spinning jenny	Churchill d.	Rameau d. Hogarth d.
1765		Young d. Goldsmith, *Traveller* Johnson, Shakespeare ed. Percy, *Reliques*	
1766	Second Chatham ministry Old Pretender d.	Goldsmith, *Vicar of Wakefield*	Lessing, *Laocoon*
1767			Telemann d.
1768	General election	Sterne d.; *Sentimental Journey*	Canaletto d. Royal Academy opens
1769	Wilkes troubles	Reynolds, *Discourses* (to 1790) Junius letters	Royal Crescent at Bath completed
1770	North ministry Cook lands at Botany Bay	Chatterton d. Goldsmith, *Deserted Village*	Tiepolo d.
1771	Etruria pottery works opens	Smollett d.; *Humphrey Clinker* Gray, d. Smart d.	

Date	Public events	Literary history	Other arts and foreign literature
1772	Cook's second voyage		
1773	Boston Tea Party	Chesterfield d. Goldsmith, *She Stoops to Conquer*	
1774	General election	Goldsmith d.	Goethe, *Werther*
1775	War of American Independence Watt's improved steam-engine	Johnson, *Journey to Western Islands* Sheridan, *Rivals*	Beaumarchais, *Le Barbier de Séville*
1776	Declaration of Independence	Hume d. Gibbon, *Decline and Fall* Smith, *Wealth of Nations* Burney, *History of Music*	
1777	Burgoyne defeated at Saratoga	Sheridan, *School for Scandal*	
1778		F. Burney, *Evelina*	Voltaire d. Rousseau d. Arne d.
1779	Cook killed Crompton's mule	Garrick d. Johnson, *Lives of Poets* (to 1781) Cowper and Newton, *Olney Hymns*	
1780	General election Gordon riots		
1781	Cornwallis surrenders at Yorktown	Sheridan, *The Critic*	
1782			Mozart, *Seraglio* R. Wilson d. J.C. Bach d.
1783	Younger Pitt in power	Crabbe, *The Village*	Capability Brown d.
1784	General election	Johnson d.	Diderot d.

Date	Public events	Literary history	Other arts and foreign literature
1785		Thomas Warton poet laureate Cowper, *Task* Boswell, *Tour to Hebrides*	
1786		Burns, Kilmarnock ed.	Mozart, *Figaro*
1787			Gluck d.
1788	Young Pretender d. Trial of Warren Hastings opens		Gainsborough d. C.P.E. Bach d.
1789	French Revolution Washington President of USA Mutiny on *Bounty*	Blake, *Songs of Innocence*	
1790	Franklin d.	H.J. Pye poet laureate Burke, *Reflections*	
1791		Wesley d. Boswell, *Life of Johnson*	Mozart d.; *Magic Flute*
1792	French Revolutionary War	Reynolds d.	R. Adam d.
1793			
1794		Gibbon d.	
1795		Boswell d.	
1796		Burns d.	
1797		Burke d. H. Walpole d.	
1798	Battle of the Nile	*Lyrical Ballads*	
1799	Washington d.		W. Boyce d.
1800		Cowper d.	

1 Introduction: the writer and society

PAT ROGERS

The self-portrait of an age rarely coincides with the likeness created by posterity. Certainly the men and women who lived in Britain 200 years ago would have been surprised by many of the labels subsequently attached to their times. That once popular but now unfashionable phrase, the age of reason, would have made a sort of sense although it was not contemporary currency. Equally, an age of political stability did not always feel quite like that to those facing dynastic struggles and constitutional upheavals; a period of agricultural improvement was experienced by many country people as a time of disruption and decline. It is only the hindsight of a revolution to come which makes 'pre-industrial' at all intelligible as a term to describe this stage in social evolution. The commonest literary or cultural label, 'Augustan', *was* used at the historical juncture to which it refers. It was originally applied to the age of Charles II, but came increasingly to cover the aspiring self-image of living writers who strove to identify themselves with imperial Rome. But it did not take long for the phrase, together with the concept it represented, to acquire an air of irony, if not downright unreality. The term survives as a textbook formula: few students of the period today would talk of the Augustan age, except as a neutral historical shorthand which enables them to point without describing or explaining. The least objectionable labels are the most modest — the Georgian era or the Hanoverian century. In fact every considerable writer who survived into the 1700s lived under one of the first three Georges.

John Dryden was not among their number. He had died with the old century, leaving some much-quoted lines on the need to begin a new age. A more significant event to mark the turn of the century, since it expressed volition, was the retirement of William Congreve. In March 1700 his *Way of the World*, which we regard as a masterpiece of witty and aristocratic comedy, had been performed at Lincoln's Inn Fields. Its author was just thirty. At this moment of high achievement he turned his back on the stage, and spent his last twenty-nine years in a life of cultivated idleness not much dignified by his government sinecures. It is true that, when William III died two years later, the last Stuart fling was still to come in the anxious reign of the gouty and muddled Queen Anne. Nevertheless, the high Stuart intensity was gone, for good or ill, and the *élan*, smartness and raffish quality of Restoration literature disappeared with the social order which gave them being. The great political divide was 1714, with the Hanoverian accession; but an identifiable eighteenth-century mode of writing starts around 1700, when Defoe, Swift, Steele and Addison (not to mention the precocious Pope) were beginning their careers. In essence this mode survived, though not without challenge or modification, for the succeeding three generations. The next real turning-point comes somewhere between the American and French revolutions. There was a twilight of the Augustan gods late in the century: all the early masters of English fiction were dead by 1770, Gray, Goldsmith and Hume were to follow in a few years, and Samuel Johnson died in 1784. The natural overlap one expects in historical evolution breaks down at this moment: Burke, Reynolds, Gibbon, Horace Walpole, Boswell and Burns had gone before the *Lyrical Ballads* came out in 1798. The energy of the eighteenth century was already dispersed by the time the Romantic movement flowered.

A few weeks after *The Way of the World* was presented, one of the most representative writers in this period was born in a remote part of the Scottish borders. This was James Thomson (1700-48), an important poet whose career might symbolize the fate of the eighteenth-century man of letters. He came from a distant and wild region, and indeed when he was born his country was still not properly confederated into the British nation. After an education that was largely theological and classical, he came up to the metropolis as a young man; he wrote of the glories of nature while tutor to a nobleman in East Barnet. Having succeeded with a poem that cunningly combined tradition and novelty (and for which a remunerative subscription was organized), he then settled down to an orthodox literary career. That is, he combined the loftiest patriotism — the words of *Rule Britannia* are his — with a fierce dislike of the entrenched Walpole government. He celebrated liberty, got into debt, struck up acquaintance with the great Mr Pope, and died in mid-century, overweight and apoplectic, in the comfortable Thames-side village of Richmond. His death was commemorated by a watery processional ode from the hand of William Collins. Predictably he ended up as the subject of one of Samuel Johnson's *Lives of the Poets*, the final accolade for one of his generation.

If Thomson's career was in some respects humdrum, his actual work was again typical — but in a more enlivening way. Near the close of his life he wrote a Spenserian burlesque entitled *The Castle of Indolence* (1748), and this is the purest expression of the entire literary context in which it was written. There is, to start with, the fact that this was an imitation of an earlier poet: Spenser enjoyed an increasing vogue throughout the period, and writers as different as Pope and Gray reveal traces of his influence. More centrally, however, the poem might be described as an allegory of Augustan values. The plot concerns a vile enchanter named Indolence whose pleasure is to hijack travellers as they pass the gates of his richly furnished mansion, set in a rich and beautiful countryside. The wizard's enchantments include visual, tactile and auditory induce-ments — all beautifully evoked — and plunge the deluded victims into a deep torpor, recalling the declared model of *The Faerie Queene* but also Pope's *Dunciad* (the most significant recent poem as Thomson was writing). In the second of the two cantos everything is put to rights by the Knight of Arts and Industry, a dynamic embodiment of will, energy and purpose. He operates as a kind of super-patron, promoting industry and agriculture, spreading peace and prosperity, reviving the arts, liberating even literature itself. It could be a portrait of the unknown Augustan patron, the sort of enlightened and public-spirited figure with whom peers liked to identify, and whom dedicators attempted to associate, more or less implausibly, with some well-heeled nonentity. The poem ends with noble redemptive gestures and the purgatorial horrors kept in reserve for those still in thrall to Indolence.

The poem is written with charm and felicity, and carries its moral theme with good humour. Yet it is easy to make fun of it, because it seems only too accurate a revelation of the 'bad' eighteenth century, as its detractors have seen it from Blake onwards. The world to be rejected, that of the foul magician, is a gorgeous and fantastic creation, rich in sensuous and imaginative life, thick with myth, legend, Oriental fable: it is, quite literally, a fairy-tale world. On the other hand we are asked to admire its destruction by an apostle of self-help, a walking (or running) personification of thrift, zeal, charity, 'social commerce'. We must give up the groves of enchantment and file neatly into the temple of communal welfare.

Faced with this, people who dislike the eighteenth century will bring up a variety of charges. They will say that there was an unhealthy distrust of the imagination, a fear of emotional freedom, and a stifling of individual feeling. Writers, they will claim, showed themselves indecently eager to accept the values of the commercial society in which they lived: idols of the market place, of the political hustings, of the over-rational latitudinarian church. All this, they might argue, is summed up in *The Castle of Indolence*, with the allegorical defeat of a tranquil and contemplative way of life by a busy, worldly and ambitious order. On one such hostile reading, Sir Industry might be taken to display yet another unattractive face of capitalism, with his restless pursuit of growth and his stimulation of constant change. Yet this would be to miss out a vital strand in the poem, which is its spiritual component. In the end, whatever Thomson's intentions, Sir Industry emerges as something very different from a munificent eighteenth-century man of affairs — the enlightened patron on the model of the Earl of Burlington or the active entrepreneur symbolized a little later by Josiah Wedgwood. The knight represents not just bridge building or credit launching or town planning, though his sphere of activity includes these things. Behind all that, he stands for disinterested energy, that is a new cardinal virtue which optimists would call Progress or Improvement. For the creed of Whiggery went beyond economic concerns to a philosophic position, and the best Whig writers — in opposition to the gloom of professional satirists —

enshrined this belief in a variety of imaginative modes. We should not be misled by the archaism of form and language in *The Castle of Indolence*. Its hero is a true Enlightenment creation, with some resemblance to Sarastro in *The Magic Flute*.

I have deliberately instanced Thomson because he comes at such a central juncture. But much the same case could be made with regard to Oliver Goldsmith (?1730-74). It means substituting Ireland for Scotland, medicine for theology, and the like consequential changes. But again there is much that is representative rather than special: a miscellaneous career and diverse output, an up-and-down relation with the book trade, a gravitation towards the established leader of the profession (now Johnson), and an art that blends conventional forms with new insights. There are personality conflicts in Thomson, but the melancholy and sense of isolation have approached nearer the surface in Goldsmith — a fact that reflects external change, for it was easier to articulate such emotions in 1770 than in 1730, with the rise of the fad for 'sentiment' and an enlarged vocabulary with which writers could explore psychological states. Less happy than Thomson with the course of agricultural 'progress' ('Where wealth accumulates, and men decay'), Goldsmith yet reaffirms the eighteenth-century dream of man and nature acting in concert. The massive Virgilian confidence of Thomson's *Seasons* (1726-30) is severely qualified by the time of *The Deserted Village* (1770), but even in the later poem there is, through the evocation of 'sweet Auburn', an image of rural content — the 'innocence and ease' destroyed by enclosure and em-parking. It is important to realize that the new conditions are symbolically presented as *decline*, with weed-choked ditches, ruined cottages and tangled hedges. Although opulence is the enemy, that is the greed of an expropriating landlord, the effect is poverty and waste as far as the villagers are concerned. Thomson admires in the present tense what Goldsmith laments in the past: but they both hold out the idea of a rural community at once prosperous and uncorrupt.

In 1759 Goldsmith devoted a part of the last number of a shortlived periodical called *The Bee* to an 'Account of the Augustan Age in England'. This contains a rapid survey of English literary history, with a strong emphasis on the development of a pure and expressive style. Goldsmith concludes that the highpoint was reached around the time of Queen Anne, 'or some years before', and it is in the era of Congreve, Prior, Addison and Bolingbroke that he locates the true 'Augustan' phase. By our standards Goldsmith seems unduly preoccupied with eloquence for its own sake, and his examples are not always those we should choose in order to establish creative merit. Nevertheless the essay tells us a good deal regarding the eighteenth century's idea of itself. Writers of the period were the first to carry the burden of the past, in the sense that they were more selfconscious and aware of their genealogy than medieval and Renaissance authors had been. Actually they were encouraged, rather than depressed, when they contemplated their historical situation. Rejecting the Middle Ages as gothic and monkish, they looked on most Renaissance literature as for the most part an amiable and blundering attempt to create an indigenous tradition. To be an Augustan, in their terms, was to be engaged in sweeping the recent past right away; it was to be a reformer and an improver. It was an urgent, highly contemporaneous enterprise; it was to be, paradoxically, modern.

The cultural map

There were, of course, high standards to be maintained and models to be studied for the purpose of ultimate emulation. In so far as the pantheon was classical, it was predominantly the grandeur of Rome rather than the glory of Greece that most appealed to readers and writers. In so far as more recent literature was concerned, there was a thin line of approved English authors: these included Shakespeare, Spenser, Ben Jonson, Milton and Dryden. But the greater challenge was provided by France, especially the writers in Louis XIV's long reign. Both theory and practice were heavily indebted to French example, and although this influence was less readily acknowledged in the middle of the eighteenth century than it had been at the start the traces can still be picked up. Modern scholarship has been inclined to qualify the extent to which classical and French models influenced taste. It has been argued that the declared allegiance to ancient writers sometimes went with a shallow knowledge of classical texts. Similarly it has been contended that a strong native tradition was always ready to carry on a resistance movement against the fashionable and Frenchified court.

However, it can scarcely be denied that most of the acknowledged masters were classical or French (apart from Cervantes, other European writers counted for little); and it would be unwise to underestimate the effect over time of this constant tutelage from outside.

As indicated, the drift of the age was Roman rather than Hellenic. It was this predisposition, producing a lack of 'poetic largeness, freedom, insight, benignity', which Matthew Arnold found most significant in 'an age of prose and reason' and which caused him to deny true classic status to Dryden and Pope. It would be going much too far to say that Greek culture was slighted. There is evidence, J.W. Johnson has observed, that Greek literature 'strongly affected' both the outlook and the productions of writers in the period. An unprecedented flow of texts and translations began in the Restoration; these were sometimes parallel Greek-Latin texts, and it was common to read major texts in a Latin version (Pope regularly did this while working on his translation of Homer). Nevertheless a great deal must have been absorbed, whether at first or second hand. Homer was a permanent touchstone of excellence in the highest of literary forms. Pindar was edited, translated and imitated; while among prose writers Plutarch kept a steady popularity. The great tragedians were comparatively little studied, but against this the historians were familiar to educated people in a way that is today almost incomprehensible — politics came into a young man's education as an adjunct of rhetoric and oratory, encountered most prominently in the pages of Thucydides, Herodotus and Polybius. It did not come into a young girl's education at all; she was not encouraged to strive after eloquence.

This being said, the overwhelming urge, particularly after 1700, was to pursue a Roman version of classicism — had it been otherwise, we should have to speak of the Alexandrian age or to write about the Peace of the Pericleans. The influence makes itself felt in scores of ways. There is the cult of Cato, whose noble suicide was seen to mark the division between a tyrannical republic and an enlightened empire. As well as the figure of Augustus himself, viewed a little unhistorically as a kind of patriot king and ideal ruler, his friend Maecenas lay at the heart of the English myth of Augustanism. His name became standard jargon for disinterested patronage, and in a wider sense he represented the things that writers believed aristocrats should be — but rarely, in practice, embodied. Loosely defined, the Augustan authors in Rome were Virgil, Horace, Ovid and Livy; occasionally their numbers were supplemented by succeeding generations, notably the first-century poets Persius and Juvenal. There was also Cicero, who did not live into the empire proper, having been proscribed and murdered by the order of 'a chill and mature terrorist' — the future Emperor Augustus, then the triumvir Octavian. It was this body of literature, transmitted directly in the classroom and diffused impalpably throughout the educated world, which so strongly conditioned eighteenth-century English literature. Virgil supplied patriotic themes and potent historical messages. Ovid afforded a refined eroticism and plangent emotional scenes with a touching elegiac colouring. Perhaps most beloved of all was Horace, with his strategies for disengagement, his easy tolerance, his worldliness, his relaxed and slightly weary tones. Cicero was a shade too earnest to command quite such general popularity, though Hume's admiration almost rivalled the 'infatuation' of Frederick the Great and Voltaire. But this is speaking in relative terms. All the writers just named comprised a major context of literary creation in themselves; their attitudes, turns of phrase, expressive mannerisms and artistic personalities were intimately known by eighteenth-century readers and writers alike.

More problematic is the degree of French influence at the start of this period (contact with the Enlightenment later on was extensive but irregular). It is clear that royalty restored in 1660 meant also France reinstated at court; Charles II brought back from his exile a number of retainers who had spent their formative years in a French-speaking culture. His own mother was French and his brother an acknowledged Roman Catholic. Throughout his reign there was a succession of visitors, for a long or short stay, helping to set the tone of court life. On a superficial level the upper echelons of Restoration society were as Francophile as they have ever been. How deeply imbued they were intellectually with Gallic ideas is a different question: it was not, in general, a notably literate or serious-minded court. It should be added that among the humbler orders of men and women the influx of Protestant refugees after the suspension of tolerance towards them in 1685 was of considerable importance: they settled in localized patches, but in London and certain areas of the provinces they made a distinct mark in the eighteenth century.

All the same, the official programme of Restoration artists was undoubtedly in some shape or form a variety of neoclassicism, and that was essentially a French phenomenon. 'Neoclassic' is another textbook epithet that has lost popularity, and there are good reasons for that. We still need a term to describe the body of critical precepts and artistic doctrines which grew up in the mid-seventeenth century. The founding father was Malherbe, the theory was refined and developed by Corneille and Saint-Évremond (who spent much of his life in England), and then came the phase of systematization and publicity carried out, with conspicuous efficiency, by Boileau, Rapin, Le Bossu and others. Put crudely, these men represented in turn the Marx, then the Lenin and Trotsky, then the Stalinists of the movement. It was not, of course, an actively repressive creed, but it did involve a measure of purging, as well as the rewriting of history. One of the features of neoclassical art is the proscriptive element: there are banned words, taboo subjects, discouraged genres. On the one side bombast, on the other low and vulgar expressions were ousted from polite usage. It makes for a special sort of literature whose power derives from the absence as well as the presence of things — for example, the peculiar intensity Racine acquires because all considerable action takes place offstage, and what we are left with are the words. Shakespeare's poetry surrounds events; Racine's poetry replaces events. Both achieve high emotional articulacy, but the underlying aesthetic is radically different in each case. Similarly with language: Donald Davie has written of the pressure we feel in Augustan poetry, mounted by words excluded from the acceptable diction, and seemingly clamouring for admission. People occasionally speak of a neoclassical 'code', and the associations of that word are just about right. It was not a draconian body of regulations. Neoclassicism offers veiled threats of ostracizing those who reject its benevolent despotism, but it proceeds through a show of consensus: all the right people, we are induced to believe, have come together to produce the agreed recommendations.

Traditionally, the pragmatic Anglo-Saxon race is unwilling to swallow any large mouthful of theory. English writers took what they wanted from the movement and discarded the rest — generally quietly, but now and then with a certain jingoistic flourish, as in Dryden and John Dennis. B.H. Bronson has even expressed doubt as to whether neoclassicism 'regarded as a distinct phase of art' ever really existed in this country. He is confident that 'a truly neoclassical work of art ... was never created in England.' That may be so, by a strict definition of terms. On the other hand the positive values of neoclassical theory — clarity, precision, order, harmony, universality — were regularly sought by British writers between 1660 and 1800. Sometimes these goals were achieved, sometimes not. What matters is that men of the age *thought* they were advancing in this regard, and were glad of it. The masters of the new plainer prose style — Tillotson, Dryden, Addison, Hume — were not trying to write ornate baroque paragraphs and failing. They were responding to deep cultural imperatives, and helping to create new imperatives. In the same way the call for 'correctness' in poetry meant a conscious withdrawal from metaphysical tangles, from syntactical involutions and from broad demotic usage. Almost to the end of our period the smallish seventeenth-century poets, Denham and Waller, were held in extraordinary esteem for having achieved 'the reform of our numbers'. This was in no sense an ironic compliment. Writers believed that they had inherited a purer and more profoundly expressive medium as a result of this intervention; the elegance and regularity of the verse form permitted them to convey their thoughts and impressions more appropriately. This is, then, the quintessence of neoclassic doctrine: it lies in the belief that the restraints of form do not repress eloquence but liberate it.

All aspects of the dogma are remote from us today, but one concept is particularly teasing — that of nature. One cannot go far in reading eighteenth-century books, or in reading about them, without meeting the word. Even people sympathetic to the period worry about this notion; scholars offering to explicate neoclassicism throw up their hands. No short formula can hope to cover everything which 'nature' once connoted. It is perhaps best to define by negatives, though still in general terms. To follow nature, then, was to avoid singularity. It was to steer clear of prejudice and pedantry; to shun personal caprice; to reject what is local or temporary. You could follow nature by telling the exact truth about the world around you, provided you chose representative rather than specialized instances. (This was not as constricting as it might sound: the story of *Tom Jones*, say, satisfies the criteria because Tom — though he has his own personal lineaments — is yet conceived through the novel as fundamentally ordinary.) On the other hand you might copy Homer or Virgil, whose practice embodied the fullest expression of nature. In the scope of the term was included what we call human nature; it did cover the 'nature' of romantic poetry — woods and rivers and mountains — but that was a relatively small component in its semantic charge. Nature also extended to the universe beyond earth, to cosmic forces and the physical operations studied by science. When Fontenelle stated that 'Nature is but a great show, resembling that of an opera', he meant more than the visual splendours of this planet and others: he had in mind a scene and its meaning — the biblical history of creation; the Newtonian sense of design; the plot, as it were, which ran through the scene. Nature was both spectacle and story. The function of art, said John Dennis in a characteristic enterprise called *The Grounds of Criticism in Poetry* (1704), was to supply 'rule and order' to our confused impressions of the world: 'The great Design of Arts is to restore the Decays that happened to human Nature by the Fall, by restoring Order.' It was the task of literature to reflect reality but also to make sense of it; to distil general laws and detect patterns in apparently random occurrences. Clearly this is a public activity, and calls for widely intelligible forms and styles. It requires an audience with a large array of shared assumptions, more concerned with the similarities between people than the things which mark off one human being as distinct from another. Not surprisingly, the forms, the language and the audience all developed in the predictable direction.

Let us take these issues in turn. The history of major literary genres will be discussed in detail later on. Here we should note that the most widely influential forms were public modes such as satire and the moral essay. They dealt for the most part with the everyday experience of men and women in society; their tone was plain and worldly, they sought to avoid a recondite air, and they addressed the reader with easy confidence. In such forms it would be difficult to attain the tortured, introspective and desperate note found in much twentieth-century writing, even supposing the authors had wanted to do that. Characteristic of such an approach, early on in the period, is Addison's paper on press advertisements in *Tatler*, No. 224 (1710), with its gentle humour, its ready allusion to diurnal experience and its frank, friendly manner. Rather later comes Matthew Green's poem *The Spleen* (1737), chatty and unhurried, picking its topics off with wry precision. At the end of the period a representative item would be a 'familiar' letter by Horace Walpole, for example his letters to Sir Horace Mann in 1784 and 1785 describing the fashionable exploits of balloonists headed by Lunardi. The three different forms exercise separate pressures, but common to them all is a blend of the conversational and the formal. None of them is truly intimate in manner; each of them is written according to what seems a long-agreed contract, covering the things that can be mentioned and those which must be left unsaid.

As for language, the stylistic ideal for prose and poetry alike was that Horatian combination, elegance united with functional efficiency. In verse, this meant avoiding specialist jargon, affected words which drew attention to themselves, vague and obscure expressions. To compass this end a custom-made poetic diction was evolved, relieving the author of the time-wasting and potentially embarrassing task (as it was seen) of devising his own idiom. In his study of Dryden in *The Lives of the Poets* (1779-81) Dr Johnson enunciated the principles with memorable force: '[a] system of words at once refined from the grossness of domestick use and free from the harshness of terms appropriated to particular arts' — *arts* refers to all kinds of human activities and occupations. Today we expect a poet to bend words or to reapply them in unexpected ways; his function is to mount a raid on the inarticulate and he is more or less required to find the vocabulary of everyday discourse insufficient for his purposes. The eighteenth-century poet was encouraged to use the language of the day, stripped of a few unacceptable elements and garnished with a selection of verbal 'beauties' along approved lines. His artistry lay in channelling his perceptions along these well-marked communicative lanes.

This does not mean that there was total uniformity of expression in all situations. On many occasions the acceptable 'middle style' was preferred, and in prose Addison came to be recognized as a master in this vein. However, epic and tragedy demanded certain heightening effects to lend dignity to the narration or impressiveness to the morality. Low forms like travesty were given an extended verbal licence; the more 'familiar' the occasion, the looser were the constraints. It is interesting that Swift's descriptions of sleazy urban living were seldom criticized on linguistic grounds. The poems themselves were found obscene or distasteful, but Swift's deployment of brisk and homely idiom was perversely decorous.

In any case the language was, as always, undergoing change. It is notorious that a peaceful and broadly conservative society will attach great importance to purity of speech, as though this guaranteed a good state of national health. In the eighteenth century writers felt genuine anxiety that the language might fall into decay; the result would be that their works would prove perishable because their meaning was lost. This was not altogether an unrealistic fear, inasmuch as the bulk of medieval authors had become impenetrable to the ordinary reader. Chaucer was still intelligible, but scholarship had not yet discerned a method in his irritating metrical madness. The need to create a bulwark against change, then, arose principally from literary considerations, though it was buttressed by insularity — the flow of French words into English went on throughout the period, especially during the time of war, and many disliked such cultural infiltration. Hence a number of projects to create an official institution along the lines of the Italian and French academies, which should act as a court of linguistic appeal. The most famous proposal was that of Swift in 1712, embodying a desire to hold grammar and vocabulary in permanent stasis. Swift's ideas did not get a very fair hearing, because they emerged in a sharply political context, but they could never have formed the basis of a realistic programme.

None the less, the call for some authority to govern these matters was still heard. In 1754 Lord Chesterfield wrote an article to recommend Dr Johnson's dictionary, published a year later, and he too deplores the absence of any 'lawful standard of our language'. As far as usage went, Johnson in large measure satisfied the demand. His work quickly achieved a magisterial position through the English-speaking world — and America is included in that phrase, until the appearance of Noah Webster's *American Dictionary* (1828), a Columbian declaration of independence. It was not that there had been no previous compilations of any merit; English dictionaries had been coming out at regular intervals since the middle of the seventeenth century, and had steadily improved in range, in accuracy of definition and in etymological understanding. Johnson brought something new to lexicography, however, and that was a profound critical mind. It was this that made his book a major instrument of literary activity. Unlike the Oxford English Dictionary, around 150 years later, Johnson's compilation is not primarily valuable to the analyst or research scholar. His instances of usage provided a kind of model anthology, and all serious users of English found their sense of the richness of the tongue immensely fortified. (The book may even have put something of a brake on the admission of loan-words, in so far as it reminded the public of the existing resources that English possessed.) Today we can only read the *Dictionary* as an archaic document; we should no more think of regulating our own usage with its aid than we should set out on a train journey by consulting a pre-war timetable. In its time Johnson's work had a more urgent relevance. Incidentally, he did supply a perfunctory grammar which was much less influential. A succession of prescriptive grammarians cast their shadow over the period; they include men as interesting (in other spheres) as the hymn writer Isaac Watts, the eccentric philosopher James Harris, the evangelist John Wesley and the critic Bishop Lowth. The consummation of this tendency arrived in the shape of Lindley Murray in 1795: his *English Grammar* reached over 200 editions and through them tens of thousands of suffering schoolchildren. It was all part of the eighteenth-century urge to sort, methodize and codify. Many of the grammarians hoped, in addition, to stabilize language; Johnson knew that his dictionary could not do that, but at least it served to ratify the accepted modes of current linguistic behaviour in polite society. He had thus performed the kind of public service an Augustan audience could appreciate.

This brings us to the third of the areas of communal assent to which I referred earlier. The eighteenth-century reading public was never exactly homogeneous, and it became less so as time went on; but it represented a fairly unified body of taste compared to that enjoyed by a modern writer. Authors and readers shared a good deal of educational experience; even if they had not studied at the two English universities (and very many had), they had read the same classical texts and had been exposed to the same rhetorical training at school. Serious literature was created for an educated public, but more importantly it was written for a relatively *settled* group of men and women, who were pleased to be confirmed in their opinions and enjoyed the pleasures of recognition. Of course, some writers obstinately refused to deliver the expected sentiments: Swift almost always, Sterne, Pope on many occasions, Gibbon more slily. Nevertheless it can hardly be denied that a high proportion of eighteenth-century literature is governed by the orthodoxies of a ruling class: whether or not one admires that class and its standards is a different question. When Addison wrote in the famous tenth number of *The Spectator* (1711) that he hoped to bring 'Philosophy out of Closets and Libraries, Schools and Colleges, to dwell in Clubs and Assemblies, at Tea-Tables, and in Coffee-Houses', he was expressing a widely felt desire. (It is just Addison's distinction that he is constantly saying what large numbers are beginning to think but have not yet found words to convey.) What might be called a secularization of taste was in progress. The ideologues, enthusiasts and Puritan sectaries were to be banished; the effective milieu of cultural exchange was to be the club room rather than the church or lecture hall.

It is a moot point how far this process is to be identified with a developing *embourgeoisement*. No one disputes that the Revolution of 1688 had led to social as well as constitutional changes. That is, along with a Whig constitutional ruler on the Dutch pattern the country inherited a Whig oligarchy on Dutch lines. The importance of the trading classes grew as financial institutions like the Bank of England (1694) came into being; the mercantile interest began to rival the court or aristocratic interest as government borrowing grew and investors in the funds had to be placated. Few considerable writers had close links with trade: Defoe, certainly, and the dramatist Lillo — Samuel Richardson is a special case owing to the fact that the commodity he produced was books, whether as tradesman (printer) or creative artist (novelist). Despite this, it is generally agreed that literature was much affected by this shift in the balance of social and political power. Richard Steele wrote plays in which leading characters proudly proclaim their commercial origins; Defoe celebrated the intermarriage of business and landed families, seeing in this the birth of a dynamic new nation. Similarly Voltaire, in his tenth letter, 'Sur le commerce', of his *Lettres philosophiques* (1733), attributed English naval and political power to the acceptance of trade by the English ruling classes, as compared with those of France in particular.

But if literature could be said to endorse the rise of the merchant, that is not the same thing as a thoroughgoing takeover of the world of letters by the middle class. Throughout the period taste was largely ruled by men and women with pretensions to breeding (whether justified or not); the private patron did not die without a fight, and George Bubb Dodington, Arthur Onslow or Lord Lyttelton were flattered into the reign of George III as obsequiously as any Maecenas of Queen Anne's day. The most conspicuous element in the reading public remained the governing class, though it may be that this class was in some respects easier to penetrate by 1760. One of the few concrete guides we have to the composition of a literary audience is provided by subscription lists. This system, whereby potential purchasers were sought in advance of publication and required to put down a deposit on the full price, came into great prominence during the eighteenth century. The first big successes had been the subscriptions mounted by the bookseller Jacob Tonson originally on behalf of a reissue of *Paradise Lost* (1688), with over 500 names, and then for Dryden's translation of Virgil (1697), with 350 subscribers including 100 who paid 5 guineas for a special illustrated edition. The most famous of all such ventures were the *Iliad* and *Odyssey* of Homer, translated by Pope, and brought out by Bernard Lintot between 1715 and 1726. As the century progressed, subscription publishing came to be used especially for multi-volume sets, large collections, encyclopedias, and the like. The lists of those subscribing have been intensively studied in recent years, and, while it is wrong to equate this group with the total literary audience, we can make certain limited deductions about the reading public at large. An inescapable conclusion emerges: for *belles-lettres* (to a greater extent than is true for scientific or theological books, say) the market was still dominated by the traditional 'bookish' classes. All considerable subscriptions are headed by aristocrats (often with a tinge of royalty), ministers, MPs, government placemen, prominent church-men, university dignitaries, professional men, and such like. There are sadly few women — I have encountered lists where they make up only one per cent of the number, and others where duchesses and countesses account for a third of the female presence. And except in very special cases, the new men of commerce and industry have receded almost out of sight.

Nor, for a long time, did the profession of letters itself undergo a real opening up to talent. Fewer authors were full-blown aristocrats, perhaps: the scornful tone Dr Johnson adopts towards poetasters like Halifax, Lansdowne and Buckingham in his *Lives of the Poets* suggests that rhyming peers were out of fashion by 1780. But though their origins were in the middle order, writers of any standing tended to become assimilated into the dominant class. This was partly a matter of educational background. As an experiment I took a sample of 100 poets within the period who are listed both in the *Dictionary of National Biography* and in the *New Cambridge Bibliography of English Literature*. Exactly a half could definitely be identified as having attended Oxford or Cambridge: 29 Oxford to 21 Cambridge. The comparable figures for Trinity College, Dublin, and Edinburgh were 5 and 4 respectively. The other Scottish universities and those on the continent supplied another 5 between them. As for schools, the list is easily headed·by the great nursery of literary talent, Westminster, with 15; followed by Eton, Merchant Taylors' and Winchester. If we restricted the count to the more eminent writers, it is certain that the concentration would be more marked. James Sutherland has calculated that out of 43 poets in Johnson's collection who worked in the eighteenth century 16 were at Oxford and 11 at Cambridge, a slightly higher proportion than my wider group reveals. Sutherland's list includes 10 Westminster products, 5 from Winchester and 4 from Eton. He continues: 'Of their parents a considerable number were either noblemen or landed gentlemen, but rather more of them were professional men — lawyers, doctors or clergymen. Eight of the poets (or about one in five) were the sons of parsons, and no less than thirteen of them (almost one in three) became parsons themselves.' It may be worth adding that my count excludes ten women who would have figured in the sample; they were of course debarred from the educational establishments.

A common education does not guarantee a shared viewpoint on every issue, though the university products tended to attend a narrow range of colleges (Christ Church and New, at Oxford; St John's and Trinity, at Cambridge), and thus to have been members of a very tight-knit group. Some of Johnson's poets got to know one another at school, as happened with Prior and Halifax — very much to the former's advantage in his subsequent life. Others became acquainted at university. Such lifelong friendships could be regarded as an accident, though the significant parallels between Addison and Steele, or even between Gray and Horace Walpole, suggest that exposure to the same scholarly exercises and the same regime — based on a narrow range of classical texts — did create a certain likemindedness among men of very different temperament. The more pervasive aspects of the system are harder to pin down, but the influence of upper-class education emphatically did not end with its direct recipients at Westminster, Christ Church or Trinity College, Dublin. The most famous peasant poet in the earlier half of the century, Stephen Duck, is one of two arguably 'proletarian' authors in my sample of 100. He was already educating himself — that is, smothering himself in the classics — when threshing in the Wiltshire fields. Given a few years' celebrity in the metropolis, a post as librarian to Queen Caroline, a Home Counties rectorship and even a stint as yeoman of the guard, Duck could deck out his mythological setpieces (as Raymond Williams tartly observes) 'with the worst of them'. His wife, née Sara Big, was employed as a guide to the Queen's allegorical waxworks at Richmond. At the age of fifty he drowned himself. It would be sentimental to imagine that Duck would have written better if he had remained untutored. He did not have the stuff of Burns in him, and anyway Burns was far from unlettered — it was only his independent Scottish will that prevented him from declining into an agreeable versifier using conventional English diction. The truth is that literature (especially poetry) was then a *learned* activity to an extent we now find it hard to imagine. Since learning was, for a variety of social and political reasons, the preserve of a ruling class, it was virtually impossible for writers completely to sever themselves from this ethos — even where they might have wished to do so.

Few writers stayed on at the universities — the academic poet or novelist is a modern development. They would have had to take orders, and many of them were not happy in their student days — Gibbon is an obvious example. Johnson was forced to leave Oxford because of financial pressure; Pope, as a Catholic, could not go there at all. Nevertheless the metropolitan élite stood at the apex of a culture which took traditional learning seriously; parliamentary oratory in the age of Burke and Sheridan exhibited by present-day standards a huge reverence for the classics. You could fault the clinical training and skill of the most celebrated medical men, but scarcely their literary taste or scholarly virtuosity. The keenest audience for new writing came from the ranks of such people: philistinism had not yet become a requisite for advancement in the world.

It is not surprising that writers should have succumbed to the prevailing ethos and should often have allied themselves (a little unrealistically) with the landed proprietors who held so much power in national life. In the opening number of *The Spectator*, when Addison is seeking to portray his spokesman as a detached and credible observer, he gives him a university background and a grand tour. As for his origins:

> I was born to a small Hereditary Estate, which, according to the Tradition of the Village where it lies, was bounded by the same Hedges and Ditches in *William* the Conqueror's Time that it is at present, and has been delivered down from Father to Son whole and entire, without the Loss or Acquisition of a single Field or Meadow, during the Space of six hundred Years.

The first words of *Gulliver's Travels* (1726) are these: 'My Father had a small Estate in *Nottinghamshire*; I was the Third of five Sons.' There follow details of a university education cut short by 'a narrow Fortune'. As for *Robinson Crusoe* (1719), the hero is once more a younger son; his father has acquired 'a good Estate' by trade and has retired from busy and vulgar Hull to dignified York. Robinson is intended for the law but of course runs away to sea. Now the writer's attitude towards his creation is different in these three cases; and the stable family background serves different moral ends. All the same, in each instance normality is represented by the life of a middling country gentleman. Adventurous heroes must rebel against such a cosy environment, as they have since fiction began. *Tom Jones* (1749) reverses the process; Tom grows into his patrimonial estate which his supposed bastardy and Blifil's machinations have denied him. In Smollett's first two novels, *Roderick Random* (1748) and *Peregrine Pickle* (1751), the hero is gradually estranged from a bickering family circle. Individual characters are allowed, so long as they are young, male and healthy, to challenge individual parents; but the larger social order is unquestioned. The wonder is that Swift, Pope, Richardson and Fielding were able to raise deep issues regarding social morality without ever truly denting the self-assurance of the polite world or damaging whatever credentials they themselves had to admission. Since the Romantic movement, to be a writer has been *ipso facto* to be a displaced person socially. It is scarcely an exaggeration to say that in the eighteenth century even the most radical spirit was, to the extent that he followed the profession of letters, an insider.

What, then, it may be said, about the dispossessed, the nonconformists and outcasts? Their voice was little heard in serious literature, partly because the forms available were little attuned to the expression of violently different states of consciousness. Street literature — broadside ballads, crude political lampoons, and the like — had little direct impact on the higher forms, and in any case tended to work along stereotyped lines. Even when an interest in earlier popular poetry began, with the ballad revival of the mid-century, nobody took contemporary folk culture very seriously. There are enough allusions to fairground drolls and country tales, sold in the market by a travelling mountebank, to make a sketchy archaelogy of eighteenth-century popular culture just about feasible. But there was no lively give-and-take between élite and mass art such as modern communications have accustomed us to. (It is the fashionable 'masquerades and operas', indeed, which recur in satire.) There again, Grub Street was inhabited by needy and far from privileged hack authors, whose life history is given lurid expression in *A Tale of a Tub* (1704), *The Dunciad* (1728) and then in the pages of Fielding and Smollett. But the dunces were not genuine outsiders: they had respectable origins, frequently spent years at the best schools and universities, and lost caste owing to the calamities of authorship. Richard Savage, by dint of Samuel Johnson's superb biography (1744) and of his friendship with Pope, came to be regarded as a hack with genius — a psychological Grubstreeter, so to speak, rather than a social failure. But even Savage was the reputed illegitimate son of aristocratic parents, and he typifies nothing. As for religious minorities challenging the hegemony of the Church of England, they had a loud voice in controversy, but a muted literary role. Few dissenters achieved prominence as writers (Samuel Richardson, contrary to many assumptions, belonged to the church). Defoe, Isaac Watts and others made some contribution, but not one proportionate to the importance of dissent within the community. Wesleyans appear in literature chiefly as objects of satire; the Evangelicals left an outstanding legacy in hymnology but only Cowper among the mainstream of eighteenth-century poets learnt to enlist their fervour. There were changes, but they were generated from within. The most extreme eighteenth-century innovators (Swift, Richardson, Christopher Smart) belonged to the broad establishment. The great new ideas came from Shaftesbury, Hume, Gibbon and Adam Smith, men nurtured in the traditional mould.

The common identification with country gentry to which I referred goes with a well-marked tradition of 'retirement' literature, in which modest rural living is contrasted with corrupt city life. Variations on this theme can be found in almost all the major writers: it is part of a recurrent Horatian dream (no poem was more frequently imitated than the epistle *Hoc erat in votis*). It is associated with the inclination towards country as against court politics, that is to say in effect a tendency to support what was still an inchoate and ill-organized opposition. In the middle of the period, with Thomson, Gray and Collins, retirement is often linked imaginatively with a spiritual refuge for the true artist, away from the deceits of the world. Later still it becomes for Cowper a way of holding on to personal identity amidst a barrage of psychological pressures. The expression varies but the gesture remains the same — an ideal of tranquillity to set against the bustle of men and affairs.

Yet this was strictly a mental escape route. Few ages have known a more thoroughly metropolitan literary élite. There is a popular notion that eighteenth-century writers were urban in outlook, and in essence the view is correct. (At this date the net migration into the capital from the country was about 8000 per year.) Characteristically writers came up to London from the provinces and stayed — witness Fielding and Smollett, Johnson and Goldsmith, Gay and Thomson. Boswell found himself a vocation and a subject in London, and though he struggled on at the Scottish bar he belongs, *qua* writer, among the metropolitan group. Sterne pined in his obscure Yorkshire village, made do for years with York, but finally achieved the recognition he craved in London society; thereafter he found it hard to stay away from the fleshpots. Swift was forced into exile, to another capital, and left his closest confederates in London. His visits to London in 1726 and 1727, when he fraternized with the highest in the land as well as resuming intimacy with Pope, Gay and Bolingbroke, were in sober truth homecomings. In the middle of the century the London nexus breaks down a little, with poets scattered around the country in anxious isolation — one symptom, in itself, of the breakdown of high Augustan culture. But it should be recalled that even at this very juncture the Johnson circle was forming in the capital. Johnson himself, Burke, Goldsmith, Reynolds, Garrick — all had provincial friends and contacts; but none of them, if we exclude Boswell, was a person of the same stature. A dreary series of letters floods in from worthy nobodies, and in the post they cross their correspondents' engaging messages from the capital.

The textbooks will tell us that provincial living attained a new amenity in the eighteenth century. We shall be reminded of the growth of spas, the spread of tourism, the rise of seaside resorts like Scarborough and Weymouth. It is true that assembly rooms were built (usually by public subscription), newspapers founded, and theatres opened. A scientific élite met regularly as the Lunar Society of Birmingham. By the mid-1740s, when a London bookseller issued the *Harleian Miscellany* with the participation of Samuel Johnson, a subscription list could include 250 provincial booksellers, with towns as small as Cranbrook, Honiton and St Neots represented. Yet all this was exceptional: only a few places amounted to anything as centres of the book trade, with publishing or wholesaling carried on. There was a subscription library in Liverpool, with a hundred members in 1758. Bath, Bristol, Norwich and York were true outposts of Augustan civilization, and some educated people were happy to spend their lives there. But it is indicative that literary men and women generally went to Bath to have a rest from writing; like the party of travellers in *Humphry Clinker*, they saw the sights and enjoyed the facilities before hastening off along the London road — the first main highway completely covered by turnpike systems. Only with Jane Austen, one might argue, do we get an in-depth study of Bath from a major writer. I do not say that educated people could not derive enjoyment from Bath or Tunbridge or Matlock; they could, but so they could at Epsom or Newmarket, where the racing engendered a special kind of social atmosphere. The fastest-growing cities, like Manchester, were busy rather than stimulating places. It is a harmless fiction that eighteenth-century life was equally rich and sustaining in remote parts of the country as in London; but the truth is that the real allegiance of contemporary intellectuals lay in a London-based culture. As modern New York dominates a vastly larger and more cosmopolitan nation (even California), through television, films, books and records, so London stood unchallenged in Georgian England.

The word 'England' here is used advisedly. None of these limiting remarks applies to Edinburgh, the 'Athens of the North', where an extraordinary efflorescence in literature, philosophy and architecture occurred as the century went on. Glasgow, too, which in 1700 was a rather mean little town, attained an independent cultural life far beyond that of English towns still more populous. We should remember that Scottish thinkers pioneered modern aesthetics, sociology and economics, besides producing distinguished work in historiography and rhetoric. Several distinguished Scotsmen were drawn up to London, where they made a full contribution to metropolitan life; but Hume, Adam Smith, Adam Ferguson, William Robertson, Lord Kames and many others stayed on. If anything, Boswell was keener to show Johnson the luminaries of Edinburgh in the autumn of 1773 than the grandeur of the Highlands. Johnson's England could rival neither.

Ireland, though it provided a stream of major writers in Swift, Congreve, Berkeley, Goldsmith and Burke, is perhaps best regarded as an offshore colony, like a less remote American nation. Politically it was separate from Britain, with its own parliament until 1801; this was a mark of subservience rather than of equality. Its church, university and other institutions were dominated by the Anglo-Irish or even appointees sent from England; an official Protestantism ran counter to a deeply entrenched Catholicism among the population at large. The only other feeble challenge to the cultural hegemony of London was mounted by the ancient universities in England. As we have seen, a considerable proportion of writers studied there, and a few (Addison, Edward Young, Thomas Warton) retained some more or less tenuous attachment. Nevertheless, Thomas Gray is unique as the only literary man of the first rank who made a career in the university. It is true that he devoted himself to miscellaneous learning and that he was more like a private research student than an academic teacher. In 1768 he was appointed to the chair of modern history, an eighteenth-century foundation which had been occupied by mediocre men and involved no defined tutorial duties. Gray at least resided in Cambridge, as his Oxford counterpart Joseph Spence (the antiquarian who assembled Pope's table-talk) never did in his twenty-five years' tenure. But Gray himself did not get round to delivering any lectures, although he laboriously compiled an inaugural address in Latin: like much else that he produced, this lecture never saw the light of day. In recent years much scorn has been poured on Matthew Arnold's comment, 'He never spoke out', as a way of describing Gray's thin output. But Arnold had some right on his side. It is not hard to think that Gray could have been stultified as a writer by his professional, or unprofessional, way of life. A man with a sinecure, permitted but not encouraged to study, safely isolated from the disruptive young — such a man is likely to survive only if he can keep his communicative urges under strong restraint. Gray could. Much of the best of himself went into private letters. By contrast Samuel Johnson seldom appears to full advantage in his correspondence; he was too busy writing — in every kind of organ on every kind of topic — to worry about being a writer. The full tide of literary existence unquestionably flowed through the capital.

The literary public

Logically prior to the question of the artist's role in society is the state of that society. In this period the nation was demographically stable; economically still agricultural for the most part; and politically a constitutional monarchy based on the rights of property. In the first half of the eighteenth century the population of England and Wales, standing originally at five and a half millions, increased at the rate of one per cent roughly every four years: it would have taken 350 years to double itself, and by 1750 had reached not more than six millions. Thereafter the curve became much steeper, and in the second half of the century population increased by about one per cent a year. By the time of the first official census in 1801 it had reached nine million and was climbing ever more rapidly. The reasons for this acceleration have been hotly debated. Some authorities put it down to increased fertility, generally associated with earlier marriage; at the start of the century women did not marry on average until the age of twenty-seven. Other writers think the birth rate stabilized around 1740 at about 35 per 1000, and attribute the change to a fall in the death rate. Numerous medical, social and economic factors have entered into the argument; but the haziness of early Hanoverian vital statistics make certainty impossible. (There were plans for a regular census in 1753, but an MP for York opposed this as subverting English liberty, and parliament agreed.) Meanwhile Scotland and Ireland followed a parallel curve, slightly out of synchronization, though they did not experience the Industrial Revolution in quite the same dramatic form. The Irish population remained at a slow rate of increase until the 1780s, when a rapid upsurge was observed. These two countries provided by far the most important body of immigrants (mostly to London); otherwise immigration into England was not on a major scale. London and its immediate environs had something like three-quarters of a million inhabitants; no other British city reached six figures. The capital stood at the centre of distribution for agricultural, as well as manufactured, goods; it dominated economic life far more completely than it has ever done since.

Throughout the period manufacturing was developing, ceasing to operate through localized cottage industry and taking on more of the features of modern large-scale production. But the changes were not rapid, to begin with; Thomas Newcomen's steam engines, invented in the first quarter of the century, were not to find wide application in factories until much later — the block was economic as much as technical. Abraham Darby (1677-1717), originally from Bristol, settled in Shropshire during Queen Anne's reign. His son perfected a method of smelting iron using iron instead of charcoal around 1735. But it was in his grandson's time that the famous Iron Bridge was built across the Severn at Coalbrookdale, and with it an era of true industrial 'revolution' could be said to be under way. The long-term result was a shift from a wood-based to a coal-based economy: the social consequences included a new distribution of the population, with the traditional densities (in the South-East, in wool counties like Wiltshire, Somerset, Norfolk and Suffolk) soon overtaken by new concentrations of people in the West Midlands,

Tyneside and later South Wales. In the eighteenth century the transformation was in an incipient stage, and even such areas as Lancashire or Staffordshire were not heavily urbanized by modern standards. But the process was under way, at least. Internal migration — up till now confined to the drift to London — became more widespread. Improved transport opened up new industrial centres and new markets: at first the schemes to make rivers more navigable were the most important; then came the development of turnpike roads; then towards the end of the period the age of canal building set in. By 1780 Bristol, Liverpool and Hull were linked by well-used inland waterways. A generation of provincial industrialists, led by Matthew Boulton (1728-1809), Josiah Wedgwood (1730-95) and Richard Arkwright (1732-92), typifies the enterprise of the mid-century. Wedgwood is particularly representative: a practical potter and an artistic creator, a research worker and a management controller, a systems engineer and a dilettante: tough-minded but liberal in outlook, more or less self-educated, a local patriot and a cosmopolite who sent dinner services to the Empress of Russia. He pioneered a kind of mass production, although most manufacture retained a strong craft element.

If men such as Wedgwood provided the basis for Adam Smith's economics, then agricultural improvers lay behind the optimistic pictures of rural England supplied by Arthur Young (1741-1820). In general Young welcomed the changes in the countryside which he observed as he toured from the 1760s. Like most people accounted good judges of the subject at that time, he approved of the marked increase of enclosures during the period, whereby the old strip system of 'open fields' was replaced by large hedged fields allotted to a single owner. Enclosures had been going on for centuries, but the remaining strongholds of the open field, in the South and Midlands, held out until the eighteenth. Rough grazing land on the downs was brought into more productive use. Another contemporary trend which agricultural observers, as opposed to peasants and poets, found easily acceptable was the influx of city men who acquired country estates. The largest landowners felt no pressure, and indeed really big estates prospered at this juncture; it was the lesser gentry and tenant farmers who found themselves squeezed. Naturally enough it was not these subsistence farmers who were most adventurous or receptive to change. Technical innovation usually started at the top and flowed downwards: Walpole's coadjutor Lord Townshend (1674-1738) is now better remembered for his turnip growing, involving the rotation of crops, than for his statesmanship. Later on the Earl of Leicester, Thomas Coke of Holkham (1752-1842), bred sheep, cattle and pigs, as well as introducing wheat to the light Norfolk soil. Just as engineers such as James Watt helped to fuel the Industrial Revolution, so its agricultural counterpart was stimulated by inventive spirits like Jethro Tull (1674-1741), a gentleman amateur who developed the seed drill and many other ways of increasing crop yield. A little later Robert Bakewell (1725-95) led major improvements in stock breeding. These things were important because a large proportion of the employed nation still depended, either directly or indirectly, on agriculture for a living; the shopkeepers, tradesmen and artisans remained in a minority.

If the demographic and economic patterns show evidence of change (slow as it was, to begin with), this is less true of the political nation. England was still a land of élites and oligarchies, where traditional patterns of authority and deference survived almost intact. Half the land under cultivation was owned by 5000 people; and almost half of *that* amount was owned by the lucky 400 families who thus took an unquestioned place in national or local affairs. (Of these about 175 were headed by a peer of the realm.) Few institutions were in any obvious sense representative of the people at large; if parliament embodied one kind of social élite, equally the local magistracy — with their wide administrative and supervisory powers, in every corner of life — performed a separate ruling-class function in the shires. Older Whig historians like to draw a picture of social harmony, with each man and woman content in his or her lot, and the asperities of class conflict softened by deep ties of kinship and communal assent. A new generation of commentators, of whom E.P. Thompson is the most eloquent, have raised many questions concerning the reality of this harmony. Certainly, no one who has spent any time ferreting through county record offices, in archives relating to quarter sessions or turnpike trusts or forest courts, could doubt that collisions between authority and populace were common occurrences. The game laws were perhaps the most frequent grounds for conflict; they defended the rights of a minority group even among landowners, and were backed by penalties so severe that, in the judgement of many, they often proved counterproductive. It is not necessary to put the rights and wrongs of these disputes where Mr Thompson does in order to agree with him that they were more pervasive than was ever allowed by the traditional account. Unfortunately for our purposes, protest was most commonly a matter of direct action, felled trees or smashed turnpike gates. The scattered anonymous letters and threats follow a ritualistic pattern. As a result, we rarely get near the submerged half of the population, the near three million men and women without land or capital, since their articulacy did not measure up to their sense of grievance. Professional writers, catering for a highly literate audience in long-sanctified forms, were totally cut off from these underground cries; the deserving poor figure in many a sentimental novel, but there was no serious attempt to find a literary language which would give such people an effective voice.

Regrettably, it is equally the case that eighteenth-century society offered a pitiful array of chances for women fully to express themselves. In this respect the most deprived classes were neither better nor worse; women probably led a marginally more brutal life, with the hazards of childbirth augmented by crude gynae-cology and surgical implements that look like instruments of refined torture. Prostitutes — estimated by one observer at 50,000 — lived a scarcely more degraded life to many eyes. How-ever, in the middle and upper orders of society, many women had enough leisure to regret their enforced idleness. Women could start salons, could become independent scholars — like the pioneer Anglo-Saxonist, Elizabeth Elstob (1683-1756) — and could even become painters in the approved style, as the case of Angelica Kauffmann (1741-1807) illustrates. They could exercise power behind the throne, as consorts or royal mistresses or society hostesses. But they were denied access to proper schooling, excluded from the universities, forbidden the professions, kept well away from the armed services (apart from the occasional disguised recruit bluffing her way to the lines), and generally confined to trivial and ornamental offices. This was a waste of intelligence and imagination which even the most enlightened thinkers chose to criticize only obliquely. Defoe, Addison, Swift and Pope were all by the standards of the day advanced in their attitudes towards female education, but they could none of them foresee a real transformation in sexual patterns. Later writers were no more able to take this particular leap in psychological conditioning. Somehow the childless Augustans seem to have been restricted to the viewpoint of a male clubman, whatever their personal characteristics. It is noteworthy that Swift, Pope, Gay, Prior, Congreve, Thomson, Gray, Collins, Horace Walpole, Johnson, Gibbon, Hume, Goldsmith and Cowper to name but a few were childless, and most of them unmarried. (The same is true of Hogarth, Reynolds and Handel.) Their sterility did not occasion their sexual attitudes — none of them, incidentally, was homosexual so far as we know — but it may have been caused, in part, by those attitudes.

As it was, a few brave spirits managed to challenge the male domination of the literary world. Eliza Haywood (1693-1756) was allotted a lively role in *The Dunciad*, and she was indeed one of the more talented denizens of Grub Street. Lady Mary Wortley Montagu (1689-1762) wrote some moving letters as well as some witty and malicious ones; an author of genuine distinction, she confined herself almost entirely to ladylike epistles and occasional verses. A little later novelists such as Sarah Fielding (1710-68), fated to go down in history as Henry's sister, and Charlotte Lennox (1720-1804) extended the compass of fiction. An important contribution to the 'gothic' novel of terror and sublimity was made by Ann Radcliffe (1764-1823). But it was left for Fanny Burney (1752-1840), a precursor of Jane Austen who lived on into Queen Victoria's reign, to achieve fame and social recognition as a result of her youthful novels — after which she relapsed into court attendance, marriage and prosiness. In all some 75 women writers of fiction are listed for this period in the *Cambridge Bibliography*. It is often asserted, without good concrete evidence in support, that women formed a large part of the new novel-reading public. If we trust the stories (and not all anecdotal testimony is suspect) then the fate of Pamela and Amelia was most eagerly followed by the female population, old and young alike. At a more abstract level we can say that the concerns of the novel suited feminine experience more aptly than the old epic battles or the exotic settings of Italianate comedy; moreover, the comparative *inwardness* of novelistic narration — as compared with the rant of heroic tragedy or the declamation of Juvenalian satire — meant that women were more easily able to accommodate themselves, as writer or reader.

All women, and the vast majority of the poor, were excluded from practical politics; the franchise approximated to adult male suffrage only in a handful of boroughs, and elsewhere the vote was providentially confined to those who knew how to use or sell it — that is the propertied class, about a quarter of a million people in all. Even in the counties, where the extreme exclusiveness of tiny boroughs like Old Sarum was absent, the electorate was often smaller than the 12,000 who were entitled to vote in the City of Westminster, or the 7000 qualified for the City of London. Most counties had about 3000 voters, though the figure for tiny Rutland was down to 800. Open contests were unknown in the constituencies with a restricted franchise and often there was no contest at all.

But politics has usually been spectacle as well as ideology; today we have television, with debates, interviews, pollsters, swingo-meters, demonstrations and other organized scuffles. Then they had processions, speeches from the hustings, fairs and general saturnalia: Hogarth's brilliant series of *Election* scenes (1754) vividly evokes the tumult, the brutality, the drunkenness, the corruption and the gaiety of such an occasion. Peaceful Georgian countryside was regularly invaded in this fashion, wherever the local magnates could not come to any cheaper accommodation. The ballot was not secret, and pollbooks were often printed with a list of votes as cast. In these circumstances the average citizen probably had more face-to-face contact with the struggle than an elector has today. The deluge of pamphlets, addresses and handbills which accompanied these contests would be perused with attention by everyone capable of reading, enfranchised or not, just because there was so little else to read — no advertising circulars arrived on the doorstep each morning. Likewise with that great mass medium, sermons: many a pulpit must have issued forth thinly disguised propaganda, its content determined by the political colouring of the individual who held the patronage of that living. Not all elections were boisterous, some were not even corrupt; but all in all the doings at Eatonswill, in Chapter 13 of *Pickwick Papers*, would not have seemed unfamiliar to eighteenth-century bystanders. The divisions in society, whose political consequences are described in the next chapter, were no matter of the closet or backroom. They were proclaimed on the streets, and the least attentive of observers knew just what the issues were. In that restricted sense, if not in others, politics belonged to everyone.

One growth area during the early Georgian period was organized crime. The London of Elizabethan and Jacobean times had, of course, teemed with coney-catchers and sharpers, but they had operated as freelances — sturdy beggars and vagrants with a knack for opportunism rather than professional criminals as we understand that phrase. London under the Georges had become big enough to make full-time gangs an economic proposition, whereas municipal policing remained that appropriate to a Tudor borough. Even if the magistrates had been well trained, the gaolkeepers uncorrupt and the parish watch properly organized, they would have been set a hard task by the enterprising Jonathan Wild (1683-1725), a truly innovative mind who devoted his talents to regularizing the return of lost (i.e. stolen) property to its owner. Since none of the conditions was met, Wild enjoyed spectacular success for many years. A businessman among pilferers and foot-pads, he naturally entered the public imagination, for *business* and *property* lay at the heart of every well-lined consciousness. Wild belongs in any Augustan pantheon, the antitype of its favourite sons. Ultimately he was brought down, partly as a result of special legislation and partly through overreaching himself in the best entrepreneurial style. His influence had spread throughout the capital and even into the adjoining counties. Though his particular system was smashed, there were imitators later, and Henry Fielding for one believed that gangsterism prevailed twenty-five years later.

Meanwhile the statute book was loaded with fresh capital offences, though pardons were bestowed in many cases and sentences commuted to transportation; sometimes it was hard to get juries to convict where the penalty seemed out of proportion to the wrong committed. Theoretically everyone was equal before the law, but the provision of 'benefit of clergy' (a literacy test) allowed latitude in desired cases to evade the full rigour. In summary, we must acknowledge that crime played a significant part in the Hanoverians' sense of their own identity. Criminals perhaps dramatized the threat of subversion for property owners; with the loss of their possessions would go, in the ultimate, their status and wellbeing. The smalltime thief — uneducated, living in a squalid tenement costing half a crown a week, amid the tumult of St Giles or Smithfield, surrounded by disease and gin-swilling — was making no conscious political point; he generally stole out of need or desperation, without challenging the law. A few men may have enjoyed the excitement that came from committing crime, but most probably sank into one miserable condition while fleeing another.

Everywhere that life was most nasty and brutish, it was generally at its shortest. The death rate in London around 1750 was about 50 per 1000, whereas the country as a whole averaged no more than 35 per 1000. It has been calculated that over 51 per cent of the infants baptized in London during the 1770s died before they reached the age of five, many of them stupefied by gin and laudanum, used as painkillers. The figures would certainly have been no better earlier in the century. In the terrible winter of 1740, when the Thames froze right across, twice as many people died in London as were born. One scourge alone, smallpox, was comparatively well contained in the capital, because of immunity developed after perpetual outbreaks. Higher up the social scale prospects were of course more favourable: there was a spectacular increase in the expectation of life among a sample of ducal families which have been studied — the male expectation went up from thirty-three to forty-five, the female from thirty-four to forty-eight, as between groups who were born at the start and the middle of the eighteenth century. It might be added that 100 male poets represented in the *Cambridge Bibliography* averaged almost fifty-five years of life; eight women poets sixty-two. Of course such persons by definition survived to maturity, and most occupied a high social rank. Eighty-four dramatists, of both sexes, average sixty-one years. The seven eighteenth-century novelists in this *Bibliography* average sixty-six years, although the one woman (Fanny Burney) tilts the scale with her score of eighty-seven. For comparison, a sample of forty leading politicians was taken, and the identical mean of sixty-six achieved.

The London mortality rate was at its highest in the 1730s, when an official report discovered 7000 retailers of strong spirits, of whom 2000 were unlicensed — this was certainly an underestimate. Gin shops used the slogan, 'Drunk for a penny, dead drunk for twopence, and straw for nothing.' Parliament tried in 1736 to limit consumption by imposing heavy duties on retailers; but attempts at total or partial prohibition seldom work. There were extensive riots against the measure in the East End, and the act never became effective, as Walpole realistically conceded. Fines and whipping did not discourage illegal hawking: over 8,000,000 gallons of spirits were produced annually by 1743. It was not until 1751 that another campaign made more headway, this time led by the polemical skills of Fielding, with *An Enquiry in the Causes of the Late Increase of Robbers*, and the starker black-and-white symbolism of Hogarth's *Beer Street / Gin Lane* diptych.

It would be wrong to leave an impression of unalloyed gloom. The harsh fate of insolvent debtors, who could be imprisoned by their creditors, was periodically alleviated, and though (as *Little Dorrit* reminds us) the practice survived into Victorian times the highest incidence appears to have occurred early in the century. Charity schools for the children of the poor were widely promoted. Penal reform was one of the slower philanthropic activities to emerge; fifty years and more after the emergence of bodies like the Society for the Propagation of the Gospel and the Society for Promoting Christian Knowledge, and some time after the growth of a rudimentary hospital system which occasionally cured more disease than it spread (see below, pp. 178-9), prisons remained dirty, infested and corruptly managed. It was the achievement of John Howard (?1726-90) to improve both the sanitary and the administrative health of city and county gaols; his *State of the Prisons* (1777) represented a major advance in thinking upon the subject. Along with men like John Bellers (1654-1725), Thomas Bray (1656-1730), Jonas Hanway (1712-86) — famous, too, for his introduction of the umbrella and opposition to tea drinking — Thomas Coram (?1668-1751), who promoted the Foundling Hospital in London, and James Oglethorpe (1696-1785), who oversaw the development of Georgia as a settlement for deprived men and women, Howard ensures that we need not enter a nil return as far as the social conscience of the age is concerned. Methodism, too, did something to improve the lot of the poor. It was by modern standards a paternalistic form of charity, but it enlisted compassion, zeal, disinterested service and genuine public spirit.

There were other social changes in the period of which space precludes any full description. For example, the older professions organized themselves better and made general headway. The legal profession was headed by judges and the handful of serjeants-at-law, with the Recorder of London holding an important and politically sensitive place. There were only about 200 barristers, virtually all based in London. A small but select group of 'civilians' had to themselves ecclesiastical law and all cases relating to matrimony or to probate. Meanwhile the old distinction between attorneys and solicitors disappeared; an act of 1729 set up, not before time, something resembling a professional code to guide this much criticized body of men. In *Tom Jones* (XVIII, vi) we hear of a debt which 'an attorney brought up by law charges from 15*s*. to £30'. This kind of abuse was not destroyed overnight, but a number of measures — including the formation of the Society of Gentleman Practisers in 1739 — helped slowly to improve the standing of the legal profession. (Not that the satirists saw much change for the better.) Two of the greatest men of the century in Britain were the Scottish-born judge Lord Mansfield (1705-93), a friend of Pope at the end of the poet's life, and Sir William Blackstone (1723-80), author of the famous *Commentaries* on the English law, which were to exercise a huge influence on subsequent thought in Britain and America. During this same period the armed services offered increasing opportunities to those sufficiently well connected or well heeled to obtain a commission. The naval establishment grew rapidly around the middle of the century, when sea power was generally the decisive factor in war. There must have been approaching 5000 regular army officers to fight in the European theatre, to assist in colonial struggles (not generally against natives but as part of the remoter conflict of major powers) or to man the garrisons. There were thirty-five garrison towns in Britain alone; an intriguing number of early novels are set in their vicinity, and Lydia Bennet was not the first young lady in English fiction to be entranced by a redcoat.

In the long run there was a larger movement in social history which took place quite outside these well-recognized modes of getting on in life. New professions, like surveyor, land agent and architect, came to prominence. The activities surrounding commerce and finance became less socially dubious, an important condition of Britain's economic take-off later in the century — only Amsterdam had anything like the sophisticated London credit market. Manufacturers were slower to find acceptance, but even this process was under way by 1780. Wedgwood was seen to be a scholar and a gentleman; Arkwright finished up high sheriff of Derbyshire; the second Robert Peel became an MP, a baronet and the father of a Tory prime minister. Nabobs with interests in India and West Indian merchants with sugar estates in the Caribbean enjoyed greater prosperity as the turns of war and diplomacy gave Britain its first great empire, with a new administrative bureaucracy replacing the old commercial venturers. Spain and the Low Countries were in decline, and the eastern European powers had not yet emerged on the world scene. France was the major trading rival, and the Utrecht settlement of 1713 had given Britain a temporary start in the richest markets: the merchant shipping fleet trebled between 1702 and 1776. The slave trade, of course, played a significant part in all this. Meanwhile, at the very top of the scale, the great Whig dynasties grew bigger, yet more cohesive. The dukeries thrived, while the squirarchy pinched and scraped. Sir Roger de Coverly (died, by Addison's hand, October 1712) would never have seen such golden times again.

The contemporary social register was delicately shaded with fine nuances which often elude our observation today. Merchants had their own elaborate caste system, while the exact distinction between the various grades of landowner, from the great magnates like the Duke of Devonshire through the various categories of gentry down to the lesser freeholders, is not always easy to draw, though the top and bottom of this scale are miles apart. Very approximately, one might say that the structure was a pyramid, with the magnates enjoying an income of £5000 upwards, up to £40,000 even; the wealthiest gentry including baronets (under 1000 of them) had £3000 or £4000 per annum; the class termed by the early demographer Gregory King 'esquires' would number some 3000, and receive around £1000 per annum; and the remaining gentry (12,000 or more in all) £250 as a minimum. The 100,000 freeholders or owner-occupiers might earn £300 and downwards, with the poorest among them not making more than £50 annually. Social prestige and influence in the country went closely in line with this economic gradation. National figures in politics needed a strong local base, and often exercised direct influence as lord lieutenant of the county. Below the magnates, but active in parliament and local affairs (e.g. turnpike trusts or canal building) came the knights of the shire. The squires were men of the stamp of Allworthy in *Tom Jones*, magistrates and church patrons, highly important people within a narrow geographic area. Below that, real power was circumscribed but gentility still strenuously maintained.

Yet despite the seeming rigidity of this social order, the hierarchy could be invaded. James Brydges, Duke of Chandos (1673-1744), one of the great literary patrons, offers a striking example. He was the younger son of an impoverished country gentleman, and younger sons generally went into the church or the army. But Brydges worked his way up the ladder of court appointments and finally obtained the remunerative post of paymaster to the forces in 1705. He had lobbied assiduously for this job — not surprisingly. The army during Marlborough's wars was clothed, fed and paid by private contractors; the government paymaster could extract bribes, put out public money at interest (for his own benefit) until it was disbursed, and generally line his pocket. In quick succession Brydges became an earl and a duke; he raised a baroque mansion outside London, whose magnificence Defoe lauds in his *Tour*, a stream of visitors wondered at, and Pope (perhaps) satirized in the picture of Timon's villa (*Epistle to Burlington*). The 'least cautious' of peers, Chandos employed Handel as his director of music, invested in all the leading funds, survived losses in the Mississippi crash and in the South Sea Bubble, engaged in speculative building in Bath and the West End of London, and dabbled in every sort of enterprise: the new Covent Garden theatre, coal mines, soap works, glass factories, oyster fisheries and much else. He still had time and money to collect books and pictures — a Maecenas who had arrived from nowhere.

The artist, then, had to find his place in a sharply graduated society, with steep divisions in status, income and power. Perhaps no writer occupied quite the same subservient position as the assistants in a painter's studio, where hired underlings were paid a small wage to fill in the costume or the background foliage in a portrait. Nor were authors in the state of dependence to dealers and connoisseurs which reduced Hogarth to embittered protest: the bookseller's hack had one employer but many readers, and this wider market gave the literary world a less anxious and incestuous quality. A writer who achieved any worthwhile success could claim an assured place in the social order — and was still content to claim it. In the lower reaches of Grub Street neither financial security nor respectability was so easy to come by. But the mood of the age, palpable long before Adam Smith codified these things, discouraged the habit of rewarding failure. Like the church, the literary profession had its acknowledged ladder of preferment, and it was up to the individual to climb from isolation and obscurity to the pinnacles of success and recognition.

Opportunities for the professional author look, with hindsight, to have burgeoned within the period. Not all contemporaries saw it that way. There is a long and unhappy tradition of fulminations against the book trade: much of this emanates from writers of moderate success, like James Ralph (?1705-62) who contributed a sour review of *The Case of Authors by Profession or Trade* (1758), but similar criticisms are found in Goldsmith and others. Ralph is much concerned with the status of authorship, and complains that whereas a man 'may plead for Money, prescribe or quack for Money, preach for Money, marry for Money, fight for Money', writers were expected to be uniquely disinterested, so that 'he who aims at Praise ought to be starved'. By such means 'the Credit and Value' of the profession had been unfairly depreciated. Ralph harks back to the favoured era at the start of the century, when Prior and Addison had benefited from 'the Link of Patronage which held the Great and Learned together'. A more refined version of this critique appears in Goldsmith's account of the Augustan age, which I quoted earlier. The reign of Queen Anne is there singled out because 'at that period there seemed to be a just balance between patronage and the press. ... The writers ... were sufficiently esteemed by the great, and not rewarded enough by booksellers, to set them above independence.' Laments over the decline of patronage are usually accompanied by bitter words directed against booksellers. Samuel Johnson is one of the few moderating voices on this issue, acknowledging that the trade was led by 'generous, liberal-minded men'.

It is difficult to assess the rights and wrongs of this matter. At the start of the period there was something of a golden age for patronage — it was relatively brief, but then golden ages always are. It happened that distinguished men of affairs were, as individuals, active bibliophiles and collectors who enjoyed the company of wits; moreover, the Whig dining society known as the Kit-Cat Club, which flourished about the time of the Marlborough wars, provided a basis for collective patronage. The famous Kneller portraits of the club show two members actually holding a book. They were the secretary, Jacob Tonson the elder, a major figure in the book trade who was associated in turn with Dryden, Congreve, Addison and Pope — he is shown with a copy of his notable edition of *Paradise Lost*; and John, Baron Somers (1651-1716), who is holding a volume of Spenser, doubtless the text edited by John Hughes and dedicated to Somers (1715). Tonson, as one would expect, had published the volume. In addition, several others among those painted by Kneller (Cobham, Newcastle, Montagu, Halifax, Dorset and Carlisle) were important patrons.

When the Hanoverians came in, the tradition of patronage did not die overnight. But a number of factors combined to divert energy, and money, elsewhere. The early Georges were keener on opera than any established literary mode. Exceptionally, George II gave Steele £500 for the dedication of a play in 1722, and Cibber £200 a few years earlier. Caroline did support a few writers, as with Stephen Duck, but her bluestocking urges led her more frequently to patronize the study of philosophy. A year after Queen Anne died, Lord Halifax (patron of Addison, Prior, Congreve and many others) followed her to the grave: one more year and it was the turn of Somers. At the very same juncture Pope's subscription *Iliad* was declaring the independence of writers from direct aristocratic tutelage; the dedication was pointedly bestowed on William Congreve, by then a retired gentleman but by no conceivable licence of speech a patrician. More generally Pope and Swift furnished an example to later authors by their studied pose of disinterest; they accepted the friendship of great men but not their pension. A few years more and surviving bibliophiles like the Earls of Sunderland and Oxford were dead. The long dominance of Robert Walpole began, and for one reason or another Walpole — a cultivated man with exquisite taste in painting — did not see his role as being Maecenas to the patriots and panegyrists of his day. He took a cynical attitude towards the journalists who supported the ministry case in public prints, and bore with robust good humour the opposition of almost every notable creative writer. Above and beyond all this, the overriding explanation for the demise of old-style patronage may be connected with nothing more remarkable than fashion. As the century unrolled, a few pockets of sub-aristocratic largesse survived, but there was no central focus like the Kit-Cat. The only comparable organization to which George Bubb Dodington — the mid-century's answer to Somers — is suspected to have joined is the group of absurd satanists known as the Hell Fire Club who cavorted on the banks of the Thames at Medmenham. The Kit-Cats were not plaster saints, but books had lain a good deal nearer the centre of their activity.

Concurrently there were gradual changes in the structure of the book trade, and also in its commercial operations. There were four main functions, if we discount ancillary tasks such as paper making and exclude the curiously ramshackle organizations which managed the university press at Oxford and Cambridge. First, there were printers, less secure and dominant in the Stationers' Company than they had been in the era of Shakespeare or Milton. Second, there were publishers, as we call them today: by contemporary usage they would be described as booksellers. So for that matter would the third class, wholesale booksellers, and the fourth, retailers of books with shop premises. These functions overlapped to a confusing extent. A publisher is effectively the man who instigates production and who owns the legal title to the proceeds. This was done by the outright sale of copyright by authors in return for a single fee; royalties were not paid at this period. Commonly the rights were owned in partnership by a number of men and women; their names might then appear on a title page in a strict order governed by their date of admission to the Stationers' Company. Printers, wholesalers or retailers might publish books in this sense, but there were specialists in this branch of the trade. The imprint is far more likely to record the name of a distributor than that of the true publisher. Thus Swift's pamphlets in his early career, such as *The Conduct of the Allies* (1711), are stated generally to be 'printed for John Morphew, near Stationers' Hall'. But Morphew was a secondary agent, probably with good warehousing facilities, who supplied retail outlets from stock. The owner of the copyright, usually Benjamin Tooke, would not be named; and neither would the printer, John Barber. As the century progressed these distributors came to be known, misleadingly for us, as 'publishers'. Hundreds of title pages carry their names, but it is a mistake to suppose that they were the leading contacts in the trade for authors. A prominent representative was Mrs Mary Cooper, whose name appears on many works in the middle of the century; she figures for instance on a work by Henry Fielding published in 1747, though we know that the printer (Strahan) charged Andrew Millar with the costs of setting up the type, and it was doubtless Millar who reimbursed Fielding for his efforts. An even more conspicuous example was James Roberts (1668/9-1754), originally a printer, who can be found associated with almost every front-rank (and second- or third-rank) writer in this age. Sometimes a 'publisher', in this sense, would own the rights to a few works; and he might also have a retail outlet of his own. But essentially he was an intermediary.

The most famous members of the trade in the eighteenth century were those who came into close touch with authors. After Jacob Tonson the elder (1656-1736), whose prosperity was partly based on lucrative official contracts, a more adventurous phase set in. Bernard Lintot (1675-1736), best known for his association with Pope, managed to stay just on the right side of the law without endearing himself to many authors. In a scabrous but intensely comic part of *The Dunciad*, Book II, where the stationers' activities during the Lord Mayor's Show are cruelly transformed into obscene athletic contests, Lintot is required to attempt a noxious obstacle course along with 'dauntless Curl'. Edmund Curll (?1684-1747) stood out in a colourful era for his flamboyance and daring. A Jonathan Wild among booksellers, he lived under constant threat of prosecution, whether for publishing obscenity, for infringing copyright, for disseminating treasonable material, for libellous advertising, or a number of other causes. The government were usually on his tail, usually for his malpractices in the trade but once because a suspected Jacobite dramatist was lodging above his shop. To mend matters Curll offered to turn informer, another Wild-like shift and the usual recourse of desperate men at the time; but he never became respectable in any degree. His bouts with Pope, ranging from crude horseplay to Chancery suits, re-enact the course of author-bookseller relations.

After Curll things could only quieten down. Prominent figures in the middle decades were Andrew Millar (1707-68), involved with Thomson, Hume, Fielding and Johnson (who stated that he had 'raised the price of literature'); Robert Dodsley (1703-64), originally a footman, who brought out notable work by Johnson and Shenstone, and launched a fine series of old plays in 1744; and Ralph Griffiths (1720-1803), a pioneer of literary journalism. Tom Davies (1712-85) has one famous act to his credit, the introduction of Boswell to Johnson in 1763, but he was a writer, actor and publisher into the bargain. Some durable trading dynasties were founded by Thomas Cadell, the Dilly brothers and Thomas Longman. Among printers the most notable was perhaps William Strahan (1715-85), who did not sell books but did take a share in many important publishing ventures (Johnson's *Dictionary*, Mackenzie's *Man of Feeling*, Hume's *History*, Adam Smith's *Wealth of Nations*, Gibbon's *Decline and Fall*) — his printing activities included novels by Smollett, Richardson and Sterne. As a typefounder William Caslon (1692-1766) is of equal importance, as is John Baskerville (1706-75) as a designer and typographer. In Glasgow Robert Foulis (1707-76) introduced a new elegance and delicacy to printing, especially for the classics. By my calculations there were about 100 London booksellers regularly engaged in publishing in 1720; the total perhaps fell a little as time went on. At this date there were about 100 printing houses in the entire kingdom, of which 70 were located in the capital.

Anonymous men continued to play a large role through the activity of publishing pirates, often based truly or ostensibly in Holland. A very common imprint is that of 'A. Moore', a kind of title-page A.N. Other masking the identity of an illegal publisher; the formula 'printed for the booksellers of London and Westminster' generally performs the same function. While the old Licensing Act had been in force, some check on piracy had operated. But this Act lapsed in 1695, and there dawned an era of cut-throat competition. There were at least twelve piracies of Defoe's *True-Born Englishman* (1701), running to 80,000 copies. King of the pirates was Henry Hills (d. 1713), who scorned such cowardly devices as anonymity. It was probably Hills's manoeuvres which led to certain provisions in the great Copyright Act of 1709, including the surviving requirement for publishers to deposit copies of their publications at major public libraries. But the main bearing of the Act lay elsewhere, and indeed a large body of piratical dealing was left unaffected by this measure. What the new law did was to give existing books a term of twenty-one years' immunity, while all future books were to be copyright for fourteen years (this was renewed for another fourteen years if the author were still alive when the first term expired). The right of literary property was explicitly confirmed as the author's, for the first time in English law; of course the right could be assigned, and normally was — in the way we have seen — by sale to a bookseller.

The Act clarified some problems but not all. It was maintained by the book trade that the new provisions had statutory force, but that their old common-law rights were left intact: in other words, they believed that so-called 'perpetual copyright' went on regardless of the tightening-up on short-term breaches. This meant that those who had been publishing Shakespeare and Milton considered that they retained an irrefragable title to go on doing so, without the threat of competition from fresh quarters. It was not until 1774 that a House of Lords ruling settled the point, and overturned the claim to perpetual copyright. From this date there was a free market in publishing any work — excluding the Bible and prayer-book — whose term of copyright, as granted in 1709, had expired. This was to be important, because an interest in earlier classics of English literature had been growing up; Bentley and others had edited Milton, the Shakespeare industry was gaining momentum, and *Hudibras* became a standard text with full critical apparatus. In 1780 the corpus of English literature was easily available to the general reader, though he might have trouble getting hold of a copy of Donne. In 1700 only antiquarians and favoured private collectors could have been sure of such access.

Quite apart from the copyright issue, the avenues open to literary aspirants were steadily increasing in number. Newspapers had their economic ups and downs, as they do today, and government stamp duty ate into their prosperity throughout the period. Nevertheless a surge in newspaper production occurred at the start of the century, possibly in connection with the popularity of coffee houses which subscribed to all the prints; and this momentum was never wholly lost. Less than 50,000 newspapers were sold a week in 1700; by 1760 the figure was around 200,000. To begin with, the most regular fodder was far from inspiring: nothing imaginable could be duller than the official *London Gazette*, with its stale foreign news ponderously presented, or the timid *Daily Courant*, famous in journalism as the first real daily paper but excruciatingly boring to read through. Things looked up with livelier tri-weeklies like the *Post-Boy* and the *Flying-Post*, which do convey much of the excitement of living in the present under Queen Anne. In the reign of George I a burst of energy lifted the weekly press, notably Applebee's *Weekly Journal*, in which Daniel Defoe took a leading part, and Mist's *Weekly Journal*, conducted by a printer named Nathaniel Mist who alone rivalled Curll in shameless defiance of all authority. Under Walpole the government line was defended by the *Daily Gazetteer*; it was heavily subsidized and Walpole got better value for money than autocrats sometimes do. Papers on both sides of the political fence were distributed partly by the system of free mail franking available to MPs. Opposition journals included *The Champion*, edited by Henry Fielding and then by James Ralph. A more lasting achievement was that of the *Daily Advertiser*, founded in 1730, which kept a businesslike course for the remainder of the century. A series of 'advertiser' papers sprang up, to be followed in due course by 'chronicles' hoping to emulate the success of the *London Chronicle*, begun with Samuel Johnson's support in 1757. These papers included the *Morning Chronicle*, starting in 1769, which under its enterprising editor William Woodfall helped to pioneer regular parliamentary reporting. William's brother Henry took a prominent part on the *Public Advertiser* over the same period, and printed the famous Junius letters there, with a consequent rise in circulation to 4000 copies at the height of the episode.

All these, apart from perhaps *The Champion*, were fundamentally organs for disseminating news, though they did carry a good deal of editorial comment. At 2*d.* a copy (later 2½*d.*) they were within the pocket of almost everyone who could read. A more important medium still, as far as writers were concerned, lay in weekly or monthly journals, where more discursive essay-type material was used. Early in the century there were political outlets, like Swift's *Examiner*, as well as freewheeling essay journals on the model of *The Spectator*. Twenty years later this branch of journalism was dominated by the opposition paper generally known as *The Craftsman*, which enlisted a team of able writers including Bolingbroke, and achieved a circulation of 10,000 at its peak around 1730. In literary, as opposed to party, politics the 1730s saw the emergence of the *Grub-Street Journal*, broadly an extension of *The*

Dunciad into the field of weekly journalism. Later still there are moral and reflective papers like Johnson's *Rambler*, political and cultural commentaries like Fielding's *Covent-Garden Journal*, and a variety of specialist organs covering the theatre, commerce and professional concerns. There were the beginnings of journalism aimed at children and a few rather frumpish magazines for ladies. But outside the newspaper proper the main impetus was provided by monthly journals. The *Gentleman's Magazine*, founded in 1731 by Edward Cave, was built around its digest of the periodical press; but it also ran competitions and printed readers' effusions, especially in verse. Its illegal forays into parliament afforded Johnson an early chance to polish his command of orotund style — he was called on to disguise the proceedings as 'debates in the senate of Magna Lilliputia', and managed to produce noble perorations from the sketchy notes delivered by undercover reporters at Westminster. The magazine retained its wide currency throughout the period, even after the appearance of specialist literary journals such as the *Monthly Review* (1749) and *Critical Review* (1756), with their superior coverage of new books.

Nearly all eighteenth-century writers had their journalistic moments; for some, the engagement was more permanent and more crucial to their artistic development. I have mentioned Johnson; others who come into this bracket include Defoe (whose *Review* sharpened his originally prolix style, and gave him a fund of political and economic information), Fielding, Smollett, Goldsmith and Boswell. Writers as unlikely as Sterne and Christopher Smart are found in their formative years, turning out weekly articles and versifying current topics of attention. It is not that the really central books of the period precisely mimic or take over the processes of journalism: rather, the case is that widening opportunities and diversified modes of expression helped to break down literary exclusiveness. Authorship was less and less confined to a separate clerisy. Writing for the public prints was not as good as creating a masterpiece, but it was a way of surviving in the profession and it extended the power of the word. There was more breathing space; a chance of freer communication.

Mention has been made of the coffee houses. These institutions have figured strongly in many accounts of the period, and have been described as the 'penny universities'. Nor is this wholly myth.

The first known in England was recorded at Oxford in 1650, but as usual it was London which experienced the full force of a social trend. Under the Commonwealth a number of coffee houses were opened, and there were always a few struggling on in the ensuing decades, having survived the Restoration, licensing laws, the Plague and the Great Fire. Around the time of the Popish Plot, *c*. 1678-9, they became suspect as the cells of treason and intrigue; government spies mingled among the customers, generally with no remarkable discoveries to show for their pains. At an early stage the coffee house was associated with news, the press and gossip-mongering. With the beginnings of a postal system at the end of the seventeenth century, the houses took on a new role as circulation centres. They even operated private mailing facilities which proved an embarrassing rival to the official Post Office. They served as a box number for advertisers in the newspapers, looking for a wife or a lost dog. Another function they performed was as commercial venues; the major companies (East India, Levant, African) held meetings there, livery companies held court, and the whole South Sea fiasco came to a climax in and around these places. As is well known, modern insurance had its origin in Lloyd's coffee house, set up by Edward Lloyd about 1690. Stockjobbers, having no home of their own from the late 1690s, settled instead on Jonathan's in Exchange Alley, off Cornhill; Garraway's, in the same small street, was frequented by goldsmiths, bankers and dealers. It was in this compact area of the business quarter that the City as a financial institution evolved; and crucial to this process, with its durable effects on social and economic life, were the humble coffee houses. This function they never lost; but increasingly through the eighteenth century they spread westwards towards the twin city of Westminster. Fashionable and artistic people took over the habit of attending the houses, and new concentrations appeared — those for lawyers around Fleet Street and the Strand, for wealthy flaneurs in St James's, for literary and theatrical folk about Covent Garden. It was to the St James's house, amusingly, that Stella was to direct her letters to Swift, on his own instructions.

Bryant Lillywhite has listed over 2000 London coffee houses open at some date between 1650 and 1850. The main concentration falls in the middle of that period, and it is clear that the highpoint occurs in the eighteenth century. Few male writers can have totally escaped their influence. Not everyone went along regularly in person, though a sizeable number did just that. The most famous of the early literary gatherings was that held in Will's, on the corner of Bow Street and Russell Street. Dryden began to frequent this establishment, convenient for the theatre, in the late 1680s, and thereafter an admiring circle built up the popularity of Will's. Even after Dryden's death in 1700 the house enjoyed exceptional renown and only a generation later did it fall from favour; in the second quarter of the century it 'steadily degenerated into a gaming-house'. Meanwhile, as a pamphlet of 1714 tells us, 'Button's is now the established Wit's Coffee House.' The moving spirit here was Addison, who set up as master of the house one Daniel Button, a servant to the Countess of Warwick (whom Addison was shortly to marry). At the end of Anne's reign, when periodical papers had an astonishing vogue in the wake of the *Tatler* and *The Spectator*, their currency was heavily dependent on the coffee houses. A sort of communal reading became the rage. In the tenth issue of *The Spectator* Addison was able to make a realistic estimate of his audience: 'My Publisher tells me, that there are already Three Thousands [copies] distributed every Day: so that if I allow Twenty Readers to every Paper, which I look upon as a modest Computation, I may reckon about Threescore Thousand Disciples in *London* and *Westminster*.' There are no solid grounds for regarding this as a serious overestimate. Two printing shops were needed to keep up daily production, since occasional numbers sold far more than 3000 — perhaps 10,000 exceptionally. More and more book-sellers joined the distribution machine, and more and more copies were dispatched to the provinces. But it was in the capital, and above all in the coffee houses, that this particular cultural revolution took place. As Alexandre Beljame put it, the coffee houses 'provided rallying-points. People met, exchanged opinions, formed groups, gathered number. It was through them, in short, that a public opinion began to evolve, which thereafter had to be reckoned with.'

At this time there were reckoned to be 3000 establishments of this kind in London, and any provincial town with the slightest pretensions had a few of its own. As the century progressed the number seems to have remained fairly steady, though mergers and splits were constantly in process. New enterprises flourished, and useful societies grew up under coffee-house auspices: the Chapter in Paternoster Row was a favourite haunt of the 'conger' or association of booksellers; it was here later in the century that a circulating library was formed, while in 1777 a meeting was held which determined on a new edition of the British Poets and commissioned Samuel Johnson to write his introductory *Lives*. Johnson, of course, was a natural habitué of the coffee houses. The celebrated 'Club' was in some degree an offshoot of tavern conviviality (an older social custom), since its origins lay in the Ivy Lane society. But it came into regular being at a coffee house, the Turk's Head in Gerrard Street, Soho, around 1764; and it was there that Reynolds, Burke, Goldsmith, Gibbon, Sheridan, Adam Smith, Malone, Dr Burney, Garrick and many others gathered along with Johnson. Boswell, who recorded the doings of its members, proudly announced his own election on 30 April 1773, having waited anxiously in the fear he might be blackballed. By 1810 the Club had admitted seventy-six members, of whom fifty-five were authors; the current strength at that date was thirty-three.

Very little of what went on in coffee houses could measure up to the Literary Club — 'a Society as can seldom be found', in Boswell's own words. Nevertheless an astonishing range of activity could be witnessed in these establishments — artistic academies were founded; a Society for the Encouragement of Learning was (rather fruitlessly) set up, in the hope of bypassing the book trade's monopoly power; freemasons formed lodges, while now and then highwaymen paraded themselves in full daylight to bask in the renown of some raffish exploit. The coffee houses were almost exclusively male preserves, but in this they followed rather than created the sexual stereotypes of the age. Those few eighteenth-century ladies who achieved some independence rarely displayed clubbable tendencies; the lone scholar is a more natural product of frustration and repression. There were collections of educated women, notably the bluestockings headed by Mrs Elizabeth Montagu (1720-1800); but it seems reasonable to say that comparatively little female resentment was directed against the clubs and coffee houses. When women articulated their grievances — and they were cautious, not to say longsuffering, in doing so — they did not fix on such matters. The coffee house, indeed, was a remarkably popular institution on all sides. From time to time satirists made an effort to link its existence with nameless depravities; and at the time of the South Sea Bubble the national mood of bitterness caught up these houses in condemining the villainous world of city sharpers. But most of the visible population — literate and polite society — thought well of the coffee house, as it promoted what I have elsewhere called the 'public intimacy' so dear to the Augustans. The unseen masses, of course, had bigger things to worry about.

The main value of the coffee houses to full-length authors, as opposed to journalists, lay in the talk about books which they encouraged. Certainly pamphlets on urgent topics of the day were passed around at Button's, the Bedford or the Smyrna. It is likely that the 'prodigious run' enjoyed by *The Conduct of the Allies*, and reported by Swift to Stella on 28 January 1712, was fostered in this way. Two months after publication, Swift could boast that 'the sixth edition of three thousand ... is sold, and the printer talks of a seventh; eleven thousand of them have been sold' (again we have evidence of confusing terminology; it would be Tooke, not the printer Barber, who authorized a further edition). Tracts concerning the Sacheverell affair sold up to 60,000 each. Bundles of the pamphlets were sent up to the shires by coach or wagon, but it was word-of-mouth currency in London which permitted these high sales. Longer books could scarcely enjoy the same kind of puff in the coffee house, if only because a casual reader could not skim through their contents in between sallies of wit and scandal. Nevertheless, even such massive enterprises as Chambers's *Cyclo-pedia Britannica* (1728) or the six-volume *Biographia Britannica* (1747-66), much plundered by Johnson and Goldsmith, were bruited abroad in such places. Proposals for subscriptions were circulated, and sometimes authors actually sat in a coffee house taking in money for their projects — Thomson was doing this at the Smyrna, in Pall Mall, around 1740. It was here too that a major new form of publicity, newspaper advertising, obtained its widest audience. The first great exponent of book promotion was Edmund Curll, whose book advertisements combine racy narrative, taunts, sneers, ripostes, insults and cunning self-display. He also contrived to mention a few books, which was good value for the two shillings or so a newspaper entry cost (half of that went in tax levied by the Stamp Act of 1712 — an attempt by Bolingbroke to hamper the opposition press). Occasionally Curll's publications seem incidental, but that is part of the sales technique.

Sales figures naturally varied according to a whole range of factors, such as the subject, the price and the mode of publication. A few examples may be cited, although they cannot be termed altogether representative. *Robinson Crusoe*, priced at 5*s.*, had six printings within four months, amounting to some 5000 copies — a large but not unprecedented number. In a more august category, the University Press issued at Oxford in 1704 the famous *History of Rebellion* by Clarendon: 2350 sets were printed, at 15*s.* or 25*s.* for the three volumes. The selling was farmed out to London booksellers: the Oxford press was bad at getting rid of its own products, and 500 copies of the *Coptic Gospels* (1716) were not finally exhausted until 1907! Later in the period Blackstone's *Commentaries* (1765-9) had regular editions of 3000 a time; the proceeds went first to Blackstone and later to booksellers who bought the rights for £4000. Poetry tended to be handled more cautiously: Roberts issued 500 copies of *Persian Eclogues* by the unknown Collins in 1742; like Gray's *Elegy* in 1751 they cost sixpence. Gray's *Odes* (1757), printed by Horace Walpole at Strawberry Hill and published by Dodsley, had an edition of 2000. (On the other hand Isaac Watts's hymns are said, on doubtful evidence, to have had an annual printing of 50,000 — a bestseller indeed!) The collected *Idler* papers of Johnson, reprinted in 1761, were priced at 5*s.* for two duodecimo volumes; 1500 copies were printed, and no further edition was called for until 1767. The great *Dictionary* had a first impression of 2000 copies, and sold up to 5000 in a decade. Its price remained fixed at £4.10*s.* Commercially more successful was Fielding's *Joseph Andrews*, priced at 6*s.* for the two-volume set; three editions (1742-3) ran to over 6000 copies. *Amelia* (1751), though greeted by a muted critical welcome, quickly sold its first impression of 1000 copies, and a second batch of 3000 was put on the market.

Sometimes books were printed at the author's own expense: this was the case with the first instalment of Sterne's *Tristram Shandy* (1759). As usual in such instances, the first printing was small: only 200 copies of the York edition were published. Much to the delight of Sterne, the work gained national and especially metropolitan renown; Dodsley bought the rights to this and succeeding instalments. For later volumes the impression size went up to 5000. As for subscription ventures, they might attract anything from 100 to 2000 buyers. The mean is around 250-300. Sheer size was not the only test: Gay did very well with his *Poems* in 1720, partly because his 365 subscribers were inordinately generous in entering their names for multiple copies. He disposed of 575 copies at 2 guineas each, or at least that was the nominal position — some heavy subscribers, like the Earl of Burlington or the Duke of Chandos with 50 apiece, had no intention of taking up all the copies for which they had paid. Pope's spectacular success on the Homer translation had much to do with the favourable terms he extracted from the bookseller Lintot, as well as the distinction of his list in social terms. The actual totals he obtained (575 subscribers for the *Iliad*, 610 for the *Odyssey*) were not particularly remarkable. Matthew Prior reached 1450 in 1718, while Addison's posthumous works (1721) attracted 980 names. Bishop Burnet got over 1200 for his *History of his own Times* (1724), although the aristocracy pointedly absented themselves for the most part. Thirty years later the undistinguished Aaron Hill, a hanger-on of Pope and Richardson, had his works issued after his death 'for the benefit of the family', and somehow 1400 subscribers were drummed up, including princesses, dukes and duchesses, marquises and earls, peers by the score — not to mention George Frederick Handel and William Hogarth.

As for book prices, they ranged from sixpence or a shilling for a pamphlet of 32 or 64 pages, through 2*s*. 6*d*. or 3*s*. per volume for novels with abut 250 pages in each, to 5*s*. or 6*s*. for a long book (these prices apply to the smaller formats, octavo or duodecimo). Nine volumes making up Warburton's edition of Pope (1751) were priced at 27*s*. the set. Books meant to make something of a splash came out in impressive quarto volumes, and would cost up to a guinea; they would be cheaper if bought 'in sheets', that is unbound. Vast tomes in folio were going out of fashion, but the scholarly public who were not aware of such fads still paid out high sums for mountainous treatises on local history or heraldry. (These often came out by subscription, and seem to have paid their way on small circulations: Wood's fairly sumptuous *Athenae Oxonienses* (1721) attracted less than 200 patrons but it may have been enough.) Books were in fact expensive, though no more so than they were to be for much of the nineteenth century.[1]

For most of the period the output of full-length books stayed pretty well constant, at around 100 per annum; a spectacular rise took place towards the end of the century. These figures are misleading in one respect, however; they take no account of the main traffic of the book trade, which went on among pamphlets, tracts, occasional effusions, versified compliments or condolences, and a whole array of ephemeral materials. All the major publishers who have been mentioned had some share in this flood of print; most of the best-known writers contributed to it. If one consults the checklist of almost any considerable author, it will be found that his *oeuvre* is largely composed of small single items, interspersed from time to time with a full-length collection or *magnum opus*. This applies to Swift, Defoe, Pope, Fielding, Johnson, Goldsmith and Boswell. There are few marked exceptions: Richardson is perhaps one. Writers like Gibbon and Burns whom we think of as producing substantial volumes were busy with smaller books too. Nor were the garrets of Grub Street a haven of idleness: 40 of Pope's Dunces average 39 separate publications each in the *Cambridge Bibliography*, and this certainly understates their activity.

The total number of separate publications during the first full year of the Hanoverian era (1715) comes out at around 75 a month, with a small dip during the summer vacation: in all, not less than

1 For comparative purposes something should be said about the general level of prices. There are difficulties here, in that there was more regional variation than would be found today. Broadly, however, it would be fair to assert that prices remained amazingly stable for the first sixty years of the eighteenth century. In fact food was cheaper in 1750 than it had been in 1700; not until the last quarter of the century were the high cereal prices of the 1690s reached again. Beef cost around 3*d.* a pound, mutton 2*d.* A few commodities were getting steadily less expensive: tea, once a luxury at £3 a pound, came down to a quarter or less of that amount. Even the choicer brands of green tea were as little as 8*d.* an ounce late in this period. A labouring family could probably make do on 10*s.* a week, of which the cost of cereals made up the greater proportion.

Wages for adult working males stood at around 10*s.* per week, although labourers in London could get half as much again. (These rates, too, climbed only slowly as the century progressed.) Skilled craftsmen might earn £1 a week, with London building masons the most favourably treated; the traditional wage for a journeyman printer was a guinea. Agricultural labour was always less well paid than unskilled work in industry, which by 1770 occupied an increasing number of

700 items in the year, mostly pamphlets. (For 1730 the total was very similar — around 710.) James Roberts by himself was involved in over 100 works, and that was a rate he maintained for the next two decades. In 1715 Baker (who published Defoe), Morphew (who published Swift), Lintot (who published Pope) and Mrs Burleigh (who published Steele) were all responsible for 40 or more items. Curll probably had a share, open or concealed, in 80 publications. By contrast the Oxford University Press was a small operation: 10 substantial books annually was as much as it generally managed, and even with proclamations and funeral programmes the tally was only 20 in 1715. But London publishing was a large-scale enterprise, and anyone who glances through the monthly lists appended to the *Gentleman's Magazine* will easily discover that the flow went on unimpeded: the total for 1750 is just under 500 items, with a peak of 78 in March. The economic viability of the trade hinged to a great extent on these submerged ephemera.

I have kept until last, among these conditions of authorship and book production, the thing that mattered most to writers: the actual rewards they obtained. Once again it is foolish to attempt very general statements: payments might be high or low according to a cluster of variables, including the branch of literature, the state of the market, the reputation of the author, the solvency of the bookseller or the caprices of the public. Particular authors knew moments of sudden grandeur or decadence: Steele, after an up-and-down career, made £1000 from a single play. But if we

both sexes. Women and children in the poorer classes were lucky to earn more than 2s. weekly. An average family income in 1750 might have reached £40 per annum. As for middle-class occupations, there would be a range from £50 for small tradesmen and shopkeepers to £300 for merchants in a large way of business. It would have been difficult to maintain serious pretensions as a gentleman with an income below £250 (though some attempted it); while the landowning classes looked for a figure more like £500 as a minimum. It might be added that a substantial farmhouse could be built for as little as £250, and cottages for less than £50. The poor could rent a hovel for £2 per year; large houses in fashionable parts of London commanded a hundred times as much. The really grand mansions (Blenheim — built at public expense; Wentworth Woodhouse; Eastbury; Houghton; Burley on the Hill) cost sums which would cause an owner to blanch even today, without making adjustment for present-day values. Robert Walpole spent £1200 (about the same as his annual wine bill) on the *trimmings* of a single bed; the Duke of Chandos had an annual wage bill which ran into four figures. £1 in 1750 was worth about £15 or $25 at 1975 prices, but of course the disparity mounts annually.

exclude for the moment authors publishing their own books, we can get a rough picture of the value booksellers put on individual works: first, from the sum paid for copyright, and, second, from the price which a share in the rights subsequently commanded. Again it should be stressed that the cases cited are not in every way representative: they are given for the sake of concrete document-ation on a topic where imprecision is useless and irritating.

We have few details for either Swift or Defoe, but Pope's earnings are more fully accessible. For his early poems he never received more than £30 or so, and the original version of *The Rape of the Lock* brought him just £7. For the revised poem he was still paid only £15, though it sold 3000 copies in four days. Things began to improve with the *Iliad* translation and then his sumptuous collected works in 1717. Ultimately, his two versions of Homer earned him by Johnson's calculations a matter of £11,000. His edition of Shakespeare (1725) was mounted for the benefit of its publisher, Tonson, and elicited a disappointing body of subscribers: none the less, Pope made £200 on it. Thereafter Pope could exact the best terms from any bookseller, confident in his appeal to the market: the letters began to appear in editions of up to 4000 at a time. While we do not have all the figures, we can be sure that he enjoyed a steady income from authorship throughout the 1730s — he even *leased* the rights of the *Essay on Man* for one year, in return for a consideration of £200. The lowest forms of hack writing were by comparison meagrely rewarded: Lintot and Tonson would pay a matter of 10 guineas for long indexes to a complicated book, while the going rate for verse translations was 1½ *d.* a line — about one-fiftieth of what Pope earned by his Homer. As stated, Pope made only a little over £200 for his edition of Shakespeare, for which the profits went mainly to Tonson; the rival edition by a leading dunce, Theobald, was three times as remunerative. Poor Rowe had earned only £35 for *his* Shakespeare in 1709.

Dramatists generally profited less from the sale of copyright (they were paid separately for theatrical performances); Rowe got £75 for *Lady Jane Grey* (1715) and Colley Cibber 100 guineas for *The Non-Juror* (1717), but the average remuneration was much lower, around £20. The major exception in the first part of the century is Gay. He had been obtaining sums of the order of £25 to £50 for his early poems. There are conflicting stories about his long-forgotten tragedy *The Captives* (1724), one suggesting that Gay gave 30 guineas from his own pocket to have it survive six nights and so bring the author a benefit night, the other asserting that Gay made £1000. But we do know that *The Beggar's Opera* (1728) yielded almost £700 in theatrical returns and another 90 guineas for its copyright (this last jointly with the *Fables*, an excellent bargain for the publisher). A sequel, *Polly* (1729), was banned from the stage, but a private subscription mounted by the Duchess of Queensberry and others totalled £1200. Gay had the play printed by William Bowyer at his own expense; more than 10,000 copies were struck off in the first year, not to mention à whole series of piracies. Exceptional popularity or notoriety could transform the condition of a struggling professional author in a short space of time.

In the next generation Fielding did as well as anyone, with a steady rise in his returns: less than £200 for *Joseph Andrews*, despite its great popularity, then £600 for *Tom Jones* (to which the grateful Millar added a further £100), and finally 800 guineas for *Amelia* — more, some thought, than it was prudent for the publisher to give. Fielding, too, entered the subscription market: his *Miscellanies* (1743) attracted 425 names, some of great eminence. Less fortunate was John Cleland, whose notorious *Memoirs* of Fanny Hill have become a modern bestseller. But in 1749 it was thought worth printing only 750 sets (there were two volumes at 6s. the set), and Cleland received a bare 20 guineas. He had recently been in the Fleet Prison for a debt of something like £800 — and, to add insult to injury, he was hauled before the Secretary of State and possibly even imprisoned for composing such a 'vile' work of pornography. Curll had known better how to make a profit from obscenity and scandal.

A much greater figure, Samuel Johnson, provides more cheerful evidence. He was paid 10 guineas for *London* (1737); it was sold at a shilling and did exceedingly well. But a decade later, when he was no longer obscure and ought to have been reaping the profits, *The Vanity of Human Wishes* yielded no more than 15 guineas. Even the great *Dictionary*, from which he made, so Boswell tells us, £1575, was by no stretch of the imagination easy money; the 'expense of amanuenses and paper, and other articles' had to be deducted, and in all the work took him eight years. Not unexpectedly, 'he had spent, during the progress of the work, the money for which he had contracted to write his Dictionary.' *Rasselas* earned him £100 from Dodsley, with £25 for a revision. We cannot be too positive about the edition of Shakespeare, because Johnson spent the subscribers' money and lost their names. But for the *Lives of the Poets* he asked 200 guineas and was paid 300: informed observers assure us that he could have held out for much more. Meanwhile Goldsmith was making 20 guineas for *The Traveller* (1764), and 100 for *The Deserted Village* (1770): the first was reasonable payment, the second very good going. A play *The Good-Natur'd Man* earned him £150; the novel (a short one), *The Vicar of Wakefield* (1766), 60 guineas, though there was some difficulty in getting booksellers to buy the three shares in the copyright. Unfortunately Goldsmith had to dispose of his popular comedy *She Stoops to Conquer* (1773) in settlement of a debt to his publisher Newbery; it sold 4000 copies within three days. (By way of compensation Goldsmith obtained £500 from three benefit per-formances.) Years earlier Newbery had paid him a retainer of £100 per annum to write his twice-weekly Chinese Letters for the *Public Ledger*. But his highest payments, as with Smollett, tended to reward what now seem the least interesting ventures — compil-ations, secondhand history, potted biography, popular abstracts, each of which might command an advance of up to £500.

History was indeed one of the most remunerative modes of writing (it was the most popular species of literature, said Gibbon, since it could 'adapt itself to the highest or the lowest capacity'). In the end David Hume made a large sum from his strange backward-marching *History of England* (1754-62), though the first volume had met with a poor reception. 'Mr Millar told me', Hume wrote, 'that in a twelvemonth he sold only forty-five copies of it. I scarcely, indeed, heard of one man in the three kingdoms, considerable for rank and learning, that could endure the book.' Previously, in 1739, Hume had seen another work fall dead from the press. This was his now famous *Treatise of Human Nature*, for which a publisher unwisely gave £50, a sum he can never have recouped. Other less eminent writers made a good thing of historical compil-ation. Robert Henry was one, with his six-volume series (1771-93); the radical Catherine Macaulay, with her eight volumes (1763-83), another. Smollett's *Complete History of England* (1757-8) made him £2000 in little over a year. It was subsequently reissued in weekly parts with energetic promotion and proved exceedingly profitable to the trade. A greater historian, Edward Gibbon, was able to arrange specially favourable terms from Strahan and Cadell. He took two-thirds of the profits earned by the *Decline and Fall*, after expenses and retailers' discount had been met. Most of the six volumes had several reprints in Gibbon's lifetime, and each time he stood to gain a considerable sum. His memoirs are too reticent to put a vulgar figure on his earnings, but they must have run into several thousands of pounds. His contemporary William Robertson, we do know, received £4500 for his study of *Charles V* (1769). I have tipped only the most tentative toe into this work, which enjoyed ten editions by 1800, but it is safe to say that no publisher today would pay such a sum for it, even though the purchasing power of one pound was at least fifteen times its current value. A final sum which merits quotation is the payment of £500 made by Strahan and Cadell to Adam Smith, for the first edition of his *Wealth of Nations* (1776); two quarto volumes were priced at £1.16s. Two years later Smith took half the profits of a second edition. Publishers are commonly depicted in literature as rogues or charlatans; it is pleasant to observe that men like Strahan did as much giving as taking, and contributed significantly to some of the great moments in Western civilization. A midwife for the muse of Hume, Johnson, Gibbon and Smith deserves to be remembered: the gynaecology of genius is an art we appear to be losing.

The literary forms

The period under review saw a fundamental reversal of literary alliances. At its beginning writers inherited, more or less untouched, a long tradition of grading various genres in a set hierarchy. There was an elaborate theoretical apparatus to justify this pecking-order, as there was indeed for most ranking systems. Much critical ink was spilled in an effort to preserve the purity of breeding in each given form. In 1711 John Dennis could take it for granted, in writing to *The Spectator*, that all good judges deplored tragicomedy. Half a century later Samuel Johnson, wanting to defend Shakespeare's use of seriousness and levity within a single play, was obliged to adopt a cautious tone: 'That this is a practice contrary to the rules of criticism will be readily allowed; but there is always an appeal open from criticism to nature.' Increasingly the public was inclined to sustain this appeal, and the doctrine of kinds grew thinner and more riddled with exceptions. Hybrid forms prospered (mock-heroic, the 'town eclogue', and so on); arguably these honoured the standard classification in the breach, but there were also new forms like secret history — a kind of scandalous political allegory — and the night-piece.

There were two great blows to the system during the period. The first was negative. Traditionally two master genres dominated the scene: epic, at the very top, and tragedy, the most noble of dramatic narratives. Now the Augustans were no good at writing either genre, and this was as obvious to them as it is to us — although not so easy to admit. They went on trying; Nicholas Rowe achieved a few passable tragedies, George Lillo and John Home pleased their contemporaries (less so posterity), and Shakespeare was trained to adopt a number of the most approved Augustan attitudes. It was the same with epic; all the critics went on reiterating the pre-eminence of this form, and the ambition to produce the definitive English epic died remarkably hard. Spenser, even Milton, could be said to have constituted English Renaissance Homers, but where was our Virgil? Dryden and Pope partially sublimated their urges by translating the *Aeneid*, the *Iliad* and the *Odyssey*; but even then Pope was not really appeased in his heart, and went on making desultory plans for a 'Brutus' poem. Unfortunately other people's schemes got as far as the printed page, with the result that epics on this legend continued to appear. (Sometimes the patriotic theme was diverted into drama: Thomson and David Mallett wrote a masque called *Alfred* (1740), Richard Glover a *Boadicia* (1753), Dr John 'Estimate' Brown an *Athelstan* (1756), William Mason a *Caractacus* (1759) — often there is some irrecoverable political point in it all.) The most striking expression of the impulse, however, can be found in the work of Sir Richard Blackmore (1653-1729). He was a medical man, and acquired his knighthood for ministrations to William III. His publications on medical topics were prolific: as Johnson put it in *The Lives of the Poets*, 'I know not whether I can enumerate all the treatises by which he has endeavoured to diffuse the art of healing; for there is scarcely any distemper, of dreadful name, which he has not taught the reader how to oppose.' Spleen, that recurrent eighteenth-century disorder (see below, p.188), is the subject of more than one essay. But to contemporaries he was best known for the work of his left hand, that is his series of epics beginning with *Prince Arthur* (1695), *King Arthur* (1697) and *Alfred* (1723). They are equipped, as all well-bred epics then were, with decent critical theorizing to hide their nakedness. As poetry they are not quite bad enough to be unreadable, but when read not quite good enough to enjoy. The wits took against Blackmore with relish, and he became the exemplar of bad poetry for a long time. This must have had a subliminal effect on the standing of epic itself.

The other great shift came with the rise of the upstart novel. At first selfconscious and defensive, it required the creative and critical intelligence of Fielding to overcome its low origins. The 'comic epic in prose', as *Joseph Andrews* was described, was yet another mixed marriage: Fielding's purpose in coining the phrase is to allot the novel a tiny hold (however precarious and jokey) on the slopes of Parnassus. Modern critics have seen the principal current of energy from the worn-out epic as flowing into the novel, in books like *Robinson Crusoe*, *Tom Jones* and *Tristram Shandy*: the comparable leakage from tragedy would go into *Clarissa* above all. This is a perfectly sensible way of reading the literary history of the period, though we should look for spillage from epic in other areas — discursive poetry (*The Seasons* and *Liberty*, by Thomson; Young's *Night Thoughts*; Cowper's *Task*), history (*The Decline and Fall of the Roman Empire*, but also in some degree Hume's *History*), and fitfully elsewhere (Defoe's *Tour* of Britain; Johnson's *Journey to the Western Islands of Scotland*; unquestionably Boswell's *Life of Johnson*). It is here, not in the strutting Brutiads, that eighteenth-century England confronted its destiny and expressed its deepest ideals.

The recognized poetic genres, at a level less exalted, included fables; verse epistles, generally on a Horatian model; formal satire; numerous versions of pastoral (located anywhere from the sea-bed to the Fleet Ditch); translation and imitation of the classics; elegy; commemorative poems on public occasions like a battle or a royal birthday (the Poet Laureate was required to supply these, but he had no monopoly, and hosts of volunteer laureates gave verbose competition); verse of a congratulatory or condoling order; epitaphs, a well-trodden path throughout the period; dialogues in verse; epigrams; instructional poems on the art of cooking or walling the streets or sugar manufacture; treatises on the subject of poetics, like Pope's *Essay on Criticism*; along with many more. Few of these kinds demand any special comment, except to note how distinct and well-established they were — imitation of a classical author, for example, was conducted along broadly agreed lines. It is this fact, as well as temperamental affinity, which allies Johnson's *London* and *Vanity of Human Wishes* to the satires and epistles of Pope. More interesting is the evolution of some genuinely new forms. The topographic poem, blending natural description, local history and moral-cum-political reflection, grew far beyond its straggly roots in Virgil's *Georgics*. It took real shape with Denham's *Cooper's Hill* (dating from the 1640s), and was given added scope in Pope's *Windsor Forest* (1713). There are offshoots, like the 'country-house' poem celebrating a particular estate and the 'hill-top' poem in which the writer describes the scenery, mythology and geography of a given area, as it is visible from a high vantage point. Again most of these elements are discernible in *The Seasons*, an omnium gatherum of poetic techniques whose blurring of the separate kinds led both Swift and Johnson to mistake its variety for formlessness.

As for the lyric strain, this goes its quiet, agreeable and mostly undistinguished way. There are a few brilliant love poems by Prior, in a tougher-minded vein than that of the Cavalier poets. But until Burns this was not an area in which eighteenth-century poets excelled. Songs were written to inject moments of pathos into rumbustious plays; rollicking choruses and jovial catches were produced, and some like 'The Roast Beef of England' survive; ballads were common, though often satiric in drift; and the elegies sometimes abandoned classical lament for direct feeling. But it was probably in the ode that eighteenth-century writers were most ready to let down their hair, or if that is an anachronism we might say to loosen their habitual stays. For a variety of reasons it was felt that odes permitted, even sanctioned, a relaxation of discipline in subject matter, in verbal decorum and in metrics. The 'wilder' themes were commonly allocated to Pindaric treatment, with the use of garish imagery and fantastically oversized events. Gray's *Bard* and *Progress of Poesy* (1757) were as puzzling to readers as his *Elegy* (1751) had been comfortably familiar in its strategies. Today neither of the odes appears notably disordered, but in the Augustan context they were as violent and dithyrambic as you could go. Some odes were written in stricter (or more obviously strict) measures, notably those of Collins. Few poets altogether abjured the form, whatever use they had for it; they gave an opportunity for heightened language and stanzaic embellishment, poetic attributes much to the taste of many writers.

All the same it was in satiric modes that the highest proportion of good verse was written. Mock-heroic, I have suggested, prospered both as it drew on the hierarchy of kinds and as it subverted this. It enjoyed a considerable boost at the very beginning of the period with Samuel Garth's *Dispensary* (1699), much tinkered with for the rest of Garth's lifetime — he died in 1719 — and popular longer than that. Pope of course exploited its highest possibilities, both in *The Rape of the Lock* (1711; 1714) and in *The Dunciad* (1728; 1743). In his hands mock-heroic ceased to be a simple misapplication of high heroic standards to a banal present-day world; it became the framework for a complex interaction of disparate ideas and values, where the present and the past, the close and the distant, the lofty and the sordid, cross and recross in a bright kaleidoscope of implication. Thereafter the form remained at the centre of literary consciousness; it turns up in prose and drama as well as verse (*The Battle of the Books, Tom Jones, The Tragedy of Tragedies*) and is always liable to crop up, look where you will — Christopher Smart, Horace Walpole, Cowper. There were shabbier cousins — burlesque, travesty, Hudibrastics — and masters of the informal style like Swift, Prior and Burns employ such deflating idiom to superb comic effect. Formal satire was perhaps less successfully prosecuted, although Charles Churchill wrote some slashing examples in the early 1760s. Better results were achieved when a direct model — Juvenal, Persius or Horace most commonly — was used as the host for the satiric parasite. The poets were happiest when they had a point of departure in earlier literature.

Most of these genres, like mock-heroic or epigram, were defined by tone, attitude and treatment. A limited number of forms, however, evolved by reference to the use of particular subject matter. One such mode was the nocturnal, generally called at this period the 'night-piece'. The first, and one of the best, of poems in this kind was *A Nocturnal Reverie* (1713), a precisely observed sketch by Anne Finch, Countess of Winchilsea (1661-1720) — the outstanding woman poet of her generation. The vein was continued by Thomas Parnell (1679-1718), a member of the Scriblerus circle: among his poems edited (and occasionally doctored) by Pope in 1722 was the famous *Night-Piece on Death*. The slight strain of morbidity in Parnell was to grow more prominent in later nocturnals, after the rise of the so-called Graveyard school. Blood, charnel-houses and ruined castles abound, as in the horror movie of today. These gothic properties are most densely packed in a poem by Robert Blair (1699-1746) entitled simply *The Grave* (1743); but they occur in weaker solutions elsewhere, e.g. Young's *Night Thoughts*, Gray's *Elegy*, and even Collins's exquisite *Ode to Evening* (1747), with its 'dreary Dells' and 'religious Gleams'. Behind most of these poems lies a recollection of *Il Penseroso*; the mood is reinforced by an onset of the English malady, discussed by G.S. Rousseau later in this book (p.180). One of the fullest evocations of this melancholia is found, inevitably, in Thomson — specifically, in 'Autumn' (lines 1004 ff.), since this was the season traditionally associated with contemplative states:

> Oh! bear me then to vast embowering shades,
> To twilight groves, and visionary vales,
> To weeping grottoes, and prophetic glooms;
> Where angel forms athwart the solemn dusk,
> Tremendous, sweep, or seem to sweep along;
> And voices more than human, through the void,
> Deep-sounding, seize the enthusiastic ear.

Prophetic glooms, indeed: for here the taste for melancholy joins the new cult of the sublime, and we hear the accents of the mid-eighteenth century in their purest form.

Not altogether unrelated is a kind that might be described as the poetry of philosophic travel. An important early example is provided by the most substantial work Richard Savage ever produced to back up his lurid life-history as the archetypal bohemian poet. This was *The Wanderer* (1729), a work in five cantos, which makes striking use of some favourite ideas of the period. There is a 'madding Maze of *Spleen*'; a number of Spenserian caves and grottoes; images of imprisonment; macabre and violent scenes. At the centre of the design is a lonely bard, perhaps based in part on Parnell's *Hermit* of seven years earlier, but shading into the romantic notion of a divinely inspired prophet. This figure was developed by Gray in *The Bard*, by Collins's *Ode on the Poetical Character* (1746) and by Joseph Warton's *Enthusiast* (1744). There is even — as one might have guessed — an obscure druid in Thomson who performs the same role of inspiration, benevolence and creativity. However, there is a more specialized line of development. This runs through Mallet's *Excursion* (1728), *The Wanderer* again, Thomson's *Liberty* (1735-6) and Goldsmith's *Traveller*. In these poems and others resembling them, the pattern is that of a wide 'prospect of society', with the observer surveying different nations or regions and encountering different versions of civilization as he goes. There are remnants of this technique as late as Cowper's *Task* (1785), though domesticity and didacticism have largely supplanted the visionary excitement of earlier examples.

In all these kinds, as Sutherland has memorably put it, the Augustans 'wrote poems' where the romantics 'wrote poetry'. Crucial to their artistic purposes was a keen sense of the fitness of a particular mode to the subject matter with which it had to deal. Most of the kinds, excluding the ode, were practised either in blank verse or in heroic couplets. The former, in eighteenth-century hands, often seems to us to encourage bad habits: laborious Miltonic effects, unconscious echoes of Shakespeare, garrulity, pomposity. Even the better practitioners, like Thomson, Akenside and Cowper, sometimes fall into this windy manner. It is quite different with the couplet, which was raised by a succession of masters to a peak of artistic resourcefulness. As we have seen, the original credit for refining verse was bestowed on Denham and Waller; Dryden was the first great exponent, and after him Prior, Pope, Johnson, Churchill, Goldsmith and Crabbe showed how wit could live with feeling, brevity with dense implication, balance with flexibility, elegance with power. The aim was to attain that '*graceful* and *dignify'd* Simplicity' sought by Pope in translating Homer, where 'Simplicity is the Mean between Ostentation and Rusticity'. The Augustans did not succeed in all their quests, but the couplet was equal to the tasks laid on it.

The media of expression in prose were still more varied. Many of them lay outside what we should regard as 'creative' territory, for it was characteristic of the age to produce much of its best work in the marginal areas of literature. This applies to the most widely practised and — to the average citizen — most prominent mode of discourse in prose, that is the sermon. Not merely were men and women exposed to orations every Sunday (and the occasion might go on for two or three hours); large numbers of sermons were published separately, and collected volumes of the famous preachers appeared year after year. Some considerable writers added to this store: Swift, Berkeley, Wesley, Sterne. Especially at the start of the period, the masters of pulpit oratory exerted a profound influence on prose style. The most admired of all was probably John Tillotson (1630-94); his unpublished sermons became the object of eager bidding after his death. As Macaulay remarks, the 2500 guineas paid for their copyright was an 'almost incredible sum' when the coinage was debased and when Dryden was thought to have been 'splendidly remunerated' by the £1300 he obtained for his Virgil. Tillotson's 250 sermons became an unrivalled model of English eloquence; at one Cambridge college 'the entire religious side of the second collegiate year was devoted to [their] study.'

Political exhortation was almost as widespread as its theological counterpart. Many leading writers worked in this branch of litera- ture, with Defoe, Fielding, Smollett, Johnson and Sheridan among the most regular exponents: perhaps only Swift and Burke exerted their fullest genius on political subjects, despite that. As we have already seen, the eighteenth-century development in journalism afforded many new opportunities to the literary profession. Review- ing, that perpetual standby of modern authors, became an available possibility during this era. More surprising to us today is the tremendous vogue for books of travel. As well as the innumerable single works in the field there were well-supported collections, of which the most famous is *A Collection of Voyages and Travels*, published by Awnsham and John Churchill (1704 and many subsequent editions). Voyages round the world, as by Anson and Byron, formed one category; so did South Sea journeys, given a great fillip by Captain Cook, and later Australasian exploring. There were also many narratives of the North-West Passage. Perhaps no one in the century ever wrote more absorbingly than Captain William Dampier (1652-1715), a privateer rather than explorer, whose *Voyages* were coming out around the turn of the eighteenth century. Defoe, as an earnest plagiarist, and Swift, as a parodist, were to make use of these popular eye-witness accounts. Inland travels became another source of literary copy, especially after the rise of picturesque tourism. Again it is an earlier work, Defoe's *Tour through the Whole Island of Great Britain*, which most graphically captures the mood of the age. The first edition (1724-6) was followed by seven others in fifty years, many of them re-edited by Samuel Richardson.

A genre more favoured than we might suppose was the art of biography. It is true that nothing approaches Boswell's *Life of Johnson* (1791), the single work which most completely renders this century to us. Boswell is more comprehensive in research, more skilled in reporting, more perceptive in judgement, more daring in coverage, than any predecessor. But he learnt much from the subject of his own book: Johnson's *Life of Savage* (1744) had shown that intimate knowledge and sympathetic understanding of psychological states could bring a human being to life inside a biographic framework. At the same time there were unwieldy collections of lives — the age was fond of large books — and the flood of instant compilations when eminent persons expired. Curll's biographies, Dr Arbuthnot ruefully observed, constituted a new terror of death. They generally ran to about 120 pages, and appeared within four to eight weeks of the subject's death. Adjoining territory was occupied by the craft of historiography, a form then thought of as intensely literary and philosophical, with no nonsense about quantification or 'research'. This was an activity that appealed both to the mass market and to a specialized scholarly audience. Popular histories of England appeared at regular intervals, fifteen at least during the period, and behind the towering figures — Hume, Robertson, Gibbon — stood a mass of diminutive scribblers. Twelve of the hacks satirized in *The Dunciad*, if not more, had composed works of history, and several were best known for this literary offence. All educated people had read voluminously on the subject; at a very rough guess, one might estimate that Laurence Sterne (whose work is often seen as a critique of the novel to date) had read twenty times more books of history than of fiction.

However, two more obviously artistic modes came to dominate endeavour during the eighteenth century. These were the moral essay and the novel. Essays were known in antiquity, and had enjoyed distinguished exponents in the Renaissance: Montaigne and Bacon remained formidable intellectual influences. At the end of the seventeenth century there had been the solemn musings of Sir William Temple, Swift's mentor — agreeable but low in pressure. Everything changed in the new century, with the growth of periodical journalism. Defoe's *Review* (1704-13) is a remarkable feat of industry, and its subject matter (anything from foreign policy to insolvency and the theatre) brings out surprising delicacy of touch in its author. However, the big step forward came with the innovations of Steele and Addison, first in the *Tatler* (1709-11) and then in the *Spectator* (1711-12). The two sides of a single sheet nicely conformed to the attention-span of an average reader; there was generally room for about 1400 words, assuming the usual number of around eight advertisements. People were ready to be amused, instructed and gently civilized; and reformation of manners was achieved without hectoring or shrillness. The finest papers are mostly the work of Addison. Disregarding the critical numbers, to which I shall return presently, the outstanding issues include *Tatler*, No. 155, on the self-important newsmonger known as the 'political upholsterer'; several witty *Spectator* papers on opera, notably Nos 5 and 13; the sonorous passage concluding *The Spectator*, No. 26, on Westminster Abbey; and the various pictures of Sir Roger de Coverly in the country. The single issue which best illustrates Addison's ideas and techniques, out of 250 numbers which he wrote, is *The Spectator*, No. 69 (19 May 1711), a visit to the Royal Exchange which becomes a paeon to mercantile life; it is one of the great set-pieces of Augustan eloquence.

The later journals conducted by Addison and Steele, separately or in concert, have less to offer, and it is in directly political papers that the form develops. Writers like Bolingbroke, Fielding, Lady Mary Wortley Montagu and Lord Chesterfield contributed to the flood of polemic in the 1730s, when constitutional issues were dissected in the weekly press and social theory was mooted in newspaper columns. The moral essay *per se* regained momentum in the middle of the century, with Johnson's stately *Rambler* (1750-2) and then his more relaxed *Idler* (1758-60). John Hawkesworth's *Adventurer* (1752-4) was another journal for which Johnson wrote a number of papers; along with Edward Moore's *World* (1753-6) and George Colman's *Connoisseur* (1754-6), it maintained something of the Addisonian irony and well-bred tolerance. The last distinguished member of this species is *The Citizen of the World* (collected 1762), in which Goldsmith brought an episodic, quasi-fictional interest to his series of papers. Thereafter, though essays were frequently republished in large assemblages, the trick was lost; the form lay low again, until Hazlitt, Charles Lamb and De Quincey gave it a new personal flavouring in the Romantic period.

Literary criticism is now, for our sins, one of the most universal forms, and one of the most unstoppable cultural tendencies. Before Rymer, it used to be said, critics were as rare in England as wolves. Thomas Rymer (1641-1713) did most of his worst work in the last decade of the seventeenth century; his vigorous prose gives a certain impression of authority to judgements of frenetic prejudice on Shakespeare and other issues. He was followed by John Dennis (1657-1734) in the emphasis laid on 'poetic justice', that is the need to make plots enact the righteous dispensation of providence. Both Rymer and Dennis have their modern admirers, and they are assuredly spirited critics who make present-day academic writing seem a pale thing indeed. However, the finest criticism in the generation after Dryden was provided not in a set treatise, such as Dennis would launch upon the world from time to time, but in a series of numbers of *The Spectator*. It was Addison's achievement to elaborate the distinction betwen true and false wit (Nos 58-63); to help initiate the ballad revival (No. 70); to write the most intelligent critique yet seen on *Paradise Lost* (eighteen Saturday papers); and above all to celebrate the pleasures of the imagination (Nos 411-21), a moment of destiny in aesthetic theory. From here derived most eighteenth-century discussion of 'taste' — the great watchword in decades to come — even if the critic is likely to pay obsequious acknowledgement to the showy ideas of Shaftesbury.

The main line of criticism is carried on by Dr Johnson, with his sturdy intelligence, his massive (though harumscarum) body of learning, his deep penetration into the psychology of literary response. Other critics are perhaps truly rhetoricians in disguise; literary history takes strong roots as the period wears on, and fashions among creative writers (Spenserian imitation; ballads; the gothic) have their analogues — sometimes their inspiration — in critical discourse. Thomas Percy's *Reliques of Ancient English Poetry* (1765) offered a semi-scholarly medievalism; Richard Hurd's *Letters on Chivalry and Romance* (1762) sabotaged the inmost structures of the classical fortress; Celtic, Norse and oriental models were suddenly in favour. In general the creative results, as in Macpherson's *Ossian* and Chatterton's Rowley poems, were happiest when the authenticity was least. The cult of sublimity evoked some remarkable theorizing by Burke but second-class writing for the most part. However, it is not the duty of criticism to supply the defects of contemporary creative art.

The rise of the novel has been much debated; but what was most remarkable was the intrinsic excellence so quickly attained in this form. Before 1719 English readers could encounter varieties of European fiction: *Don Quixote*, always the biggest single influence, in the lively translation by Motteux (1700-3); *The Comical Works of Quevedo* (1707), including *La Vida del Buscón*; Rabelais; French seventeenth-century romance; the *Letters of a Portuguese Nun*, translated by Sir Roger L'Estrange out of French (1678), and frequently reprinted; while Lesage was just appearing in English. That is an interesting body of writing, but nothing in it prepares us for Defoe. With *Robinson Crusoe* the pleasures of the adventure story are wedded to those of the moral fable. An inward quest propels the external narrative; we share Crusoe's self-communing exile, and we are as close to his dreams, visions and delusions as we are to his stockade and his cave. Similarly in *Moll Flanders*, an uncertain but marvellously vivid presentation of the heroine's tough psychology. Even in *A Journal of the Plague Year*, now often read as the epic of a city under siege, it is the saddler H.F. whose consciousness controls the angle of observation. Now it is not that Defoe was the first writer to render individual states of mind; as we have been told often enough in recent years, the Puritan spiritual autobiography had devised narrative means to just this end. No: what Defoe did was to entwine this spiritual course in the secular trammels of everyday living. He found a style which could render the excitement of diurnal experience; he is a dramatist of the inner struggles of social man.

That description could be applied to Samuel Richardson, though society here is more devious in its pressures. Instead of economic wellbeing, Richardson uses sex as a metaphor of personal survival. For Pamela, it is technical 'purity' which has to be guarded if the fulfilment of marriage is to be attained; for Clarissa, her very identity is in question when rape threatens. The shut-off atmosphere engendered by the fragile contact of letters brilliantly conveys this existential clash. (*Pamela* and *Clarissa* are the trail of a comet: over a thousand epistolary fictions in the Augustan age.) By contrast Fielding uses a wide scene for his action, together with an expansive narrative manner and a whole range of literary reflectors (parody, allusion, travesty) to throw the story into relief. *Tom Jones* is about as symmetrical in construction as a book can be without needing to be wound up by the reader. Defoe and Richardson were somewhat untutored pioneers; Fielding affords the novel the protection and good name of an established genre.

A similar contrast could be drawn between Smollett, businesslike and sometimes brutal, galumphing about the country, and Sterne, tremulous, self-aware and mercurial. *Humphrey Clinker* shows the novel in confident touch with everyday reality, its characters seeing sights and making a show of themselves as they go. *Tristram Shandy* by comparison is going nowhere: the essential traffic passes between the narrator and ourselves as readers. Things do happen to the hero, but a bigger drama altogether surrounds Tristram's efforts to apprise us of these — efforts that are subverted by digressions, distractions, discontinuities. The warm comedy that suffuses the book proceeds mainly from this losing struggle with the means of communication. Words, ideas, memories and chapters arrive at the wrong moment; it is as though a Feydeau farce were taking place in the narrator's head.

The books that are regularly collected as 'shorter fiction' provide a different sort of enjoyment. Johnson's *Rasselas* (1759) is morally deep but to some tastes fictionally rather leaden. Horace Walpole's *Castle of Otranto* (1764) has the dubious distinction of instigating the minor form of gothic fiction; it is as well that this historical interest remains, because the novel itself is outright hokum. William Beckford's *Vathek* (1786), originally in French, exercised a great power over the Romantic mind and is indeed an enjoyable work with touches of Hollywood silliness. Henry Mackenzie's *Man of Feeling* (1771) has some importance in the history of taste, for its portrayal of the sentimentalist hero, but again it marks no particular advance in the technique of the novel. If we exclude the Rousseau-esque and radical novels popular at the end of the century (Godwin's *Caleb Williams*, 1794, is the best known), then there remain the gentle social comedies of Fanny Burney and the undeniable, if fragile, charm of *The Vicar of Wakefield* (1766). The great masters had done so much, so quickly, within half a century of the novel's emergence; it was only with Scott and Jane Austen that any further expressive advance occurred.

Finally, drama: if it was not a period of the highest creative achievement, at least the theatres of Georgian England were busy and reasonably prosperous. The Licensing Act of 1737 put a brake on political satire, but not much else. Heroic tragedy soon fizzled out at the beginning of the century, and the 'she-tragedies' of Nicholas Rowe (1674-1718) substitute an introspective poetry for the rant and rhetoric. George Lillo (1693-1739) extended the range of character to include a higher proportion of ordinary men and women; he manages the odd moment of genuine pathos. Things were more auspicious in the comic field. Few are now attracted to sentimental comedy, whether early (Steele, incongruously) or late (Hugh Kelly), based as it is on virtuous suffering, hapless misunderstandings and exaggerated scruples. But there is still a huge amount of enjoyment to be obtained from the plays of Fielding, Goldsmith and Sheridan. *The School for Scandal* (1777) is deeply implicated in eighteenth-century thought — as for example the merits of spontaneous impulse against those of prudence — but it is above all a brilliant stage play, full of colour, wit and movement. It was an age of remarkable impresarios, headed by Colley Cibber (1671-1757), Poet Laureate and Pope's king of the dunces; John Rich (?1692-1761), who specialized in exotic entertainments; David Garrick (1717-79), a great actor and an important theatrical manager; and George Colman (1732-94), dramatist and playhouse director. Literary intellectuals affected to see the rise of these showmen as destructive of serious drama, but the evidence will not support this view unambiguously. Apart from provincial centres like Bath, Bristol and York, the London stage boasted two or three major theatres continuously with a succession of fringe institutions, like the Little Theatre in the Haymarket where Fielding's company operated. Drury Lane, Covent Garden and the King's opera house, Haymarket, stood at the centre of theatrical life. They were mostly well administered, though finances were always short and subscription campaigns did not often prosper: opera and pantomime might increase audiences but were expensive to mount. By 1740 it needed something like £75,000 a year to keep the London theatres going. It should be added that a popular counter-culture existed in the garish spectacle of drolls put on in fairground booths throughout the country.

The repertoire included standard modern works, such as *The Beggar's Opera* and *The London Merchant*, interspersed with such new plays as satisfied the managers — one or two performances would be enough to judge their success. Among older playwrights Congreve retained extensive currency, while Dryden, Lee and Otway held the boards. But it was Shakespeare who was performed most of all; the London stage was built around his work.[2] Fashions changed but almost all the plays were revived at one time or another — special favourites were *Hamlet*, *The Merry Wives* and *Othello*. (On the other hand *The Winter's Tale* and *Coriolanus* were seldom put on, while *Antony and Cleopatra* never reached the London stage between 1700 and 1750.) Noted characterizations included Macklin's villainous Shylock, Garrick's tumultuous Richard III and Quin's extravagant Falstaff. It is true that audiences very often saw a doctored version, like Cibber's 'improved' *Richard III*

---

2 Total performances in London between 1700 and 1750 are charted by C. B. Hogan, *Shakespeare in the Theatre 1701-1800* (Oxford, 1952), pp. 460-1. Additional information can be obtained from *The London Stage 1660-1800*, 11 vols (Carbondale, Ill., 1960-8), a primary reference book for the period. Hogan's figures are as follows (adaptations such as Tate's *Lear* are included in the count):

Hamlet	358	*Midsummer Night's Dream*	51
Macbeth	287	*Henry V*	49
Othello	265	*Much Ado About Nothing*	47
1 Henry IV	214	*King John*	43
Merry Wives of Windsor	202	*Cymbeline*	25
Richard III	200	*Richard II*	25
Tempest	186	*All's Well that Ends Well*	22
King Lear	186	*Twelfth Night*	18
Julius Caesar	163	*Titus Andronicus*	16
Henry VIII	136	*Winter's Tale*	14
Taming of the Shrew	124	*Coriolanus*	13
Merchant of Venice	115	*Comedy of Errors*	12
Romeo and Juliet	96	*Troilus and Cressida*	10
As You Like It	95	*2 Henry VI*	9
Timon of Athens	89	*Pericles*	3
2 Henry IV	88	*1 Henry VI*	1
Measure for Measure	69	*3 Henry VI*	1

Not performed: *Antony and Cleopatra*, *Love's Labour's Lost*, *Two Gentlemen of Verona*.

(1700), Tate's happy-ending *Lear* (1681) or Lansdowne's *Jew of Venice* (1701). We are likely to be appalled by the transmogrification of *The Taming of the Shrew*, 'alter'd and improv'd' into *Sawney the Scot*, but the Augustan point of view was that such recensions demonstrated a lively contemporary involvement with Shakespeare. This was the period in which serious Shakespearian scholarship began; Rowe brought out his edition in 1709, followed by numerous others — Pope, Theobald, Hanmer, Warburton, Johnson, Capell, Steevens, finally Malone in 1790. If the age began the manufacture of apocryphal episodes, forgeries and fake relics, if the great Stratford Jubilee in 1769 was a washout (enlivened by Boswell's appearance as a Corsican chieftain), then at least the business of editing was carried through with zeal. Malone remains the prince of Shakespearians. And since our own productions of Shakespeare are not invariably models of fidelity or discretion, we should not be too scornful of the eighteenth century. Men and women of the time unquestionably loved Shakespeare in their fashion.

The reference to opera should remind us that this was an intensely musical era, too — England had not yet become the land without music. Without high genius in native composers, after the sad death of Purcell in 1695, the British had the good sense to import talented foreigners. Orchestral musicians from Germany, singers from Italy, librettists from France and a Swiss impresario came to the fore. Handel settled in London in 1712 and for the remainder of his life he dominated the scene, first in opera seria and then in oratorio. Italian opera had to face a barrage of criticism, but it kept its popularity for many years and enjoyed notable patronage from royal and aristocratic quarters. The finest virtuoso singers of Europe were employed in the London houses during

---

The dominance of the tragedies is evident, along with the low ranking of problem plays and romances. It is instructive to note that *Timon of Athens* was performed during Swift's maturity more often than any play in these two groups, excluding *The Tempest*. A. H. Scouten estimates that in the periods of highest popularity (around 1720 and then again around 1740) from 17 to 25 per cent of performances in the London theatre were devoted to Shakespeare: see *The London Stage*, III, i, cxlix-cl. The ratio never fell below 10 per cent. For a good account of the reception and treatment of the plays in this era, see Brian Vickers (ed.), *Shakespeare: The Critical Heritage*, Vol. II: 1693-1733 (London, 1974), pp. 1-21. Finally, it should be noted that *Antony and Cleopatra* had sunk without trace largely because of the currency enjoyed by Dryden's rescension, *All for Love* (1677).

Handel's operatic period. A star system evolved, with artists paid up to £3000 — a huge sum then — for a single season lasting from November to June. Later another German composer, J.C. Bach (youngest son of Johann Sebastian), took a similarly prominent part in the musical life of the 1770s. No Englishman of comparable stature emerged, but Arne and Boyce were considerable figures in their own right; music at court retained high standards, theatrical music was often inventive (with ballad opera a popular innovation) and serious musicology began with Dr Burney and Sir John Hawkins. Up and down the country concerts, glee-clubs and pleasure-gardens gave signs of abundant national interest. Cathedrals played their part, as indicated by the foundation of the Three Choirs' Festival in 1724. It was natural for the young prodigy Mozart to visit London in 1764; he spent over a year there. At the end of the century Haydn passed long periods in the capital, and English poets — Milton and Thomson — afforded the inspiration for *The Creation* (1799) and *The Seasons* (1800).

The Augustan prospect

The essays which follow describe principal features of the landscape of the age. They supply a context for the literature, not in the sense of some inert background against which the real business of writing goes on, but as part of the very fabric of life, from which no author could isolate himself. Poems, novels and plays in the eighteenth century stayed unusually close to the actual and the normal; to recover something of the age is to understand the workings (as well as the content) of its literary products. That may sound daunting, but really it makes for an encouraging state of affairs — you can learn a great deal about Victorian society and then find the best authors of the day resolutely turning their back on it all, their eyes fixed on distant visions of a lost paradise. In many respects the Augustans are more accessible: their finest books take us *into* the age, not away from it.

It is a commonplace that politics entered into every corner of national life at this time: there were rival cliques of Whigs and Tories in the playhouse (as on the famous first night of Addison's *Cato* in 1713), contending factions in the coffee houses, publishers of one persuasion or another. W.A. Speck shows how these divisions in society grew up, and how the nature of political conflict changed over the course of this century. He discusses the changes that took place around 1714 and 1760, and explains the grudge which (rightly or wrongly) many authors harboured against 'machine' politicians like Walpole. In a period when even a minor place in the customs depended on the favour of executive (or the influence of a well-placed outsider), writers were naturally interested in the fluctuating relations between the crown and the ministry; some, like Chesterfield, were caught up in the struggle. Dr Speck illuminates the electoral contests which crop up so prominently in literature, and traces the beginnings of the movement for parliamentary reform. Above all, he reanimates the dead issues which stirred men and women in the days of Marlborough, Bolingbroke, Walpole, Wilkes and the elder Pitt. We can hardly care as much about these matters today, but we shall enjoy Swift, Fielding and Johnson more fully if we know a little of the passions that stirred an eighteenth-century breast.

In the realm of ideas and beliefs, John Valdimir Price begins with the continuing debt to Hobbes, Locke and Newton, and shows how orthodox churchmen and freethinkers alike drew from these sources. The varieties of religious belief in the period were wider than used to be supposed: we have pietist movements, the evangelical appeal of Wesley and Whitefield, deists and apostles of 'natural religion', sturdy dissenting sects, French prophets, Quakers, freemasons and other occult societies (the first Grand Lodge was founded in London in 1717), and every kind of fringe religion. The notion that eighteenth-century theology starts and ends with men like Bishop Hoadly — plump, affable, well fed as he appears in Hogarth's portrait, his soft white hands just emerging from the lawn sleeves — is now rightly seen as a myth. Dr Price traces the beginnings of aesthetic theory in Shaftesbury, Hutcheson and others; he places Adam Smith's economic views within the development of thought; and he describes the achievement of Berkeley and Hume, the greatest thinkers of the age. We commonly think of the Hanoverians as practical men, agricultural improvers rather than metaphysicians; but the truth is that the most influential 'pure' philosophers Britain has produced are these two men along with Locke.

Science, as G.S. Rousseau observes, is often unduly neglected in surveys of the past. This is a serious omission because men and women in 1700 — and for the succeeding decades — were intensely excited about the nature of the universe, as revealed by the telescope and explained by Newton. As well as cosmological speculation, there was an attempt to apply scientific and mathematical discoveries to everyday living, a process associated with the Royal Society. Professor Rousseau moves on to discuss the course of medicine, both clinical advances and social effects, as in the provision of hospitals for physical and mental disorders. This leads into issues such as the Augustan attitude towards madness, the onset of the 'English malady' (melancholia), the growth of interest in neurology and psychology — a whole congeries of medico-scientific developments, casting great light on Sterne, Smollett, Smart, Cowper and others. Professor Rousseau makes telling use of primary sources but never forgets the literary bearings of the material he is describing.

Finally Peter Willis considers the visual arts, in a period which saw the dominance of the great estates, a fashion for the grand tour (only a few writers actually performed one, but the others were conscious of an omission), and the cult of the antique. He discusses architecture in the context of town planning, since the idea of the *urban* way of life is particularly central to the period. He moves on to painting, sculpture and the decorative arts, and then to that characteristic eighteenth-century obsession, the theory and practice of landscape gardening. The nature of 'taste' as this became the touchstone of artistic endeavour is applicable to all the forms considered. Dr Willis, once more, is able to show the immediate involvement of several writers in these developments. Again we are given not a distant background to literature, but rather a heightened foreground with the details intelligible and the references explained.

No single work will exemplify every single aspect of the period. However, it is true that the greatest books seem richest in Augustan implication; they *include* more of what people said, saw, heard, thought, believed, admired. I have frequently used *The Spectator* to illustrate points, and this is certainly an excellent guide to attitudes early in the period — in the manner of presentation as in content. *Gulliver's Travels* is actually constructed in part around the dichotomies in ideas traced in this volume: the first two voyages enact political and social conflicts, the third animates the problems and controversies to which scientific and economic progress had given rise; the last voyage takes us into the moral and religious debates of early Hanoverian England. Thomson's *Seasons*, less assured in literary quality, does nevertheless embrace a very wide range of contemporary themes. The loose-knit structure enables Thomson to write about nature and the universe, science, the sublime and the beautiful, landowners, humanitarian causes, the plight of the poor, Whig politics, travel and discovery, melancholy — and a great deal more. *Tom Jones* raises central moral and critical questions at every turn, including attitudes to sex, property and the family. So we could go on: Hume's *Essays*, Gray's *Elegy*, Goldsmith's *Deserted Village*, Johnson's *Journey to the Western Islands*, Gibbon's *Decline and Fall*, Sheridan's *School for Scandal*, Boswell's *Life of Johnson* — each operates within the context here described and makes something rich and enticing from the encounter. This is not to say, of course, that the literary merit of the book derives in any simple sense from its relevance to primary concerns of the age. Nevertheless these are works of high distinction which were almost always very perspicuous to contemporary readers: they achieve their purposes while sticking close to things the eighteenth century considered important (this applies even to Gibbon). Since then artists have tended to find their ultimate values in the realm of private fantasy. The Augustan vision was shared, to a large degree, by audience and writer.

The final version of Pope's *Dunciad* in four books (1743) splendidly unites many disparate strands. The first book sets the theme of authors in society, with the appointment of a new Poet Laureate. We are confronted by the cultural influence of the court, the power of the press, and the pressures of modern urban living: madness and poverty lie cheek by jowl. In the second book we witness the competitive enterprises of Grub Street, with journalists literally raking in the mud and decadent patrons getting touched up by obsequious clients. Book III is a vision of the coming of a new barbarism, with startling use made of imagery drawn from garish theatrical spectacles then drawing a large audience: the impresarios and the fairground drolls are much in evidence. The final book takes on a succession of current themes — opera, education, classical scholarship, the grand tour, confident freethinking and shallow metaphysics, acquisitive collectors, dull academics, foolish scientists. The great yawn of Queen Dulness envelops every aspect of national life, from George II and Walpole through the church and parliament to the armed forces. Religion, philosophy, science, art, morality — everything that the Augustans cleaved to — all perishes before the onset of a gothic anti-civilization:

> Thy hand, great Anarch! lets the curtain fall;
> And Universal Darkness buries all.

This superb rhetoric makes the eighteenth century immortal even as it prophesies the doom of the order that sustained it. Pope gives us a moving threnody for the hopes, beliefs, ideals, institutions and ways of life charted in this volume. He shows, about fifty years early, eighteenth-century civilization confronting its own demise.

The tone of *The Dunciad* is too questioning to be wholly typical of the age, even if Pope takes delight in his satiric creation. A more positive note is struck by James Thomson in this excerpt from 'Summer', first published as part of *The Seasons* in 1727 (although I quote the revised text of 1746: in this case the punctuation is normalized to avoid an unduly 'antiquated' look).

> These are the haunts of meditation, these
> The scenes where ancient bards the inspiring breath
> Ecstatic felt, and from this world retired,
> Conversed with angels and immortal forms,
> On gracious errands bent — to save the fall
> Of virtue struggling on the brink of vice;
> In waking whispers and repeated dreams
> To hint pure thought, and warn the favoured soul,
> For future trials fated, to prepare;
> To prompt the poet, who devoted gives
> His muse to better themes; to soothe the pangs
> Of dying worth, and from the patriot's breast
> (Backward to mingle in detested war,
> But foremost when engaged) to turn the death;
> And numberless such offices of love,
> Daily and nightly, zealous to perform.

Thomson is portraying a solemn night-time scene in silent woods, with the aim of showing nature as a nurse of moral virtue and of sublime religious feeling. The 'bards' who inhabit these groves are probably druids, for Thomson was one of many writers to be impressed by the poetic archaeology of William Stukeley (1687-1765), founder of the cult of druidism as the 'aboriginal patriarchal religion'. Stukeley, successively doctor and clergyman, had even argued that Stonehenge was a druid construction. This cult becomes associated in the eighteenth-century imagination with the idea of a noble British past, with liberty and the absence of corruption, and with pure literary inspiration. In Thomson *virtue* and *vice* are cant terms, expressing the attributes of opposition and ministerial parties. However, the political message is overlaid by an allegory of artistic creation, in which writing is presented as a kind of entranced and privileged prophecy. It is sometimes supposed that the Augustans disparaged poetry; on the contrary, the claims made for the poet in the middle of the century were almost extravagantly inflated. William Collins's 'Ode on the Poetical Character' (*c.* 1746) is a case in point. Thomson sees the making of poetry as a deeply responsible act, almost a sacerdotal function. His vocabulary is full of reverent and aspiring words (*meditation / inspiring / ecstatic / gracious / pure / favoured soul / devoted / worth / offices of love*). The syntax and movement create a nervous intensity along with the grave dignity; we respond to the flow of ideas not just as pious sentiments but also as a warm evocation of true creative fervour. The language is by modern standards latinate, but there is nothing frozen about the emotional content: Thomson commands an *energetic* eloquence and a taut, almost witty, form of expression ('waking whispers and repeated dreams'). There is a generous, outgoing quality in the manner of his poetic statement.

It would be better, however, to end on a note less studied in its eloquence. Here, then, is a typical passage from Daniel Defoe's *Tour* of Britain, a work which (like the nation) underwent a good deal of change and 'improvement' as the decades went by:

> I find none has spoken of what I call the distant Glory of all these Buildings: There is a Beauty in these Things at a distance, taking them *en Passant*, and in *Perspective*, which few People value, and fewer understand; and yet here they are more truly great, than in all their Private Beauties whatsoever; Here they reflect Beauty, and Magnificence upon

the whole Country, and give a kind of Character to the Island of *Great Britain* in general . . . . Take them in a remote view, the fine Seats shine among the Trees as Jewels shine in a rich Coronet; in a *near sight* they are meer Pictures and Paintings; *at a distance* they are all Nature, *near hand* all Art; But both in the extreamest Beauty.

In a Word, nothing can be more Beautiful; here is a plain and pleasant Country, a rich fertile Soil, cultivated and enclosed to the utmost perfection of Husbandry, then bespangled with Villages; those Villages fill'd with these Houses, and the Houses surrounded with Gardens, Walks, Vistas, Avenues, representing all the Beauties of Building, and all the Pleasures of Planting: It is impossible to view these Countries from any rising Ground, and not be ravish'd with the delightful Prospect.

Defoe goes on to describe the settlements on the Surrey bank of the Thames in the vicinity of Clapham, concluding that 'this glorious Show of Wealth and Plenty, is really a view of the Luxuriant Age which we live in.' This is more than vulgar materialism, just as the assertion that neither Paris nor Vienna nor Turin can equal the sight is more than crude jingoism: the total effect is more nearly lyrical than boastful. Of course Defoe was well aware of the seamy side of London life, and his mind soon reverts to the 'catastrophe' of the South Sea Bubble four years earlier (see below, pp.99-100). But his prose instinctively traps some of the energy and extroversion of his time. The lapidary images, the orderly progression of his syntax ('those Villages fill'd with these Houses, and the Houses surrounded ...'), the freedom with which he moves from close to distant focus — these could be said to be evidence of 'the control of the Augustan mind sought over its experiences, and ... the hallmark of that confident civilisation which the twentieth century in many ways envies and admires' (A.R. Humphreys). For a brief moment nature and art seemed to have joined in happy complicity; for some of the population, at least, public and private values merged. It could not last; but it made possible a peculiarly affirmative, amenable and convivial art for the best part of a century.

Select bibliography

Society

Baugh, D.A. (ed.) *Artistocratic Government and Society in Eighteenth Century England.* Paperback ed. New York, 1975. (Reprints eight standard sources.)

Clifford, J.L. (ed.) *Man versus Society in Eighteenth-Century Britain.* Cambridge, 1968. (Chapters on political man, economic status, churchman, artist, composer and writer.)

George, D. *London Life in the Eighteenth Century.* Paperback ed. Harmondsworth, 1966.

Marshall, D. *The English Poor in the Eighteenth Century.* London, 1926; repr. 1969.

_____ *English People in the Eighteenth Century.* London, 1956.

Mingay, G.E. *English Landed Society in the Eighteenth Century.* London, 1963.

Radzinowicz, L. *A History of English Criminal Law.* London, 1948-68.

Thompson, E.P. *Whigs and Hunters.* London, 1975.

Turberville, A.S. (ed.) *Johnson's England.* Oxford, 1933. (Chapters covering most of the topics discussed in this book.)

Economics

Ashton, T.S. *The Industrial Revolution 1760-1830.* Paperback ed. Oxford, 1968.

_____ *An Economic History of England: The Eighteenth Century.* Paperback ed. London, 1972.

Carswell, J. *The South Sea Bubble.* London, 1960.

Dickson, P.G.M. *The Financial Revolution in England 1688-1756.* London, 1967.

Hill, C. *Reformation to Industrial Revolution.* Paperback ed. Harmondsworth, 1969.

Mathias, P. *The First Industrial Nation.* Paperback ed. London, 1969.

Parry, J.H. *Trade and Dominion: European Overseas Empires in the Eighteenth Century.* Paperback ed. London, 1974. (Readable and informative.)

Wilson, C. *England's Apprenticeship 1603-1763.* Paperback ed. London, 1971.

Literary history

Dobrée, B. *English Literature in the Early Eighteenth Century 1700-1740.* Oxford 1959.

Greene, D. *The Age of Exuberance.* Paperback ed. New York, 1970.

Loftis, J., *et al. The Revels History of Drama in English.* Vol. 5. London, 1976.

Lonsdale, R. (ed.) *Dryden to Johnson*. Paperback ed. London, 1971. (Excellent coverage of Pope, Fielding, Sterne and others.)

Rogers, P. *The Augustan Vision*. Paperback ed. London, 1974.

Sherburn, G., and Bond, D.F. *The Restoration and the Eighteenth Century*. Paperback ed. London, 1967.

Sutherland, J. *A Preface to Eighteenth Century Poetry*. Paperback ed. Oxford, 1963. (An outstanding work.)

Williams, K. (ed.) *Backgrounds to Eighteenth-Century Literature*. Paperback ed. Scranton, Pa., 1971. (Reprints thirteen major studies from books and journals.)

Criticism and analysis

Bate, W.J. *From Classic to Romantic: Premises of Taste in Eighteenth-Century England*. Paperback ed. New York, 1961.

Fussell, P. *The Rhetorical World of Augustan Humanism*. Paperback ed. Oxford, 1969.

Jack, I. *Augustan Satire*. Paperback ed. Oxford, 1966.

Johnson, J.W. *The Formation of English Neo-Classical Thought*. Princeton, NJ, 1967.

Price, M. *To the Palace of Wisdom*. Paperback ed. New York, 1965.

Tillotson, G. *Augustan Poetic Diction*. Paperback ed. London, 1964.

Wimsatt, W.K., and Brooks, C. *Neo-Classical Criticism*. Paperback ed. London, 1970.

Books and readers

Beljame, A. *Men of Letters and the English Public in the Eighteenth Century*. English trans. London, 1948.

Collins, A.S. *Authorship in the Days of Johnson*. London, 1928.

Foss, M. *The Age of Patronage*. London, 1971. (A provocative account.)

Humphreys, A.R. *The Augustan World*. London, 1954. (The best single introduction to the period.)

Rogers, P. *Grub Street: Studies in a Subculture*. London, 1972.

Saunders, J.W. *The Profession of English Letters*. London, 1964. (Chapters 6 and 7 on the period: not wholly accurate.)

Stephen, L. *English Literature and Society in the Eighteenth Century*. Paperback ed. London, 1963. (A classic work based on the Ford lectures of 1903.)

Watt, I. *The Rise of the Novel*. Paperback ed. Harmondsworth, 1963. (See especially Chapter 2, on the reading public.)

––––––– (ed.) *The Augustan Age*. Paperback ed. Greenwich, Conn., 1968. (Reprints important material with a valuable introduction.)

2 Politics

W. A. SPECK

Studies of eighteenth-century politics, and consequently of Augustan literature, can be distorted if one approaches them as though they were all of a piece throughout. In fact, during this period, the world of politics went through at least three phases, to some extent demarcated by royal deaths. Thus the demise of Queen Anne was a major watershed, and the death of George II, while not, as some historians have argued, a similar turning point, was nevertheless more the end of an epoch than some recent scholars have been prepared to accept. These changing political contexts must be appreciated if we are to understand the reactions to them of, say, Pope and Swift, who lived through the first two phases, or of Dr Johnson, whose literary career spanned the last two. Too often these writers have been placed in a fixed context, with subsequent failure to appreciate fully the nature of some of their writings.

The reign of Anne

The very start of the century marked a realignment of politics after a state of flux in the 1690s. This was mainly due to a resurgence of issues which had divided Tory from Whig since the Exclusion crisis of Charles II's reign, but which had been largely set aside in the Revolution settlement. Perhaps the most outstanding of these issues concerned the succession. Tories had traditionally subscribed to the notion of indefeasible hereditary right to the crown, while the Whigs had been advocates of parliamentary title to the throne. The events of 1688-9 had in effect seen the triumph of the Whig view as the hereditary ruler, James II, and his son and heir James Edward, were laid aside, while William and Mary had been declared King and Queen. At the time it must have seemed that the issue had been settled once and for all. Only a handful of Tories refused to take the oaths to the new monarchs, though these non-jurors, as they were called, included prominent men in church and state. Otherwise the bulk of the political nation appeared to have accepted, however reluctantly, the new order of succession laid down in the Bill of Rights. In fact, however, none of the three heirs named in the bill produced a child to succeed them, and when this became clear, with the death in July 1700 of Anne's only child to survive infancy, it also became obvious that further provision would have to be made for the succession. Appropriate measures were taken in the Act of Settlement in 1701, when over fifty claimants with a better hereditary title to the throne were overlooked in favour of the house of Hanover. The triumph of the Whig view of parliamentary monarchy was upheld, but the misgivings of many Tories were obvious, especially when they were called upon to abjure the Pretender, as James Edward was called after the death of James II in 1701.

Most Tories had reluctantly acquiesced in the laying aside of James II because as a Catholic he had jeopardized their beloved Church of England. Thus the religious question was inextricably interwoven with the succession problem, a point driven home by the provision in the Act of Settlement that all future monarchs must be Anglicans. At the Revolution the position of the Anglican church relative to other denominations had been apparently settled with the Toleration Act of 1689. This had guaranteed freedom of worship to Protestant dissenters who accepted the doctrine of the Trinity. Yet it had also upheld the concept of an established church, by insisting on the payment of tithes to the Church of England by everybody. Moreover it had even sanctioned the Anglican monopoly of office in both local and national government by specifically reinforcing the Corporation and Test Acts, statutes passed under Charles II which restricted town councils and royal officials to communicating Anglicans. Another safeguard of the established church which survived the Revolution was the Licensing

Act, whereby writings had to be approved by state censors before they could be published. Thus only religious works which were in line with Anglican orthodoxy could be officially printed. Towards the end of the 1690s, however, these bastions of privilege were undermined. The practice known as occasional conformity, whereby Protestant dissenters communicated with the Church of England as the Corporation and Test Acts prescribed, effectively circumvented that legislation, since the rest of the time they could frequent their own conventicles. Then the lapsing of the Licensing Act in 1695 removed the official censorship, and released a spate of heterodox publications which would never have been approved under the old system. The result was that many clergymen and their Tory sympathizers began to argue that the church was in danger, and to demand action to reinforce the old safeguards. To combat occasional conformity, legislation was demanded which would penalize the practice. To stem the rising tide of writings attacking Anglicans and championing their opponents a meeting of Convocation, unsummoned since 1689, was urged. These demands obtained results after the turn of the century. In 1701 Convocation met, while in 1702 a bill to outlaw occasional conformity was introduced by the Tories into the House of Commons.

Although such bills were introduced in each of the three sessions of Anne's first parliament, they failed to pass into law thanks to opposition in the upper house, where the Whigs had a majority. Events from 1688 onwards had brought about the change in the composition of the House of Lords, since Charles II had been able to use it to block the Exclusion bills. Among the most important of these was the remodelling of the bishops' bench as a consequence of the Revolution. The refusal of several of the bishops to take the oaths to the new regime, together with some timely deaths, meant that William had to appoint no fewer than sixteen men to the twenty-six bishoprics within the space of two years. At the time most of these men were moderate Tories rather than Whigs; but as the conflict over 'the church in danger' developed during the late 1690s it polarized the clergy into high and low church parties. Those moderate churchmen who were not prepared to sanction the continued proscription of dissent formed the low church party. Although they were a minority among the inferior clergy they had a majority among the episcopate, as the debates in Convocation revealed when it met in 1701. The bulk of the Williamite bishops formed the backbone of the low church party in the upper house of Convocation. They also voted with the Whigs in the House of Lords on most major issues. This gave the Whig party a solid phalanx of support on the episcopal bench which was enough to provide the edge in the debates on the occasional conformity bills in Anne's first parliament.

The defeat of their pet project convinced high churchmen that the church was indeed in danger. Their fears concerning this issue were reinforced by the fanatical sermons of Dr Henry Sacheverell, which were brilliantly parodied by Defoe in *The Shortest Way with the Dissenters* (1702), and by the attempt of the more extreme Tories to force the third bill through the House of Lords by 'tacking' it on to a money bill in November 1704. This device was used because it was a constitutional convention that the peers could not alter a money bill but could only pass or reject it qutright. Fortunately for the government and the war effort the 'tack' was defeated by 251 votes to 134, the 134 tackers representing the hard core of the high church Tories in Anne's first parliament. Although the ministry tried to keep them out of parliament in the general election of 1705, enough of them got back in to keep alive the cry 'the church in danger', until in December of that year a resolution was passed condemning those who maintained that proposition. This proscription did not prevent Sacheverell from repeating the charge in his sermons, until eventually in November 1709 he so flagrantly defied the resolutions in a sermon delivered in St Paul's Cathedral that the government felt obliged to prosecute him. In *The Perils of False Brethren* Sacheverell argued that not only the church but the state itself was in danger from a predominantly Whig ministry. He also upheld the old Tory doctrines of passive obedience and non-resistance to the extent of denying that they were incompatible with the Revolution of 1688, by asserting that there had been no resistance to James II. Such provocative allegations obliged the government to bring him before the House of Lords in 1710 to answer four articles of impeachment, the main one of which was that he had impugned the necessity and justice of the measures taken against James II in 1688. The impeachment caused an uproar largely because it seemed to many Anglican clergymen that Sacheverell was being prosecuted for having the courage to preach publicly what many of them believed in private. It produced a deluge of pamphlets in his defence and did more than anything else to procure a Tory majority at the polls in the general election of 1710.

The last four years of Anne's reign were characterized by a high church reaction, which found expression in the final passing of an Occasional Conformity Act in 1711 and culminated in the Schism Act of 1714. The aim of the Schism Act was to eradicate dissent at source by making illegal the education of dissenters in separate schools. It was meant to come into operation on 1 August, ironically the very day of Anne's death, and thus remained ineffective until it was repealed in 1719. Anne's death, therefore, dashed high church hopes just as surely as her accession had raised them.

The revival of the twin problems of the succession and the church on the eve of Anne's reign was largely responsible for the resurgence of Tory and Whig animosities. To these was added a third issue, that of England's role in the War of the Spanish Succession, which also assisted the polarization of politics. From the start Tories insisted that England should play the part of an auxiliary in the hostilities, devoting her main effort to the war at sea, which, they argued, was the more appropriate element for a maritime power. The Whigs, however, urged that England should act as a principal, and contribute in full measure to the Continental campaign against Louis XIV. As the war went on, party attitudes towards it hardened. This was because the war aims of the allies became more precise and at the same time more difficult to realize. The main development in this direction was the treaty of 1703 which brought Portugal into the Grand Alliance, for one of the terms upon which the Portuguese insisted was that the Habsburg claimant should be seated on the Spanish throne. Since the Bourbon candidate, Philip V, was in effective possession of Spain, this committed the allies to a strategically hopeless cause. At first this was obscured by Marlborough's great victories against the French and their allies in central Europe and the Netherlands. The Battle of Blenheim in 1704, which stopped a direct attack upon the Austrian empire, and the Battle of Ramillies in 1706, which yielded the Spanish Nether-lands to the Grand Alliance, eloquently justified Whig advocacy of Continental warfare. But the defeat at Almanza in 1707 was an ominous blow to the allied cause in Spain. Tories thereafter began to insist on withdrawal from the Iberian peninsula, while the Whigs stood by their commitment to the Habsburg claimant with the slogan 'No peace without Spain'. Further successes in the Low Countries, notably the victory at Oudenarde in 1708, stifled Tory frustration for a while. After the breakdown of peace negotiations in the winter of 1708-9, which the Tories attributed to Whig insistence upon 'No peace without Spain', their demands for more realistic peace initiatives grew. It seemed as though the war was becoming endless in 1709, especially after the Battle of Malplaquet which many saw as a high price to pay in human life for a small return. It was even rumoured that Marlborough and the Whigs were deliberately prolonging the war for their own ends, a rumour which the duke did little to scotch by imprudently asking Anne to make him Captain-General for life. By the winter of 1709-10, therefore, Tory demands for peace were becoming so vociferous that Swift, with pardonable exaggeration, later wrote in his *History of the Last Four Years of the Queen* that the only difference between the parties which mattered was that the Tories were lovers of peace while the Whigs were lovers of war.

It was this mood that helped to bring to power in 1710 a ministry under Robert Harley determined to conclude peace with France. By the autumn of 1711 preliminaries of peace had been thrashed out, and an intense publicity campaign was launched to make the terms acceptable to parliament. The *chef de propagande* in this campaign was Jonathan Swift, whose *Conduct of the Allies* was far and away the most formidable contribution to the debate over the preliminaries. In the event they were accepted by the Commons but rejected by the Lords, who insisted by a narrow majority upon the old Whig slogan 'No peace without Spain'. Harley redeemed the situation by persuading the Queen to promote a dozen peers to swing the balance in the Lords from a Whig to a Tory majority. He also obtained the dismissal of the Duke of Marlborough and led the parliamentary attack on the duke and on Robert Walpole which culminated in the former Captain-General's leaving England and the former Secretary at War's expulsion from the Commons and imprisonment in the Tower. As he embarked on a more vigorous course he aroused the misgivings of some Tory backbenchers who began to have second thoughts about the desirability of what was virtually a separate peace. Their ranks were swollen by those who showed their dissatisfaction with the 'restraining orders' given to the Duke of Ormonde, Marlborough's successor, which commanded him to withdraw British troops from fighting in the summer campaign of 1712. Once peace was signed at Utrecht in 1713, the number of discontented Tories became formidable, and when a bill to make good a commercial treaty with France was introduced in June 1713 enough of them voted with the Whigs to defeat the measure. As Bolingbroke put it, 'The very work which ought to have been the basis of our strength, was in part demolished before our eyes, and we were stoned with the ruins of it.'

To some extent these different attitudes towards the war reflected the different interests which the parties represented. The Tory party counted overwhelmingly on the landed gentry and the country clergy. These were the principal subscribers to the land tax which, after 1693, was the main form of direct taxation. Originally devised as a levy on all incomes, it had for all practical purposes become a rate on land based on an assessment of rental value. In wartime the rate was fixed at 4*s.* in the pound, and although the incidence was uneven this represented the highest rate of direct taxation until the twentieth century. The economic plight of the gentry and clergy, aggravated by the land tax, stiffened their Toryism in these years. While the woes of the gentry were to some extent exaggerated, those of the bulk of the inferior clergy were real enough to persuade the government to mitigate it in 1704 by remitting clerical taxes to augment inadequate stipends in the scheme known as Queen Anne's bounty.

Whig strength was drawn from urban rather than from rural areas, though the party could rely on the support of a number of aristocrats and country gentlemen even in the most rural shires. In any House of Commons the majority of members were gentry, and the Whig party, like the Tories, enrolled a significant proportion of them in their ranks. But the Whigs had a noticeably greater proportion of the other occupations undertaken by MPs, especially among the professions of the law and the armed forces. Again it would be totally misleading to imply that either party drew exclusively from any social group, and there were a number of Tory merchants in any House. Thus the 'Old' East India Company was largely Tory until its merger with the 'New' into the United East India Company in 1709, while the South Sea Company, set up in 1711, was a deliberately Tory institution intended to offset the Whiggish Bank of England as a financial corporation. Nevertheless, Whig claims to represent mercantile interests — above all their boast that they represented the monied interest — find confirmation in the political allegiances of the bulk of the merchants and financiers who found their way into the Commons under Anne. These interests were less directly affected by war taxation. Indeed those among them with surplus capital to invest in loans to the government could actually profit from demands for money during the wars, since it was in these years that the machinery of public credit was set up to service the national debt and, at least until the South Sea Bubble, seemed to make investments in 'the funds', as they were called, as secure and certainly more profitable than investments in land. Hence there arose Tory accusations that Whigs were intent on prolonging the war in order to feather their own nests and to destroy the landed interest, themes emphasized in Swift's contributions to Tory propaganda after 1710.

The Tories, then, lamented the necessity for parliamentary monarchy, championed the Church of England, and begrudged the commitment to Continental war and the consequent financial burden on the landed interest. The Whigs, on the other hand, welcomed the advent of the Protestant succession, sought to protect dissenters from the adverse results of the privileged position claimed by the Church of England in the state, and accepted complete involvement in the War of the Spanish Succession, with the financial necessities this entailed.

These attitudes polarized the two parties in the opening months of the eighteenth century after a decade in which the party alignments had often been obscured by more immediate issues. At Anne's accession the bulk of the members of both Houses were marshalled under Whig or Tory leaders. By then the indisputable heads of the Whig party were the five peers who formed the so-called Junto. Lord Halifax was the financial wizard of the Junto; Lord Orford was its naval genius; Lord Somers was one of the outstanding lawyers of the day; Lord Sunderland was to make his mark as Prime Minister under George I; and Lord Wharton, the butt of many sallies by Swift after 1710, was its indefatigable electioneer. Together their diversified talents added up to a formidable team of Whig leaders. The Tory party could boast no such united leadership, perhaps because the Tories themselves were more fissile than their rivals. Certainly at the start of the century they could be divided into at least two groups: the high church Tories and the moderates. As we have seen, the high church Tories put the defence of the Anglican establishment before all other considerations, and were prepared to jeopardize even the war effort to put the church out of danger. At Anne's accession various politicians could be identified as aspirants to the leadership of the high church wing of the party, including the Earls of Nottingham and Rochester in the Lords, and William Bromley and Henry St John in the Commons.

It is tempting to put three of the most conspicuous politicians of Anne's reign, Lord Godolphin, Robert Harley and the Duke of Marlborough, among the moderate Tories at this time; but to do so is to distort the reality of politics under Anne. Godolphin and Marlborough, it is true, had been regarded as Tories and even suspected as Jacobites under William, though Harley had begun his political career as a Revolution Whig, and, while he associated more with Tories in the late nineties, it is disputable to what extent he became one. But under Anne these party labels obscure the true role of 'the triumvirate' as they were known until they parted company in 1708. They were essentially not party politicians, but agents, or brokers, or managers who negotiated between the crown and the parties.

For although there were two major parties this does not mean to say that there was a two-party system. Far from it; for standing above the parties was the monarch, and neither William nor Anne was prepared to concede power to either Tories or Whigs. They regarded party politics as a threat to their position, since organized bodies of politicians intent on gaining power were a direct challenge to the royal prerogatives of appointing or dismissing ministers at pleasure, and even of declaring war and making peace. It must not be forgotten that, despite the bill of rights, the Revolution settlement of 1689 left considerable powers to the crown, and both William and Anne were not prepared to surrender them without a struggle. They were the last monarchs to use the royal veto on bills which had passed both Houses of Parliament, and they fought hard to retain the maximum freedom of manoeuvre between the enlisted men on both sides.

In this they were helped by the fact that, although most politicians were so enlisted, there was a significant number in both Houses who could reasonably be expected to put their loyalty to the crown above their loyalty to a party. These were, primarily, placemen — peers and MPs who had positions under the crown. For the crown used its patronage in the household, the treasury and other departments of state to reward politicians with a variety of places from such key administrative posts as Lord Treasurer, Secretary of State and Chancellor of the Exchequer, to such sinecures as the Clerks Comptrollers of the Green Cloth and the Farmer of the Green Wax. The House of Lords had a total membership of about 160, but the votes rarely added up to 100, and peers in place were often in a majority. The larger House of Commons had a total membership of 513 before the Union with Scotland added a further 45, but an attendance of over 400 was unusual, so that the presence of about 120 placemen presented a formidable block of voters. The votes of placemen were not completely reliable in Anne's reign, for in any major division in either House there would be a significant minority who mutinied or deserted. Nevertheless there was a hard core of peers and common-ers who could be relied upon to vote for the court, whatever the party political complexion of the ministry happened to be at the time. This element, once referred to by Godolphin as 'the Queen's servants', militated against the emergence of a two-party system under Anne. It was the task of her managers to attach to this nucleus as many politicians as they could persuade to put their duty to the Queen above their attachment to the Tories or the Whigs, in attempts to build up a court party which could command a parliamentary majority. An essential role committed to propagand-ists whom the government employed at this time, such as Defoe and Swift, was to appeal to this element, which is why a 'non-partisan' attitude features so largely in the *Review* and the *Examiner*.

Another way in which the crown could influence the alignment of parties at Westminster was by its intervention in parliamentary elections. The electoral system in Anne's reign was far from democratic, for about 300,000 men had the right to vote, or a mere

5 per cent of the total population, albeit perhaps 22 per cent of the adult males. Nor were these equally distributed into equal electoral districts. On the contrary, of the 269 constituencies in England and Wales about a third had over 500 voters, another third between 100 and 500, and the remaining third under 100. The smaller constituencies were wide open to the exploitation of patronage, and this enabled the crown to exert pressure. There was a handful of boroughs in which the government itself could directly influence the outcome of elections, including Harwich, where the Post Office had considerable patronage; Rochester and Queenborough, where the nearby dockyards at Chatham and garrison at Sheerness respectively gave the navy and the army a major interest; the Cinque Ports; the boroughs on the Isle of Wight; and anywhere that the crown was a principal element in the local economy. But the direct influence of the crown only returned at most twenty members under Anne. More important was its indirect influence either on the patrons of small boroughs or on the sentiments of the electors in more open constituencies. Thus in areas where rival Tory and Whig magnates were struggling to control the representation of local boroughs, as happened in Cornwall, the backing of the crown could tip the scales in favour of one or the other as they were able to employ royal patronage to attract support.

In large boroughs and in counties, where the voters were too numerous to succumb entirely to patrons, knowledge that the crown was in favour of a particular party could often sway the uncommitted or floating voter to support that side in a general election. Again propagandists were employed to carry the crown's message to the electorate, Defoe's *Review*, for example, doing stalwart service in the election of 1705.

Thus directly and indirectly the crown was able to influence the outcome of elections to a considerable extent, so much so that some historians have argued that the government never lost an election in the eighteenth century. Such a claim is, however, not justified before 1715. Late in 1701, for instance, William III dispensed with the services of several Tory ministers and appointed Whigs, and otherwise indicated that he supported the Whig party in the general election that took place in December, yet the Whigs were unable to control the Commons when the new parliament met. Anne was rather more successful, though even she could not manipulate elections to the degree her ministers would have liked. By and large they preferred neither party to have an overall majority so that the placemen could achieve a balance, but this happy outcome was only realized in 1705. After the general election of 1708 the Commons contained far more Whigs than Anne wanted, forcing her to concede more power to the Junto than she had been prepared to do. Again in 1710 more Tories were returned than Robert Harley, her Prime Minister, had bargained for.

This was because the degree to which the outcome of elections could be controlled was very limited under Anne. For one thing, thanks to the Triennial Act of 1694, more general elections took place than under the Georges after the Septennial Act was passed in 1716. Between 1700 and 1715 there were no fewer than eight general elections, a total not achieved after 1715 until 1768. For another thing there were far more contests in the early eighteenth century than in the middle. This was because the great battle to control the smaller constituencies was still being fought. It was not until well into the reign of George II that oligarchy finally triumphed, and the bulk of the smaller boroughs succumbed to patrons. Until that happened many of the 300,000 voters exercised their right to vote with an independence not realized until recent times. Under Anne politicians ignored at their peril an active and volatile electorate.

The age of Walpole

Walpole's world was a very different one from that of Queen Anne. His very survival for twenty years as Prime Minister is to some extent a measure of this, for the political scene had changed far more rapidly before his rise to power. The political stability over which he presided is now regarded as one of the major achievements of the early Hanoverian era. Its origins have been sought in the turbulent period which preceded it, and there can be little doubt that there were forces making for a more stable system even at the height of the rage of party under Anne. The machinery of government became more complex as the state mobilized unprecedented resources for the conflict against Louis XIV, and its very complexity contributed to the growth of political stability as it created vested interests dependent upon the survival of the Revolution settlement.

The growth of oligarchy had already commenced in the constituencies, though this was to proceed apace after 1716 when the
Septennial Act made the tenure of a seat in parliament a much
more attractive investment. Thus not only was Walpole less
dependent upon the whims of the electorate than his predecessors
had been, since he need only call an election every seven years, but
the voters themselves were less independent and more subservient
to patrons, a phenomenon reflected in the diminishing number of
contests in smaller boroughs as the period went on.

Although there are signs of increasing stability before 1714, its
development was by no means assured on the death of Anne. The
main contribution to the transition from an age of party strife to a
more tranquil era was the cooling off of the political issues which
had divided Tory from Whig since the Exclusion crisis and which
had kept passions at boiling point.

Of course the great issues involving foreign policy, the church
and the succession, which had done so much to divide Tory from
Whig in the past, did not disappear overnight on Anne's death.
But by 1720 they were no longer the major questions in English
politics. Although the Whigs continued to inveigh against the
Peace of Utrecht as a betrayal of the Grand Alliance and a
capitulation to France, diplomatic realities in the opening years of
George I's reign led his ministers to sign a treaty with France in
1716 to guarantee the Utrecht settlement. This *rapprochement*
with the French was to be the cornerstone of English diplomacy for
over twenty years. It effectively defused the party debate over
foreign policy.

The church issue also became less explosive in the opening years
of George I's reign. Quite why this happened is not entirely clear,
for the suppression of Convocation in 1717 and the repeal of the
Occasional Conformity and Schism Acts in 1719 might have been
expected to keep alive the old cry 'the church in danger'. Yet,
although dissenters were even protected from prosecutions under
the test and corporation acts by a series of indemnity acts, which
became annual under Walpole, his opponents never raised the
charge against him. Perhaps this was because the alleged danger
from dissent became less obvious a threat as their numbers shrank
and they were themselves rent apart by a controversy between
Unitarians and Trinitarians in their midst. Perhaps also it was

because there was a revival of moderate churchmanship which to some extent healed the breach between high and low church that had exacerbated ecclesiastical politics under Anne. They closed ranks in the first years of George I's reign in response to challenges to their respective positions from their own extremists. Thus the high church position was attacked by the nonjurors who were no longer prepared to communicate with the Anglican church, on the grounds that it was in schism and had broken the apostolic succession which they, of course, maintained. The most outspoken response to this came from Benjamin Hoadly, Bishop of Bangor, one of the leading low church apologists in Anne's reign. In a pamphlet of 1716 and a sermon preached before the King in 1717 he argued that the apostolic succession had been broken anyway, and virtually maintained that an established church was unnecessary. These criticisms infuriated both high and low churchmen, who, whatever their differences, shared the common belief that the Church of England was both apostolic and necessary. It was to forestall an attack on Hoadly's sermon — and not one mounted by high church clerics alone — that Convocation was suppressed in 1717. Apart from a brief meeting in 1741, it never met again to do canonical business until the nineteenth century. Meanwhile the former rancour between high and low church had long since ceased to be relevant to English politics.

The succession problem survived more obstinately, and indeed the spectre of a Jacobite restoration was only finally exorcized five years after Convocation's brief resurrection. But long before the rebellion of 1745 it had almost disappeared as a live political force south of the Cheviots, and with it the Tory party of Anne's reign.

The Tories had been split on the succession before Anne's death. Those who had opposed the commercial treaty with France came out strongly in favour of the Protestant succession, while a substantial minority made no secret of the fact that the option of a Jacobite restoration was open as far as they were concerned. These looked to Henry St John, Viscount Bolingbroke, for a lead, and he was prepared to go along with them. Bolingbroke was thus ready to take a desperate gamble. A Jacobite restoration would be opposed by the Whigs, probably with armed force. It was against the wishes of the Queen, of most Tories and even, unless the Pretender changed his religion, of the majority of those who were prepared to consider it. To remove all these obstacles would take time, and time was not on Bolingbroke's side. Yet the Hanoverian successor was so opposed to all who had supported the Treaty of Utrecht, and so attached to those who had resisted it, that in the long run it seemed to be the only way of ensuring for himself a future in English politics. In the short run the only alternative as he saw it was to destroy the basis of the Whig party's power and to build up that of the Tory party, so that he might at least make it necessary for the Hanoverian successor to come to terms with him.

The main obstacle to such a programme was Robert Harley, now Earl of Oxford and Prime Minister. He would never approve of a wholehearted attack on the Whigs to bolster the power of the Tories; and so Bolingbroke determined to persuade Anne to remove him. Unfortunately the Queen was more slowmoving and reluctant to take decisions than ever, and she let Oxford cling to power until July 1714. Bolingbroke's hour had come too late, for within days Anne herself was dead, and the initiative had been seized by the moderate Tories and Whigs in the privy council. Bolingbroke's hopes, and the Tory party's prospects of retaining power, died with the Queen. As Bolingbroke wrote to Swift of the short interval between the dismissal of Harley and the death of the Queen, 'What a world this is! and how does fortune banter us.' He also realized immediately the political implications. 'The grief of my soul is this,' he informed Atterbury. 'I see plainly that the Tory party is gone.' And so it proved. Although under the first two Georges contemporaries recognized the separate identity of 'tories', they rarely referred to a tory *party*. Tories came to be seen as but part of an opposition or country party.

The Tories put all they could into the general election of 1715, hoping to secure a majority which would oblige the King to take notice of them. Unfortunately for themselves they were beaten at the polls by the Whigs. After this defeat Bolingbroke realized that the fight was hopeless, and, fully aware that the Whigs would use their majority to attack the former ministers, he fled to the court of the Pretender in France.

Bolingbroke's flight played into the hands of the Whigs since it provided evidence that the Tories were indeed Jacobites. Later in the year another episode caused the accusations to be even more widely believed when a Jacobite rebellion broke out in Scotland.

Although it met with some success initially in Scotland, in England the rebellion was a complete fiasco. An attempt to raise support in the West Country got absolutely nowhere. Some Jacobites rose in the North and, after joining in the Scottish rising, marched south into Lancashire, where they were easily overcome at Preston. The rebellion was the last nail in the coffin of the Tory party of Anne's reign. Though the rebels were treated with surprising leniency, prominent Hanoverian Tories still in the government pleaded for even more clemency and were dismissed. This left the ministry entirely in the hands of the Whigs. The Tory party, once the stronger, became the lost cause of a minority and ceased to be a serious rival to the Whigs in the struggle for power.

The Whigs, therefore, were promised a period of unquestioned ascendancy. They assured this situation for themselves immediately by passing the Septennial Act, to defer a general election by making it unnecessary for the King to dissolve parliament in 1718, as was prescribed by the Triennial Act of 1694. In future seven years could elapse between dissolutions. In fact the next general election was deferred until 1722, and meanwhile the Whigs had consolidated their hold on power.

By 1722, however, the pattern of politics had been almost completely transformed. In addition to the collapse of the Tories, this was due to divisions in Whig ranks which were partly a throwback to earlier disputes between court and country Whigs, and partly to a schism in the body of the court Whigs themselves.

Just as the great issues of Anne's reign did not disappear overnight, so the disputes between court and country did not emerge fresh after the accession of George I. On the contrary they can to some extent be traced back to the reign of Charles II and even to that of his father. Thus there was tension between backbenchers in the Commons and ministerialists over the limitations of executive power and this could create serious political antagonisms. These stemmed from differing views of constitutional practice which started with basic agreement about the nature of the Constitution itself. By 1715, if not earlier, the bulk of the political nation accepted that England was a mixed monarchy. That is, the old Tory notion of the sovereignty of the prerogative was now almost completely discredited, and there was general agreement that the powers of the crown were limited by the Lords and the

Commons in parliament assembled. Indeed men not only accepted this but boasted about it. It became axiomatic that England had found the right balance between monarchy, aristocracy and democracy by having a mixture of all three, which ensured that there was no oppression. Such a happy arrangement was alleged to secure the lives and liberties of Englishmen better than any other regime in the world, a somewhat complacent attitude which Swift set out to puncture in *Gulliver's Travels*. Yet although men were agreed about the nature of the Constitution, they disagreed over the methods necessary to preserve its perfect balance. Thus ministers argued that a strong executive was a necessary safeguard against the enemies of the Revolution settlement both at home and abroad, while country politicians, Whigs as well as Tories, were convinced that such post-Revolution developments as the growth of a standing army, and the increase in the organs of state required to service it, were a major threat to the constitutional equilibrium. One very noticeable product of the expansion of the military machine and of the revenue system needed to sustain it was an increase in the number of places which the executive could use to reward members of parliament. To prevent the encroachment of the executive on the independence of the Commons the country opposition demanded a reduction in the armed forces and the elimination of placemen from the Commons. This campaign really got under way in William's reign, and although it was eclipsed by the party battles of Anne's reign it by no means completely disappeared. The gradual elimination of the great party issues after 1714 brought it once again into prominence.

Some upheaval in the Whig leadership was probably inevitable as the Junto dissolved with the deaths of three of its members — Halifax, Somers and Wharton — before the end of 1716, and the consequent struggle to fill the vacuum left by them. The other two members, Orford and Sunderland, parted company in the ensuing conflict, Orford siding with Robert Walpole and his brother-in-law Lord Townshend, and Sunderland going into partnership with James Stanhope, a veteran soldier of Anne's reign and chief architect of the diplomatic structure which consolidated the Anglo-French *entente* under George I. Indeed it was this betrayal of Whig principles in foreign policy which led to the disagreement between the rival groups. It was the first major exchange in a dispute, which became perennial under the first two Georges, over the extent to which British foreign policy was being subordinated to the interests of the electorate of Hanover. When Townshend objected to the alignment with France he was at first demoted from Secretary of State to Lord Lieutenant of Ireland, and then dismissed in April 1717, Walpole leaving office with him. In the reconstruction of the ministry which followed Stanhope became effectively Prime Minister, Sunderland became principal Secretary of State, while Joseph Addison was the rather surprising choice for the second secretaryship.

In opposition Walpole's determination to get back into office displayed itself in the most opportunistic parliamentary stratagems, in which he sided with Tories even to the point of supporting the dropping of charges of impeachment against the Earl of Oxford, when he had previously been the most intransigent opponent of the fallen Prime Minister. The dispute between the two factions of court Whigs was also extremely rancorous, so that pamphlets on both sides spared nothing in their attempts to heap blame and abuse on each other. The prospect of Whig leaders engaged in such an unedifying dogfight probably did as much to break down the old party battle lines as the downfall of the Tory party and the resurgence of the conflict between court and country.

Walpole and Townshend succeeded in their tactics of getting back into office by outmanoeuvring Stanhope and Sunderland in parliament, especially over the Peerage Bill. This was a measure dear to Stanhope's heart by which he hoped to freeze the status quo in the House of Lords by restricting the royal prerogative of creating peers. In future the monarch was to create peerages only to make up for extinct lines. George I was ready to go along with this because it would hurt his son, with whom he had just quarrelled, more than himself. The bill thus aggrieved the Prince of Wales and all those gentry families who hoped one day to become ennobled. Walpole killed the fears of both with one stone when he opposed the bill in the Commons and contributed more than anybody to its defeat in 1719. The debate over the measure incidentally found the old partners Addison and Steele on different sides for the first time, Addison supporting it in *The Old Whig* and Steele opposing it in *The Plebeian*. The defeat of the bill obliged the King to take Walpole and Townshend back into the ministry, though he drove a hard bargain, giving them posts junior to those they had left.

It was not until 1721 that Walpole became again Chancellor of the Exchequer and First Lord of the Treasury.

What facilitated Walpole's climb back to the top was the South Sea Bubble. The scheme for converting that part of the national debt held by annuitants into South Sea stock was formulated while he was in opposition, so that he had the good fortune not to be associated with its origins, and indeed was on record as favouring a similar scheme proposed by the bank. His earlier opposition, therefore, could be projected as a case of 'I told you so' when the bubble burst. In reality Walpole was not farsighted about the scheme, and was actually prepared to invest after stock had 'peaked' in the summer of 1720. However, unlike Sunderland, his hands were clean and he could pose as the saviour of the nation's finances. Not that this role automatically brought him to the premiership. He was also fortunate in that the deaths of Stanhope and Sunderland removed the two greatest obstacles in his path.

The South Sea Bubble was a major watershed between the political worlds of Anne and Walpole. For one thing it merged the separate interests which had previously polarized into Tory and Whig. All sections of society with any surplus capital, Tory as well as Whig, country gentlemen as well as city businessmen, Oxford colleges as well as inns of court, seem to have been playing the stockmarket in 1720, unlike previous years when the exchange had been dominated by a London-based plutocracy. Just as a great variety of investors were involved in speculation, so they suffered a common misfortune in the crash. Peers and businessmen, gentry and clergy, shared the general calamity. This in itself brought together divergent interests, a process that was furthered by a tendency of the investing public to hedge their bets and purchase land as well as stock in order to have greater security against a similar collapse.

As important for politics was the fact that charges of corruption replaced accusations that the church was being endangered as the most effective rallying cries. There was plenty of substance in these charges, since South Sea Company directors, leading politicians and even the King's household had been prepared to give and receive presents of stock as inducements in 1720. Moreover, once back in power, Walpole tried to screen the highest in the land from investigations into their dealings with the company, for which he earned the nickname of 'screen-master general'. His motive was to get on the right side of the King, a vital move in an aspiring politician at a time when the favour of the crown was necessary to retain power. But it lost him a great deal of popularity. Hostile publicity recalled how he himself had once been expelled from the Commons and imprisoned in the Tower on charges of corruption, forgetting that he had been treated with scandalous partisanship by a Tory House of Commons.

Indeed this was a time for forgetting past animosities in the general hue and cry about corruption. Nothing helped to erase old distinctions between Tory and Whig and to cement the Tories and country Whigs into a country party more than the allegation of corruption in high places. So fundamental was this notion in country ideology that it forms an inexhaustible theme of invective and innuendo in the opposition propaganda under Walpole. Tories and country Whigs could unite on a platform to argue that corruption was the greatest threat to the Constitution and to the health of the body politic. Corruption it was which more than any other force unbalanced the perfect equilibrium of the Revolution settlement. It also spread down from on high to affect all classes, including professional men and businessmen. Unless stopped it would infest the entire nation and render it fit for arbitrary power and slavery. It could only be stopped at its source, the court. Such was the message repeated *ad nauseam* in country effusions such as the *Craftsman*. It also informed less ephemeral literature such as Gay's *Beggar's Opera* (1728) and Johnson's *London* (1738). Despite attempts to curb opposition propaganda, such as a heavy stamp duty imposed in 1725, and the censorship of plays by the Lord Chamberlain, begun in 1737, criticism of Walpole's regime continued unabated. It ranged in quality from the most obscene scurrility to lofty political philosophy.

The philosophical case against Walpole involved a mythology which has been called 'the politics of nostalgia'. According to the country philosophy England had known a golden age in which she had been ruled by a hereditary landed aristocracy, which knew instinctively how to govern in the country's best interests. Unfortunately the rise of the monied interest that had been necessary to fight the wars against Louis XIV had made politics dependent upon the city, and this in turn had brought about an unscrupulous alliance between upstart politicians and *nouveaux riches* monied men to turn the simple art of government into an unintelligible craft. These sinister new elements had usurped the role of the hereditary aristocracy, and were fast consolidating their hold upon the nation by corruption. In order to eradicate this threat a return to the simpler economy of the golden age, and the rule by disinterested lords and gentry, i.e. by the men who formed the backbone of the country party, was necessary. To some extent the country philosophers were calling for a return to paternalism away from the new creed of Mammon which they claimed had come to power with Walpole. Bolingbroke was to argue this theme loftily in his *Idea of a Patriot King*. It can also be found in Swift's *Gulliver's Travels*; for in many ways Brobdingnag is England with the ideals of the opposition realized — no standing army, but a militia; government a simple art, not a cunning craft. And one could say that in his *Moral Essays* Pope is offering an example of the old paternalism in the Man of Ross and of the new, tasteless Mammonism in Timon.

All this was fine rhetoric, but was based on the myth that there had been a political age of innocence, on the libel that Walpole kept himself in power entirely by corruption, and on the absurdity that the country politicians would, if they replaced him, be more idealistic. The machinery of government had, admittedly, become more complex since the Revolution, but there was nothing necessarily sinister in this development as the country politicians implied. It did not produce a machine which rode roughshod over the provisions and safeguards of the Revolution settlement. It is true that Walpole, the machine politician *par excellence*, indulged in a far more systematic exploitation of patronage than had been undertaken in Anne's reign. One result of this was that, where her ministers could count on at most 120 placemen in the Commons, he boosted the total to around 185. During the first four decades of the eighteenth century, therefore, the proportion of placemen in the Lower House increased from less than a quarter to about a third. Placemen can be identified from their posts, but there is now no way of telling how many members were bribed with pensions, though if the *Craftsman* were to be believed Walpole could control the votes of more than 300 members. This was, however, a grotesque distortion of the extent to which influence could control the Commons. At its height all those who were dependent upon the court never reached a majority. At all times the bulk of the Lower House consisted of independents, who amounted in any parliament to some 250 members. If these had united into a bloc against the court, then the Commons would have been completely unmanageable. Fortunately for Walpole they were divided. Some of them were in more or less permanent opposition, the 100-150 Tories sitting in the House forming the backbone of this group, though they included country Whigs in their ranks. The others were inclined to support the court on the grounds that opposition was disloyal, but this could change if they could be persuaded that ministers were invading the liberties of Englishmen. This was the group for whose allegiance ministerial and opposition politicians fought.

In previous reigns these backbenchers had been divided into Tories and Whigs. Walpole tried to keep them so divided, while the opposition attempted to forge them into a united country party. Walpole's main gambit in perpetuating party divisions among the independent members was to harp on the theme of Jacobitism, to scare Whigs among them by branding the Tories in their ranks as traitors. He did this most successfully at the outset of his career as Premier when he persuaded parliament that Francis Atterbury, the high church Bishop of Rochester, was implicated in a Jacobite plot. In 1723 Atterbury was sent into perpetual banishment. The same year Bolingbroke was allowed to return to England, and Walpole used his services for the Pretender to keep alive the identification of Toryism with Jacobitism, though with diminishing results as the years went by.

In reply to Walpole's constant harping on the Jacobite theme, opposition politicians argued that the old party labels had become meaningless, and that Tories and country Whigs now had more in common in mutual resistance to the encroachments of the executive. To eliminate the dangers from the 'Robinocracy', as they dubbed Walpole's system, they called for shorter parliaments, the reduction of the number of placemen in the Commons, and the diminution if not the demobilization of the standing army.

By and large these appeals were unsuccessful. One reason for the relative ineffectiveness of the opposition to Walpole was that their accusations were ingenuous. For while they could be devastatingly detailed in their attacks on corruption, they were singularly vague on what kind of system would replace the 'Robinocracy'. The notion that if Walpole was to be removed and they were to replace him all would be well was, to say the least, unconvincing. For Bolingbroke, who had corruptly profited from office under Anne, to pose as the altruistic patriot under George II made the opposition's case implausible.

Only once during the whole of his career as Prime Minister was Walpole seriously challenged by the country opposition: in 1733 he found resistance to a scheme for transferring customs duties on tobacco and wine to inland excises so fierce that he felt obliged to abandon it. Walpole had hoped that the excise scheme would in fact be popular with independent country gentlemen, since he tried to sell it to them by presenting it as an alternative to the land tax. He thus held out the prospect of keeping the land tax at the low rate of 1*s*. in the pound or even of abolishing it altogether. So far from appealing to the backbenchers, however, the scheme produced an uproar. The opposition argued that ultimately all taxes fell on land, which took the edge off Walpole's offer to shift the incidence from direct to indirect taxation. More tellingly, they conjured up a picture of a vast army of excisemen which would further invade English liberties, and increase the executive's scope for patronage. Such arguments so thoroughly alarmed the independents that the opposition rose to over 200 votes in the Commons. Even so Walpole kept his majority, although it slumped from 61 votes on the first division to 17 on the last, the result more of abstentions by members who usually supported him than of conversions to the opposition. Nevertheless the erosion of his majority was serious enough to persuade him to drop the measure.

Delighted as the opposition was with the success of its campaign against the excise scheme inside the House of Commons, they were overjoyed at the agitation that it stirred up outside parliament. Even before the scheme was introduced, an impressive number of constituencies had instructed their members to oppose it. During the debates demonstrations against the scheme had mounted, culminating in a petition from the City of London, which was the immediate occasion of its being dropped. After its abandonment celebrations were held in many cities and towns. The opposition hoped to exploit this resistance to the measure to defeat Walpole in the general election of 1734. In this, however, they were disappointed, for although the counties and large boroughs where public opinion counted almost all came out strongly against the ministry, the government more than held its own in the more numerous small boroughs. By this time patronage and oligarchy had really got a grip on many of the lesser constituencies, making it impossible for any opposition to topple a ministry by a popular campaign alone. In this respect Walpole's opponents had a legitimate grievance that, although they had public opinion behind them, they could make little headway against the great man. Yet they never proposed the obvious solution, parliamentary reform, but instead merely advocated the end of bribery in elections and a return to triennial parliaments. They were essentially reactionaries, looking back to the allegedly golden days of Queen Anne, not radicals anticipating the reforming movements of the next reign.

In the event Walpole was toppled not by an assault of the opposition so much as by defections within the court party itself. The first serious loss was that of his Scottish supporters, who normally delivered forty-five docile votes in the Commons. These were so angered by his punitive treatment of Edinburgh after the Porteous riots of 1736, however, that they came out against him, and he lost heavily in the Scottish elections of 1741. He also fared badly in that election in Cornwall, normally a court preserve, but largely at the disposal of the opposition after 1737 when the Prince of Wales, who had the main patronage in the county, quarrelled with his father and joined forces with Walpole's enemies. These were losses which left Walpole with such an insecure majority that he decided the game was not worth the candle and resigned in 1742.

More important than the defection of the Scots and the Prince in persuading Walpole to resign was the fact that he no longer saw eye to eye with the King over foreign policy. His own inclination was to prevent England from becoming embroiled in Continental conflicts, and by and large he had managed to avoid hostilities for nearly twenty years. His aversion to war was almost entirely conditioned by its probable impact on domestic politics. He had lived through the War of the Spanish Succession and had seen how it had exacerbated the party struggle under Anne. Part of his determination to keep the land tax low was the result of that experience. He was also afraid that war would assist the Pretender. The pacific foreign policy which these considerations dictated, however, was not always welcome to his monarch or his Cabinet colleagues. Twice he dismissed Secretaries of State with more ambitious schemes for England's role in Europe, dispensing with the services of Lord Carteret in 1724 and of his brother-in-law Townshend in 1730. His refusal to intervene in the War of the Polish Succession in 1733 irritated the King and Queen, but Walpole justified it on the grounds that going to war on the eve of the election would hurt the government which was already badly shaken by the excise crisis. He was probably right to suspect that war would be unpopular then, but he failed to realize that a rising generation which had not known the Spanish war did not sympathize with his pacifism, but on the contrary held it to be unpatriotic. They were anxious to use warfare to protect and even advance English trade, and regarded it as an insult when Spain interfered with the legitimate and even the illicit activities of English traders in the West Indies. Their demands for reprisals found sympathetic echoes at court and in the Cabinet, forcing Walpole reluctantly to go to war with Spain in 1739. Next year the same pressures obliged him to intervene in the War of the Austrian Succession. These disagreements over foreign policy were irksome to Walpole, because the support of the monarch had been absolutely vital in maintaining his position for so long. Thus when George II had come to the throne in 1727 he had almost got rid of Walpole, who would have fallen but for the support of Queen Caroline. Her death in 1737 was a blow to his influence with the tetchy and petulant King. Although George was reluctant to see him go, it is hard to imagine how Walpole could have long presided over a foreign policy with which at heart he disagreed.

Walpole had been at least partly right about the impact of war on English politics. The cost of intervention in the Austrian war was far greater than the financial burden of the Spanish war, there was a recurrence of the political instability which had characterized the era before the 'Robinocracy', and in 1745 the Young Pretender, Prince Charles Edward, landed in Scotland and advanced as far south as Derby. What Walpole had not foreseen, however, was that the dynasty and the political system were now strong enough to take all these in their stride. England absorbed the increase of her national debt from £47 millions to £76 millions, the political upheaval was shortlived, and the Young Pretender was defeated at Culloden in 1746.

The political instability reflected a constitutional impasse. The fact that for the best part of twenty years Walpole had enjoyed both the favour of the crown and the support of a parliamentary majority had concealed the dilemma that could develop when these two sources of power were not enjoyed by the same minister. The problem quickly emerged after Walpole's fall, when the King's favour was bestowed on Carteret, while control of the Commons remained in the hands of Walpole's lieutenants, the Duke of Newcastle and his brother Henry Pelham, who led the court party which over the years had come to be known as 'the old corps'. The result was a showdown between the rival politicians in 1746 which the Pelhams won. Although George II insisted that they had forced his hand, events were to show that they needed the King as much as he needed them. Before the end of the war the King was giving the Pelhams his full support. When they persuaded him to dissolve parliament in 1747 — a full year before an election was necessary under the Septennial Act — they caught the opposition (which still included the Prince of Wales) napping, and pulled off the quietest electoral victory of the reign.

After the war ended in 1748 Henry Pelham quickly reduced the financial burden on the country. By 1750 expenditure had fallen from £12 millions to £7 millions a year, by 1752 the land tax was down from 4s. to 2s. in the pound, and the rate of interest was reduced to 3 per cent. Small wonder that George regarded Pelham as a better financier than Walpole, and sighed on his death in 1754 'Now I shall have no more peace.'

The King's hunch was correct. Once again the situation arose whereby the favour of the crown and the support of the Commons were divided. George gave his backing to Pelham's brother, the Duke of Newcastle, thus breaking with the convention established by Walpole of the Prime Minister's being a member of the House of Commons. Although this need not necessarily have presented insuperable difficulties, at very least Newcastle needed an able lieutenant in the Lower House to manage the government's business there for him. Unfortunately for the duke he failed to find one, and lost the confidence of the Commons to William Pitt.

Newcastle did not lose the confidence of the Commons because he lost a general election. On the contrary, the results of the 1754 election, over which he presided, were more favourable to the ministry than those of 1747, producing a government majority of over 200, the largest in the century. But, as Pitt warned the duke, 'The inside of the House must be considered in other respects besides merely numbers, or the reins of government will soon slip out of any minister's hands.' They slipped in fact into Pitt's own hands when the disasters attendant upon the opening of the Seven Years War in 1756 gave him substantial issues on which to attack the Prime Minister, who, in a characteristic panic, resigned. Yet the ministry formed to replace him, which included Pitt, did not last long. Although Pitt could probably bank on the support of the Commons, he could certainly count on the hostility of the King. Thus the impasse reached in the previous war arrived again, and was not resolved until Newcastle and Pitt agreed to form a joint ministry in 1757. Having the confidence of both King and Commons, and lacking any opposition, this was to prove the strongest ministry of the century.

With stability assured at home, abroad these were among the most dynamic years in British history, culminating in the 'wonderful year' of 1759, with successes in Guadeloupe, Quebec, Lagos and Quiberon Bay. In 1760 the whole of Canada was obtained with the acquisition of Montreal. Belle Isle, Dominica, Martinique and Grenada were added to the list of conquests in 1761 and 1762. By the time of the Peace of Paris in 1763, however, the political world of George II had been transformed.

From Chatham to the Younger Pitt

George III, who succeeded in 1760, was the grandson of George II, his own father, Frederick, having died in 1751. Like his father he disliked the ageing George II, and so the continuing quarrels in the royal family prepared men for changes in 1760. They were not, however, fully prepared for the extent of them.

George wanted as his Prime Minister his 'dearest friend', the Earl of Bute. The relationship between the earl, a botanist and scholar, whose literary interests secured a pension for Dr Johnson, and the guilt-ridden and impressionable young King thus became a major threat to the Elder Pitt. Not that George felt able to remove the popular Pitt overnight, and so Bute was initially made Groom of the Stole. What enabled the King to dispense with Pitt was his determination to end the war and conclude peace with France, for the Prime Minister disapproved of the peace terms and left office in 1761, to be followed by Newcastle the following year. In 1763 the duke's supporters were also purged in what was known as 'the massacre of the Pelhamite innocents', when scores of men whom Newcastle had placed in all levels of the administration during the previous forty years lost their jobs. George and Bute replaced Newcastle's veterans with their own followers, who were known as 'the King's friends'.

The political world was not prepared for such sweeping changes. Thirty-three years had passed since George II's accession, the longest period without a change of ruler since the death of Queen Elizabeth in 1603. Moreover, the death of George I had not permanently dislodged Walpole, and after a third of a century it seemed to have made no difference at all to the great man's career. George III, on the other hand, dislodged the great commoner at the height of his power and reputation, and dispensed with the services of the Duke of Newcastle, who epitomized the Whig oligarchs who had been ruling England since the Hanoverian accession. Moreover, he replaced both with an upstart Scots careerist. This seemed to many at the time, and to Whig historians of the nineteenth century, to be a sinister reassertion of the power of the crown. According to the Whig view, George was intent on overturning the constitutional conventions of his immediate predecessor, whereby only those ministers were appointed who enjoyed the support of the Commons, to revert to the earlier practice of having full prerogative to appoint whom he pleased. Bute was blamed for imbuing the King with these unconstitutional principles, providing his young tutee with unsuitable reading matter such as Blackstone's *Commentaries* and Bolingbroke's *The Idea of a Patriot King*. In the *Patriot King* Bolingbroke had expounded the thesis that the only way to rescue England from the corruption and depravity into which it had sunk under Walpole was by the succession of a truly virtuous prince, who would stand above parties and rule a united nation at the head of a pure and uncorrupt administration. George was said to have undertaken to implement this programme in 1760. Thus he exhibited his own patriotism when he described Hanover as 'the horrid electorate' and when he boasted that he gloried in the name of Britain, while his determination to stand above parties was exhibited when he included Tories as well as Whigs among the 'King's friends'.

The whole Whig thesis has been dismissed as a myth by most modern historians following its debunking by Sir Lewis Namier, who demonstrated that the idea of George's being imbued with unconstitutional principles was entirely fictitious, and moreover that the very nature of the Constitution as it had developed under the Hanoverians had been misunderstood by Whig historians. It was not a dress rehearsal for the Victorian system, whereby a monarch was obliged to choose a Prime Minister from the party which succeeded in winning a general election. On the contrary, the power of the crown was still strong enough to ensure that under the early Hanoverians no ministry lost an election. Friction could arise if a ministry disintegrated between elections, as occurred after 1741 and again after 1754. Even then the King's room for manoeuvre was great, since, although his ministers needed the confidence of the Commons, they also needed his support just as much. In fact a situation parallel with George II's difficulties with the Pelhams or with Pitt did not arise in the case of Bute, for the court had just won the general election of 1761, and when Bute resigned in 1763 it was due to panic rather than to a defeat in the Commons.

The difficulty about accepting the Namierite view in its entirety is that it fails to take sufficiently into account the degree to which George interfered with the convention of ministerial responsibility when he announced that he was going to be his own First Minister. The convention was that the King could do no wrong, and that his ministers were responsible to parliament. But such a distinction was difficult if not impossible when the King took government into his own hands, as George avowedly did in 1760.

Whatever the constitutional propriety of the scheme, there can be no doubt that it was unpopular. Bute was hated and reviled at all levels of English society. Much of his unpopularity was inspired by crude detestation of Scots by the English. Scottish politicians were suspected, quite inconsistently, either of being slavish supporters of the court or of being rank Jacobites. This hatred of the Scots underlay the more outspoken attacks upon Bute, particularly those published by Wilkes in *The North Briton*, the very title of which meant Scot in the eighteenth century. Indeed, Wilkes was specifically replying to the Scottish Tobias Smollett's pro-Bute *True Briton*. It was not the popular press which brought Bute down, however, but an unpopular tax which he placed on cider. This aroused a storm of opposition from the City and the apple-growing counties reminiscent of the excise crisis which rocked Walpole's government in 1733. Although Bute rode the storm until the cider bill received the royal assent, it plainly unnerved him, and on 8 April 1763 he resigned.

The failure of Bute proved once and for all that no minister could long survive without the support of the Commons. At the same time the power of the crown was still so strong that a minister needed its support too. The outstanding problem of the first decade of George III's reign was to find a man who could keep the confidence of both.

In the early 1760s parliament was still under the influence of the great Whig aristocrats whose power the King himself wanted to break. Even after Bute's fall he tried to avoid dependence upon them, and appointed George Grenville as his First Minister. Grenville succeeded in securing the support of the Commons with the budget he introduced in 1764, but he failed to keep the confidence of the King. For one thing he resented being used as a screen behind which Bute could still advise George. For another he offended the King by his manner, particularly over his handling of the Regency Bill in 1765. In that year George III suffered the first attack of an illness which was eventually to incapacitate him completely. Though its symptoms were mental derangement, the disease itself has been skilfully diagnosed as a rare bodily complaint, porphyria. A Regency Act was considered necessary in case another attack made the King unfit to rule, and against George's will Grenville excluded his mother from the list of regents before the bill was presented to parliament. The minister's clumsy handling of a delicate matter affecting the royal family led George to dismiss him on the first possible occasion.

The trouble was that there were few other politicians to whom he could turn without giving power to one of the great Whig aristocrats. Pitt stood aloof from them, but attempts to reconcile him to the King failed. There was nothing for it, therefore, but to come to terms with one of the magnates, and in 1765 George made Lord Rockingham, the heir to the Newcastle connection, First Minister. But if Bute's career had shown that a ministry needed the support of parliament, Rockingham's demonstrated that it could not survive long without the backing of the crown, and it broke up, as ministers would rather resign than carry on without the King's confidence.

In 1766, therefore, George turned once again to the man who had led the most successful ministry since Walpole's resignation. This time Pitt accepted, but his second ministry was a miserable fiasco in contrast with his former triumphs, largely on account of his own personal failure. His very choice of ministerial colleagues was whimsical. As Edmund Burke put it, 'Here a bit of black stone, and there a bit of white; patriots and courtiers, king's friends and republicans, whigs and tories, treacherous friends and open enemies...indeed a very curious show.' Pitt's acceptance of a peerage, whereby he became Earl of Chatham, lost him a great deal of popularity, and made it more difficult for him to influence the House of Commons. Finally his mental balance, always precarious, now became quite unstable, and his inability to control affairs thus led him to resign in 1768.

Chatham's resignation left the Duke of Grafton at the head of the ministry. It was not a position he enjoyed, as he had little aptitude for politics. His ineptitude was ridiculed in some of the most vitriolic satires of the century, the mysterious *Letters of Junius*. Clearly here was not the man to shield the King from the Whig clans. By this time, however, the generation of politicians who had dominated politics under George's grandfather was being steadily removed by death. When Grafton resigned in 1770 the political scene was very different from that which George had inherited in 1760. By now, too, he had found his ideal politician in Lord North. North enjoyed the necessary confidence of both King and Commons. A former protégé of Pitt, he became a personal friend of the King, while in the Commons he earned the respect not only of the court and treasury party but also of the independent country gentlemen, who admired his financial skill. Until he lost their support twelve years later, he provided the stable government which George III had been seeking since his accession. In that respect 1770 was perhaps as much of a turning point as 1714 and 1760.

Lord North's ministry was shaken by the growth of radicalism, and then shattered by the War of American Independence. Both these developments had their origins in the 1760s. Radicalism in the first years of George III's reign was indelibly linked with the name of John Wilkes — a rakehell on the fringe of the political establishment who immortalized himself as 'that devil Wilkes'. He first sprang to prominence as editor of *The North Briton*, the chief scourge of Bute in the press. When Bute resigned it seemed as though the object of the paper had been achieved, and it nearly ceased publication. But when George III made a speech to parliament in praise of the Peace of Paris another issue, the forty-fifth, was brought out. In No. 45 Wilkes attacked the policies put forward by the King as 'the most odious measures and the most unjustifiable public declarations from the throne'. Although he tried to cover himself by claiming that he held the ministers and not the King responsible for the peace, George III took it as a personal attack. The government acted promptly by issuing a warrant for the arrest of 'the authors, printers and publishers of a seditious and treasonable paper, entitled the *North Briton*, number 45'. On the authority of this warrant Wilkes was committed to the Tower.

The arrest of John Wilkes on a warrant in which he was not named began a process by which a notorious rake became one of the heroes of English liberty. He established the illegality of such general warrants, championed the rights of the electors against those of the House of Commons, and got parliament to allow the publication of its debates.

Wilkes challenged the validity of general warrants by suing the Under-Secretary of State who had arrested him. The case was tried in 1763, and the judgement went in Wilkes's favour, whereat he was awarded £1000 in damages for wrongful arrest. This was one of a whole series of cases brought against the government by the press, in which the power of ordering arrests and searches of authors, publishers and printers, which had been exercised by Secretaries of State for nearly a century and had never before been challenged, was declared to be illegal.

Wilkes escaped an action for libel on the grounds that as MP for Aylesbury he was immune from arrest, since members could only be arrested during sessions on charges of treason, felony or breach of the peace. The crown therefore asked the House to remove the privilege of freedom from arrest from members involved with seditious libel, and to expel Wilkes. The Commons duly obliged, and further proceedings for libel were brought against him, this time for printing an obscene parody of Pope's *Essay on Man* entitled *An Essay on Woman*. Anticipating arrest for this, Wilkes fled to Paris.

The general election of 1768 gave him the opportunity to get back into parliament, and so he returned to England and offered himself as a candidate in both London and Middlesex. In the City he came bottom of the poll, but he topped it in the county. His election, however, did not end his tribulations, for although his outlawry was reversed he was fined £1000, sentenced to two years in gaol, and again expelled from the Commons. His second expulsion was an affront to the Middlesex electors who had voted for him, and he was readopted as candidate for the vacant seat in the ensuing by-election. There followed a running battle between the electors and the House of Commons. Three times they returned Wilkes and three times he was expelled. On the first two occasions he was unopposed, but at the third by-election Henry Lawes Luttrell stood against him. Though Wilkes polled over 1000 votes and Luttrell under 300, the House of Commons rejected Wilkes and declared his opponent duly elected.

Legally the Commons was in the right to adjudicate on elections, but the quashing of the expressed wishes of a majority of the Middlesex electors raised important political issues. When a majority of members returned for tiny boroughs could decide who was to be the representative of a populous county the notion gained ground that parliament should be more representative. The social support for this demand can be seen in the profile of the freeholders who voted for Wilkes in Middlesex. By and large the substantial gentry, and the clergy, supported the ministerial candidates in the various elections, while the Wilkites came from the less well-to-do voters, especially those in parishes close to or in the metropolis. Such men, the rabble in the eyes of the establishment, campaigned across the country for parliamentary reform. Eighteen counties and twelve boroughs petitioned the King, requesting the dissolution of parliament on the grounds that it was unrepresentative. Wilkites in London founded the Society for the Supporters of the Bill of Rights.

The society helped to gain for the press the right to publish proceedings in parliament, which until then the Commons had strictly forbidden. Reports of debates had earlier appeared in some periodicals, but the words put into members' mouths, for instance in Dr Johnson's contributions to the *Gentleman's Magazine*, were almost entirely fictitious. The growing interest in parliamentary proceedings revealed by the Wilkes case, however, led to demands for more authentic reports. The Bill of Rights society protected printers who incurred the wrath of the Commons as a result of catering for this demand. Thus in 1771 the Lord Mayor of London, who was a member of the society, discharged a printer ordered into custody by the Commons for printing its debates. Though the House proceeded against the mayor for infringing its privileges it took no further action against the printer, and thereafter rarely tried to prevent the reporting of its proceedings.

The society's agitation for parliamentary reform, however, was much less successful. Though it raised the issue in the general election of 1774, the results outside London were meagre. Wilkes got back in, and moved for a bill to make parliament more representative, but the motion was defeated. Not even the opposition was interested, Burke speaking for most of them in his *Thoughts on the Cause of the Present Discontents* wherein he argued that the influence of the government rather than the unrepresentative nature of the electoral system was the real culprit in the Constitution.

After 1774 Wilkes became less influential in the reforming movement. He himself concentrated more and more on reversing the resolutions of the House of Commons in 1769 which had declared him incapable of taking his seat as member for Middlesex. In 1782 he finally succeeded, and thereafter the Commons no longer claimed to declare ineligible a candidate eligible by law and returned by a majority of the voters. This was a victory for the right of the electors, but meanwhile the agitation for reform had been taken up by others, in particular the Rev. Christopher Wyvill.

In 1779 Wyvill founded the Yorkshire Association for promoting parliamentary reform, which pressed for annual parliaments, equal electoral districts and 100 more county members. It was perhaps appropriate that Yorkshire should take the lead in the reform movement. The population changes of the eighteenth century had altered the balance of people between South and North, and such industrial centres as Leeds and Sheffield, which had no members of parliament, had grown, while many a borough in the South which returned two MPs had shrunk into insignificance. Yorkshire's lead was not taken up in the North, however, but in the South-East, which had always been under-represented in comparison with the South-West, where Cornwall, for instance, had forty-four members, only one less than the whole of Scotland. London radicalism was more extreme than the Yorkshire Association, as was shown in the Society for Constitutional Information, founded in 1780, which in addition to Wyvill's proposals demanded manhood suffrage and the secret ballot. Both organizations hoped for impressive results from the general election of 1780. As in 1774, however, the results of radical efforts at the polls were disappointing.

So frustrated were the reformers at making any headway through the unreformed system that they came dangerously close to making revolutionary proposals. Wyvill, for instance, at one time tried to claim that the Yorkshire Association was a truer representative than parliament. Such frustration found some sympathy in the Commons itself, where a motion proposed by John Dunning, a former associate of Wilkes, that the influence of the crown had increased, was increasing and ought to be diminished, was actually passed in 1780. But this did not mark, as has been argued, a radical threat to Lord North. The members who supported Dunning's motion were not advocating electoral reform but a reduction of the patronage of the crown. Electoral reform was not popular among parliament-arians in the year of the Gordon Riots. The parliamentary reform movement came close to disturbing the old system, but it quickly backed off. Wyvill himself denounced extremists in his own ranks, and never seriously threatened to dislodge North. Although the Yorkshire Association was never formally disbanded, it ceased to operate after 1785.

What toppled Lord North was not the radical agitation outside parliament but an upheaval inside the Commons in protest against the conduct of the government in the War of American Independence. As with the radical movement, the war had its origins in the opening years of the reign.

Although there was friction between the North American

colonies and England long before the reign of George III, the immediate cause of war was the Peace of Paris of 1763, which virtually removed the French from North America, making the presence of troops to protect the colonies less necessary. At the same time, largely because of the unprecedented increase in the national debt caused by the Seven Years War, it was decided by the British government to tax the colonies in order to pay for their own defence. The decision provoked the response 'No taxation without representation' and precipitated a train of events on the American continent which led to war in 1774, the Declaration of Independence in 1776, and the defeat of the British at Yorktown in 1781.

It was not North's intransigence in the face of colonial defiance which led to his downfall. On the contrary, although some members, particularly Burke, urged reconciliation, most shared the views expressed in Dr Johnson's tract *Taxation no Tyranny*. Rebellion had simply to be crushed as far as the majority of MPs was concerned. What dismayed them was the military defeat. All Lord North's political skills could not save him from the news of Yorktown. It produced a revolt among his own backbenchers which lost him control of parliament, and he had to resign in 1782.

The two years that followed the fall of Lord North were characterized by political instability such as had marked the opening of George III's reign. Once again the King was in the grip of factions. Lord Rockingham came to power, with his henchmen Lord Shelburne and Charles James Fox. This was a vigorous ministry, which pushed through measures to reduce the crown's influence over the House of Commons and made peace with the rebellious American colonies. But its stay in power was shortlived, for Rockingham died a few months after taking office. Shelburne and Fox struggled for the leadership, a contest which the King decided by making Shelburne chief minister. Fox therefore went into opposition, and shocked the political world by joining with Lord North, formerly his bitter enemy, to work for the removal of Shelburne. This manoeuvre succeeded, and resulted in the formation of the most remarkable of George III's ministries, the Fox-North coalition. George was the most shocked of all at this outcome and tried desperately to avert its consequences. At one time he even thought of abdication. Eventually, however, he was able to bring about the defeat in the Lords of a major measure concerning India which the coalition put forward. The very next day he removed the obnoxious ministers and persuaded William Pitt, Chatham's twenty-four-year-old son, to form a ministry.

At first Pitt could not command a majority in the House of Commons, but early in 1784 parliament was dissolved and a general election held, three years before one was necessary under the Septennial Act. This was the ultimate answer to those who held that the King could not appoint a minister who lacked the confidence of the Commons, for the influence of the crown was sufficient in many small constituencies to ensure a majority for his Prime Minister. On this occasion, however, even in constituencies where there was a large number of voters, Pitt's supporters proved to be popular candidates. Court and country therefore united to give him a majority. This was the happy combination which George III had been seeking since his accession. It was to last until the end of the century.

Pitt's ministry was eventually to be seen as the first of a series of Tory governments, while the opposition, led by Charles James Fox, was to be regarded for the most part as Whig. Towards the end of the eighteenth century, therefore, the pattern of politics was once more in the mould of two conflicting parties. The three political eras of the period can consequently be very approximately characterized thus: the first was dominated by the Tories and the Whigs, the second by court and country, while the third witnessed again the rise of party. Chronologically they overlap, though the second stage had definitely replaced the first by the time of Walpole's ascendancy, while the rise of the Rockinghamites has recently been regarded as the major force in transforming the second into the third.

It was not, however, a case of the tail simply going into the mouth. Augustan political history cannot be described as a full circle from one two-party system to another. The first phase was in many ways a hangover from the seventeenth century, where the world was conceived in religious terms. Politicians justified their actions by appeals to God, or at least to the law of nature. The second phase saw a secular reaction, typified in the supremely pragmatic Walpole, who openly boasted that he was 'no Saint, no Spartan, no Reformer'. When parties arose again under George III they appealed once more to conflicting ideologies, but the appeal was to philosophical rather than to religious concepts. These phases are reflected in the ideological writings of the period. The world of Defoe and Swift was based on religious presuppositions; that of Bolingbroke, Fielding, Gay and Johnson was essentially secular, the contrast between Swift's *Tale of a Tub* and *Gulliver's Travels* being some indication of the transition; finally Burke's universe was based on metaphysical sanctions, but they were very different from those of Anne's reign.

To what extent the political writings of the era had any impact cannot be accurately measured, merely estimated. Between 1701 and 1715, when the government had relatively little control over parliamentary debates, and the electorate went to the polls on average every two years, there was more scope for propagandists, and there is some evidence of their concerns being shared by voters in general elections. From 1720 to 1760 the court controlled a much more efficient parliamentary machine, while there were only seven general elections in those forty years. This meant that 'public opinion' could be mobilized much less frequently, though it had some effect during crises such as that generated by Walpole's excise scheme in 1733. During the 1760s Wilkes found a popular constituency for his brand of radicalism, and his skilful exploitation of opinion 'out of doors', recently described as 'the commercialization of politics', inaugurated an era when propagandists could again bring pressure to bear on politics by appeals to a wide audience.

Select bibliography

Bennett, G.V. *The Tory Crisis in Church and State.* Oxford, 1975. (A biography of Francis Atterbury, essential for the eclipse of the Tories and the extent of Jacobitism under George I.)

Brewer, J. *Party Ideology and Popular Politics at the Accession of George III.* Cambridge, 1976. (A trendy revisionist study of the 1760s.)

Butterfield, H. *George III, Lord North and the People 1779-80.* London, 1949.

Cannon, J. *Parliamentary Reform 1640-1832.* Cambridge, 1973. (The best introduction to its subject.)

Christie, I.R. *Wilkes, Wyvill and Reform.* London, 1962.

———*Myth and Reality in Late Eighteenth-Century British Politics.* London, 1970.

Dickinson, H.T. *Bolingbroke.* London, 1970.

_____*Walpole*. London, 1973.
_____ *Politics and Literature in the Eighteenth Century*. London, 1974.
_____ *Liberty and Property: Political Ideology in Eighteenth-Century Britain*. London, 1977.
Foot, M. *The Pen and the Sword*. London, 1956.
Hill, B.W. *The Growth of Parliamentary Parties 1689-1742*. London, 1976.
Holmes, G. *British Politics in the Age of Anne*. London, 1967. (The definitive study.)
_____ *The Trial of Dr Sacheverell*. London, 1973.
_____ (ed.) *Britain after the Glorious Revolution*. London, 1969. (A useful collection of essays summarizing recent scholarship on the period 1688-1714.
_____ and Speck, W.A. *The Divided Society: Party Conflict in England 1694-1716*. London, 1967. (Documents and commentary.)
Kramnick, I. *Bolingbroke and his Circle: The Politics of Nostalgia in the Age of Walpole*. Cambridge, Mass., 1968.
Langford, P. *The Excise Crisis*. Oxford, 1975.
_____ *British Foreign Policy in the Eighteenth Century*. London, 1976. (A clear introduction to complex diplomacy.)
Namier, L. *The Structure of Politics at the Accession of George III*. 2nd ed. London, 1957.
_____ *England in the Age of the American Revolution*. 2nd ed. London, 1961.
(Sir Lewis Namier's works were the most influential studies of eighteenth-century politics to be published in this century.)
O'Gorman, F. *Edmund Burke: His Political Philosophy*. London, 1973.
_____ *The Rise of Party in England: The Rockingham Whigs 1760-1782*. London, 1975.
Owen, J.B. *The Rise of the Pelhams*. London, 1957.
_____ *The Eighteenth Century*. London, 1974.
Pares, R. *King George III and the Politicians*. Oxford, 1954.
Plumb, J.H. *Sir Robert Walpole*. 2 vols. London, 1956, 1960. (The standard life, a third volume 'in active preparation'.)
_____ *The Growth of Political Stability in England 1675-1725*. London, 1967. (The most original contribution by the period's leading historian.)
Rudé, G. *Wilkes and Liberty*. Oxford, 1962.
Speck, W.A. *Tory and Whig: The Struggle in the Constituencies 1701-1715*. London, 1970.
Thompson, E.P. *Whigs and Hunters*. London, 1975. (The Waltham Black Act of 1723 seen as a brutal act of oppression by a Whig ruling class.)
Trevelyan, G.M. *England in the Reign of Queen Anne*. 3 vols. London, 1903-4. (Still the best narrative of the years 1702-14.)
_____ *Stability and Strife: England 1714-1760*. London, 1977.

3 Religion and ideas

JOHN VLADIMIR PRICE

The legacy of Locke

The interplay of religion and ideas in the eighteenth century owes much to three seventeenth-century thinkers: Thomas Hobbes (1588-1679), John Locke (1632-1704) and Isaac Newton (1642-1727), two philosophers and 'the greatest and rarest genius that ever arose for the ornament and instruction of the species' (Hume, *History*, VIII). Fittingly for the age, the most accomplished theologian of the three was Newton, and his theological works exhibit orthodox piety but none of the world-changing discoveries or insights found in his *Principia* (1687) and *Opticks* (1704). Although Hobbes died well before the beginning of the eighteenth century, he was never very much out of the minds of theologians and other thinkers in the century; anyone interested in religion and ideas during this period had to come to terms with Hobbes's 'materialism'.

In the last decade of the seventeenth century, Locke published three works which affected eighteenth-century life and thought as much as Newton's discoveries changed the orientation of the physical sciences; they were *An Essay concerning Humane Understanding* (1690), *Some Thoughts concerning Education* (1693) and *The Reasonableness of Christianity* (1695). Had these three works never been written, it is safe to say that religious and philosophical thought, as well as educational theory and practice, would have developed quite differently. The difference between the manner of thinking in Locke's *Essay* and that of earlier philosophers can be inferred from Locke's stated purpose in the introduction to his first chapter: 'to enquire into the Original, Certainty, and Extent of humane Knowledge; together, with the Grounds and Degrees of Belief, Opinion, and Assent ...' Compared to Francis Bacon's claim 100 years earlier in his *Letter to Lord Burleigh* (1592) — 'I have taken all knowledge to be my province' — Locke's purpose is not only modest but, more importantly, implies some uncertainty about the composition and limits of knowledge as well as a curiosity about its relationship to the mind's supplementary powers of faith and acceptance. Moreover, Locke's *Essay* exhibits a systematic thoroughness that cannot be associated with any previous British philosophical thought, but only with Newton's inquiries and, of more structural importance, theological writings of his time. Thus, Locke's *Essay* combines the rigorous empiricism of Newtonian methodology with the systematic structuralism of late seventeenth-century theology, as exemplified in the writings of the so-called Cambridge Platonists.[1]

Locke's *Essay* is divided into four books, the very titles of which indicate the modern quality of his approach to philosophical and intellectual problems: 'Of Innate Notions', 'Of Ideas', 'Of Words' and 'Of Knowledge and Opinion'. Locke's attack upon innate ideas opens the *Essay*. It is commonly assumed, he says, that 'certain Principles both *Speculative* and *Practical*' (I, ii) exist prior to our apprehension of them; thus all mankind come into the world stocked with 'innate ideas' that are not derived from experience. Experience may confirm them but cannot create them. Against this universal assumption, Locke deploys a considerable barrage of tough-minded empiricism, and it is probably safe to say that since Locke few philosophers have been interested in trying to prove the existence of innate ideas.

---

1 A loosely defined group of theologians and philosophers located for the most part at Emmanuel College, Cambridge; among it most prominent were Ralph Cudworth, Nathanael Culverwell, Henry More, John Smith and Benjamin Whichcote. Influential during the latter half of the seventeenth century, they opposed Hobbesian materialism on the one hand and Calvinistic authoritarianism on the other. Selections from the more important works can be found in *The Cambridge Platonists*, ed. Gerald R. Cragg (Oxford, 1968), and *The Cambridge Platonists*, ed. C. A. Patrides (London, 1969).

Locke maintains that our ideas are derived from sensation, or sensory perception, and from an awareness or perception of the operation of our own minds. If all knowledge comes from ideas, and all ideas from experience, then it is evident we can have no knowledge without experience. (It is also evident, I think, that Locke's argument is tautological.) Despite problems, Locke's argument is, to a Western mind, unanswerable, and the very difficulties that we have in formulating a rebuttal are a measure not only of the accuracy of Locke's position but of the pervasiveness of his influence.

Locke's theory of knowledge thus assumes that the mind is at birth a *tabula rasa* on which all kinds of information can be written. The metaphor is important, as it conveys the empirical, sensational (in its literal sense) quality of Locke's thinking, of his extreme nominalism when writing about 'General Terms' ('universals' in philosophical jargon), of his indifference to metaphysics, and, ultimately, of his attempt to see the operations of the mind in a series of minute but important discriminations. In a section added to the fourth (and last lifetime) edition of the *Essay* in 1700, 'Of the Association of Ideas', he enlarged upon suggestions in Hobbes's *Leviathan* about the operation of the mind in creating links between dissimilar perceptions. Locke was clearly aware of the power of ideas to influence and direct behaviour, and he was probably the first to perceive so clearly the way in which an unformed mind could be influenced by words and ideas.

One of the most satisfying qualities of Locke's theoretical and philosophical speculations is the practical use to which he put them. For example, the sections in the *Essay* dealing with the operations of the mind and with the association of ideas are important to Locke's educational theories; in the education of children, care should be taken to prevent unfortunate associations of ideas from being made. Equally, the tyranny that words, particularly abstract universals, have from time to time exercised over mankind, the abuses to which misunderstandings of words have led, did in part produce his famous *Epistola de Tolerantia* (1689; English translation the following year), a document with few rivals in the history of liberal thought.

Locke was not alone in seeking to promote a practical application of his philosophical and political ideas. When Joseph Addison declared in *The Spectator*, No. 10 (12 March 1711), that he proposed to bring 'Philosophy out of Closets and Libraries, Schools and Colleges, to dwell in Clubs and Assemblies, at Tea-Tables, and in Coffee-Houses' (see above,p.15) one of the philosophers whose ideas he most assiduously propagated was Locke. The whole of Addison's writings in *The Spectator* are informed by Lockean philosophy, and several issues were devoted entirely to popularized explanation of Locke. In No. 62 (11 May 1711), enlarging upon Locke's distinction between wit and judgement,[2] Addison insists that surprise should be added to resemblance of ideas to have real wit: 'Thus when a Poet tells us, the Bosom of his Mistress is as white as Snow, there is no Wit in the Comparison; but when he adds, with a Sigh, that it is as cold too, it then grows into Wit.' Had Locke not distinguished between wit and judgement, had he not commented upon the effect in the mind of a resemblance between ideas, Addison could never have chosen such a shrewd example.

Though greatly influential during the eighteenth century, Locke was not always received rapturously by his contemporaries. In the *Letter on Toleration* Locke had denied that Christianity could be sustained by force, had argued the necessity of distinguishing between the proper activities of the civil government and the business of religion, and, while he excluded atheists and Roman Catholics from the right to political liberty, he nevertheless began to encounter some rather vigorous attacks on his writings and ideas. When he published *The Reasonableness of Christianity* in 1695, in which he rejected the notion of original sin and claimed that the 'message' of the gospels was accessible to anyone through the exercise of reason, he found himself submersed in controversy for most of the rest of his life. He was besieged from several sides, most notably from the extreme Calvinist John Edwards (1637-1716), and a series of attacks and counter-attacks ensued.

The Reasonableness of Christianity probably contains the most

---

2 'For *Wit* lying most in the assemblage of *Ideas*, and putting those together with quickness and variety, wherein can be found any resemblance or congruity, thereby to make up pleasant Pictures, and agreeable Visions in the Fancy: *Judgment*, on the contrary, lies quite on the other side, in separating carefully, one from another, *Ideas*, wherein can be found the least difference, thereby to avoid being misled by Similitude, and by affinity to take one thing for another.' Locke, *Essay* (Bk II, Ch. xi).

succinct statement of the idea of 'natural religion' (as distinct from 'revealed religion') to be found at the end of the seventeenth century. It had appeared in earlier writers, most notably in Joseph Glanvil (1636-80) and also in less obvious theorists such as William Sherlock (?1641-1707), but Locke's short book encapsulated the most telling arguments. It was followed a year later by an even more influential (and better-written) work, John Toland's *Christianity not Mysterious*. Toland (1670-1722) accepts without question Locke's theory of knowledge; its relevance to Christianity is straightforward: knowledge is acquired by the comparing and contrasting activity of the mind with data derived from experience — a process called reasoning. It is unlikely that the word of God would not exhibit similar characteristics; therefore, the Bible must be reasonable. Toland's sceptical doubts about the argument that revelation offers knowledge that is unobtainable by reason is expressed in a famous rhetorical question: 'Could that person justly value himself upon being wiser than his neighbors, who having infallible assurance that some thing called Blictri had a being in nature, in the mean time knew not what this Blictri was?' Toland has no time for the spurious metaphysics which argues that we cannot know the 'real essence' of things; we do not know the 'real essence' of a blade of grass but that does not make it a mystery to us. The only mysteries to which the Bible refers are not things unknowable but the products of the ignorance that must precede knowledge or even revelation.

In many ways Toland seems an ideal man to have precipitated the controversy between those of a deistic, unitarian persuasion like himself, who exalted the authority of reason and nature in theological matters, and the more orthodox divines. Toland was christened Junius Janus, but he was urged by his schoolmaster to adopt 'John' as his Christian name in order to prevent mischief from his classmates. He was rumoured to be the illegitimate son of a Catholic priest, and, though brought up as a Catholic, he became a Protestant at sixteen; schooled in Ireland at Redcastle near Londonderry, he attended university in Glasgow and Edinburgh, receiving an MA from the latter in 1690. Further studies on the Continent and at Oxford steered him into freethinking and deism, and when, at the age of twenty-six, he published *Christianity not Mysterious* as his first work, he seems to have been destined to stir up a theological hornets' nest. Though he 'apologized' later for his indiscretion in publishing this work, his later writings give little evidence of his having renounced his earlier ideas. The difficulties he experienced, probably because of his seeming heterodoxy, in finding a suitable position, and in being accepted by his own church, are a paradigm for the lives of future eighteenth-century sceptics and freethinkers.

Locke and Toland, then, are the most conspicuous figures in what might be called the 'revolt against revelation' in eighteenth-century thought. Starting from philosophy, Locke arrives at a theological position that is radically new. Locke does not ask his reader, any more than Newton did, to accept his arguments and insights on the basis of authority but, rather, to look within himself for confirmation from his own experience and perceptions of the *general* accuracy of Locke's reasonings. Toland, as Locke did, begins with philosophy and argues that anything as important as the subject matter of religion must be understandable to anyone willing to use his reason. Both recognized that, if religion insisted on obedience to its laws in terms of authority, tradition and revelation, it would be only a short time before it became the cultural and intellectual laughing-stock of Britain. The Restoration of Charles II in 1660 and the Glorious Revolution in 1688 had permanently changed ways of life in Britain, not least in the likelihood that no power group would be able to command obedience by authority or tradition alone.

As intellectual innovators, Locke and Toland do not stand quite alone, but they are the obvious figures in the landscape. Toland brought to religious discourse a spirit of secularism that has not since been absent from Anglican theology. The controversies that ensued from his and Locke's publications were far-reaching and productive. Once again, the church became an outlet for ideas, for innovation and for experimentation. These trends and qualities are best exemplified in what has come to be called 'the Bangorian Controversy'.

Its beginnings can be traced back to the early years of the century. In 1702 Benjamin Hoadly (1676-1761) published *A Letter to Mr Fleetwood occasioned by his Essay on Miracles,* in which Hoadly doubts the ability of the angels to perform certain miracles. This was not a point of view likely to win friends and influence bishops. For several years, Hoadly continued in this semi-dissenting vein, though many of his other views were more orthodox than not. At the death of Queen Anne, he was advanced to the royal chaplaincy and was later consecrated Bishop of Bangor on 18 March 1716. In this year he also published his *Preservative against the Principles and Practices of the Nonjurors both in Church and State*. The tone of the argument here is drawn very much from Ecclesiastes, but Hoadly's contention that an individual is entitled to God's favour through the sincerity with which he conducts his conscience was verging on the heretical. He exacerbated matters the next year in his famous sermon 'The Nature of the Kingdom of Church of Christ' (preached before the King and published by royal command). The text of this sermon ('My kingdom is not of this world') provided a point of departure for some startling conclusions. Hoadly vehemently denied that there was any authority inherent in the role of a priest; Christ alone had the prerogative of judging who is to receive blame, who reward, and this prerogative cannot by usurped by any alleged representative of Christ. In essence, Hoadly was ready to dispense with the established church, ecclesiastical preferment, sacerdotalism, religious discipline, and virtually all the trappings of Christianity. Christianity was transformed into a one-to-one relationship between the individual and God, with individual conscience acting not only as guide but as judge in religious matters.

This sermon provoked over 200 replies within two or three years, and few clergymen can ever have been so disliked by other clergymen as Hoadly was. Yet at this distance in time, the passions engendered by the controversy are almost impossible to imagine, much less reconstruct. Indeed, it is difficult to tell now who is attacking and who is defending, so trivial and tedious do the issues seem. Historically, the important thing is the extensiveness and the public nature of the controversy. Virtually for the first time since the Middle Ages, religious debate was no longer the property of the ecclesiastical establishment. (There are echoes of this dispute in Fielding's *Joseph Andrews*, I, xvii.) The church, while losing some of its authority and seeming infallibility, was acquiring a humanity and awareness that had hitherto been unknown. The new empiricism ensured that theological doctrines had to gain acceptance by an inductive process.

Not all the interesting or important thinkers came from the church or from a clerical background, however; the Lords Temporal — the 'Second Estate' — had contributions to make. Of all the thinkers in the eighteenth century, Anthony Ashley Cooper, third Earl of Shaftesbury (1671-1713), is the most difficult to reconcile to the eighteenth-century temper. Unlike most of the writers with whom we are concerned, Shaftesbury's primary interest is not so much in ideas and concepts but in attitudes and habits. He has been described in the eighteenth century as 'that excellent author', in the nineteenth as 'a valuable critic and stimulator of thought', and more recently as a man who understood 'the philosopher's need for inspiration in the highest reaches of thought'.[3] His influence in the eighteenth century was diverse and far-reaching, but today he is very difficult to read; neither his way of thinking nor his literary style is amenable to the twentieth-century temper, and his popularity in the eighteenth century is hard to credit.

This having been said, Shaftesbury has much to offer. For example, his notion that ridicule was a method of exposing sham, deceit and hypocrisy — in short, a means to 'truth' — is bound to strike a sympathetic response in readers today who are weekly, if not hourly, exposed to the ludicrous point-scoring of politicians and the extravagantly conflicting claims of various pressure groups. One instinctively sympathizes with observations such as this:

> Truth, 'tis suppos'd, may bear *all* Lights: and *one* of those principal Lights or natural Mediums, by which Things are to be view'd, in order to a thorow Recognition, is *Ridicule* it-self, or that Manner of Proof by which we discern whatever is liable to just Raillery in any Subject.... The gravest Gentle-men, even in the gravest Subjects, are suppos'd to acknowleg this: and can have no Right, 'tis thought, to deny others the Freedom of this Appeal ...

This is not to suggest that Shaftesbury supports the undisciplined or frivolous use of ridicule; his ideal is the man of good humour, not

3 By David Hume in his essay 'On the Independency of Parliament', in *Essays, Moral and Political* (Edinburgh, 1741), p. 80; by Sir Leslie Stephen in *History of English Thought in the Eighteenth Century* (London, 1876), Ch. IX, para. 20; and by Stanley Green in *Shaftesbury's Philosophy of Religion and Ethics* (Ohio, 1967), p. 258.

the iconoclastic scoffer or opportunist ridiculer. The properly philosophical man tries to achieve an attitude of detachment and contemplation, in harmony with the structure of the universe.

Shaftesbury is also associated with the coining of the phrase 'moral sense' (in 'An Inquiry concerning Virtue and Merit') and the founding of the 'moral sense' school of philosophy, which was to be of such importance in Scottish philosophy of the later eighteenth century. He argued that man (like other creatures) was aware of a fitting rightness or wrongness in respect of various actions and activities and that 'There is in reality no rational Creature whatsoever, but knows that when he voluntarily offends or does harm to any one, he cannot fail to create an Apprehension and Fear of like harm, and consequently a Resentment and Animosity in every Creature who observes him.' Though the argument is couched in metaphysical terms (which, ironically, Shaftesbury scorned), it does seem from time to time as if Shaftesbury is convinced that there is a kind of moral imprinting on the central nervous system; hence his discussion of moral sense as a 'natural' phenomenon. Unlike Locke or Berkeley, who would have advanced some empirical argument, or adduced evidence from experience, Shaftesbury restricts his commentary to exhortation and observation.

Indeed, it must be said that a great deal of the persuasiveness of Shaftesbury lies in his concern with behaviour rather than with thinking. He observes that "'Tis the Habit alone of Reasoning that can make *a Reasoner'* and steadfastly refuses to separate a rational or intellectual process from the person undertaking it. In that sense, he is as fastidiously empirical as any of the eighteenth-century empiricists. Yet, in contrast, he is always more likely to construct an Identikit portrait of the urbane, sophisticated cultivator of sensibility and virtue. The reader is enjoined to cultivate refined conversation (with, to be sure, 'Mankind of the better sort'), to avoid 'enthusiasm' in religion as well as politics, and to emulate the life patterns of certain ancients, particularly the Stoics. He is far more interested in the result of education and training, with the improvement of the men who make up society, than in the ideas that animate or inspire them. Religion, for example, has more utilitarian value than it has truth: in so far as religion has the power to discipline unruly passions and exalt civilized behaviour Shaftesbury finds it valuable; too often, however, it gives rise to petty disputes or large-scale bloodshed and must therefore be contemned. One of the charms of Shaftesbury's writing is the adroit and tactful way in which he takes the majesty and authority of religion and transforms it into a branch of the social sciences. A skilful polemicist, he convinces without necessarily converting the reader.

Intellectual history is not as full of chance meetings and coincidences as scholars would like to think; in our present context it would be interesting to know what Shaftesbury would have thought of Samuel Clarke (1675-1729). It seems unlikely that he would have had much sympathy for the rather sterile intellectualism that has come to be associated with Clarke, who regarded himself (and was regarded) as the Newton of theology. Clarke made his reputation in 1704-5 with sermons given in a lecture series established by Robert Boyle and usually referred to as the Boyle Lectures (see below, p.159). The sermons were published in two volumes (1705-6) as *A Demonstration of the Being and Attributes of God* and went through innumerable editions in the eighteenth century. Clarke is famous, or notorious, as the chief proponent of the *a priori* argument for the existence of God. He begins his *Demonstration* with an incontestable proposition, *'Something has existed from all Eternity'* and from this he infers a necessarily self-existent being who has been for all time and whose non-existence would logically entail a contradiction. This ontological proof of the existence of God then moves into a cosmological one, with Clarke arguing, for example, 'that Colours, Sounds, and the like, which are not Qualities of Unintelligent Bodies, but Perceptions of Mind, can no more be caused by, or arise from mere Unintelligent Figure, and Motion, than Colour can be a Triangle, or Sound a Square, or Something caused by Nothing.' Having said this, Clarke then has the problem of fusing these *a priori* propositions into a continuum with the historical evidence of Christianity. Here the influence of Newton is clear, as Clarke draws an analogy between the usefulness of pure mathematics to Newton in arriving at universal physical laws of nature and the usefulness of *a priori* abstractions in setting forth the laws of Christianity with absolute historical veracity.

The pursuit of this analogical method, however, requires of metaphysics something as empirically testable as Newton's third axiom ('To every Action there is always opposed an Equal Reaction: or the mutual actions of two bodies upon each other are always equal, and directed to contrary parts'). For Clarke, that something is revelation: 'Consequently, considering the manifold Wants and Necessities of Men, and the abundant Goodness and Mercy of God, there is great Ground from right Reason and the Light of Nature, to believe, that God would not always leave Men wholly destitute of so needful an Assistance, but would at some time or other actually afford it them.' Clarke goes on hastily to assert that God is not obliged to make such a revelation, but, having admitted the utility of it, he concedes the paucity of the ontological argument with all but the most astute (and previously committed) minds. Revelation provides for the 'vulgar' a proof of the existence, omnipotence and goodness of God in much the same way that the promise of a future life conditions their moral behaviour in this. Thus, while one admires the vigour of Clarke's mind and his formidable scholarship, one ultimately feels that he has expended considerable energy on a largely sophistical argument composed of two irreconcilable disciplines.

Clarke has been concerned to show, among other things, that the necessary existence of God led inevitably to the Christian ethic, and he was not unique in this respect. His name was often linked, particularly in the nineteenth century, with that of William Wollaston (1660-1724). Yet Wollaston does not handle Christianity, morality and the existence of God so monolithically. His chief publication, *The Religion of Nature Delineated* (1722), opens with the pronouncement, 'The foundation of religion lies in that difference between the acts of men, which distinguishes them into *good, evil, indifferent.* For if there is such a difference, there must be religion; & *contra.*' Wollaston then proceeds to infer a Christian system of morality with very little reference to the documents and doctrines of Christianity, a procedure that scandalized his contemporaries. By defining religion as 'nothing else but an obligation to do ... what ought not to be omitted, and to *forbear* what ought not to be done', he created a system that would seem to do away entirely with revelation, salvation or, for that matter, belief in a deity. Not so. If man can distinguish between good, evil and indifferent, he does so by means of his reasoning process. The reasoning process is not observed to take place on quite the same level throughout the rest of nature, and, while one responds to physical nature, one does not attribute to the stars or to the trees an ability to reason. Man's reasoning abilities must therefore arise from something other than pure chance or accident, and since it is unlikely that any putative creator would endow man with a faculty that he, the creator, did not have, there must be a being of infinitely greater reasoning ability than man, that is, a supreme intelligence. While reason can discover the existence of the Almighty, nevertheless one cannot conceive the manner in which God operates. Thus the implied analogy between man's reasoning ability and God's is not total, but the method enables us to arrive at knowledge of God's existence and his attributes without being able to reify them. For example, if one reads a book that is well organized, well written, and well reasoned but then comes to a few pages written in an unfamiliar language, one still infers that these pages would exhibit the same good sense hitherto encountered, especially when there were prior considerations to suggest that the author was the same person.

One admires and responds to Wollaston's considerable ingenuity in deploying the argument from analogy in support of the existence of God though he also relies on what might be called the Argument from Awe — who-can-survey-all-this-and-not-believe-in-God? One of the pleasures of reading the work is in observing Wollaston's ability to surprise the reader with sudden shifts of argument and insight, such as his naming prudence the 'queen of virtues' and defining it as the means of choosing and using 'the most reasonable means to obtain some end, that is reasonable'. He also gives ample scope to the role of the passions in human behaviour, asserting that if the passions are 'watched, and well examind; if *reason* is on their side, or stands neuter, they are to be hard ... ' Surprises and *aperçus* such as these make Wollaston's discussion of religion, particularly natural religion as opposed to revealed religion, noteworthy and attractive both as philosophy and as theology.

The fusion of philosophy and theology is carried about as far as it can be in the works of Bishop George Berkeley (1685-1753). In an age when clerics regularly charged each other with apostasy, heresy, blasphemy and other sorts of heterodoxy, Berkeley was concerned to find propositions about God, his nature and his existence, to which all men could assent and from which Christians could derive a theology, a morality and a world-view. Immanuel Kant christened him the father of idealism, that is, the creator of a philosophical approach denying the real existence of the material world and maintaining the superior real-ness of ideas. Most of Berkeley's best work was published when he was quite young, though he produced some remarkable works in his late forties; in the last ten years of his life he extolled the medicinal virtues of tar water.

Berkeley's most recurrent philosophical notion can be both adumbrated and summarized in the Latin tag, *esse est percipi*, to be is to be perceived. This idea and its development are presented in their most attractive form in *Three Dialogues between Hylas and Philonous* (1713), the former representing an empirically minded man of common sense, while the latter espouses Berkeley's ideas. Shrewdly using the dialogue form, Berkeley engages our sympathies on the side of Philonous when Hylas expostulates with Philonous for maintaining that there is no such thing as material substance in the world: 'What! can any Thing be more fantastical, more repugnant to common Sense, or a more manifest Piece of Scepticism, than to believe there is no such Thing as *Matter?*' Philonous proceeds to analyse what we mean by matter or material substance and Hylas is forced to agree that we associate a number of qualities with certain physical attributes that we might otherwise separate. When we have an idea of pain, or of colour, or of sound, we have an immediate sense datum from the world outside our bodies; ideas may also occur when we remember or imagine something. If we accept this, Philonous asks, how can we be certain that qualities continue to exist when they are not present to our minds? If we are not perceiving an item, in what manner can it be said to exist?

The reply of Hylas is that which we would all make: 'If it comes to that, the Point will soon be decided. What more easy than to conceive a Tree or House existing by itself, independent of, and unperceived by, any Mind whatsoever?' To which Philonous replies, 'How say you, *Hylas*, can you see a thing, which is at the same time unseen?' And Hylas is forced to admit that it would be a contradiction. Little by little, Hylas is led to conclude that there is no logically, empirically verifiable way of proving that a tree he saw ten minutes ago still exists.

Philonous admits that he is not prepared to argue that this

putative tree pops in and out of existence when we are not perceiving it. God does that job for us: 'The real Tree existing without [my] Mind is truly known and comprehended by (that is, *exists in*) the infinite Mind of God.' This argument is a brilliant conflation of the necessary existence of God and the continuity of the physical world. Were it not for God perceiving trees, flowers and philosophers, their existence and continuity would be uncertain; the Christian has no hesitation in acknowledging that God perceives and the world endures.

This argument has been wittily versified in two limericks attributed to Ronald Knox:

> There was a young man who said, 'God
> Must think it exceedingly odd
>   If he finds that this tree
>   Continues to be
> When there's no one about in the Quad.'

God's reply was as follows:

> Dear Sir:
>   Your astonishment's odd:
> *I* am always about in the Quad.
>   And that's why the tree
>   Will continue to be,
> Since observed by
>   Yours faithfully,
>   GOD.

Berkeley's arguments about matter and perception in the *Three Dialogues* are largely a refinement and re-presentation of ideas found in his earlier *Principles of Human Knowledge* (1710). That he chooses to elaborate them in the dialogue form indicates something of his sensitivity to the literary taste of the time, when there was a surprising interest in abstract philosophy. Addison had indeed brought philosophy out of the closets and on to the coffee tables, and many philosophical writers endeavoured to find accessible literary forms for their ideas and speculations. In 1732 Berkeley published his *Alciphron: Or the Minute Philosopher*, which was at least as influential as his earlier works. Written while Berkeley was in America, it gives considerable attention to a believable structure, even to the extent of having the minute Philosopher, Alciphron, standing with his 'head reclined on the left shoulder in the posture of a Man meditating ... and after two or three Minutes [he] uttered these words, oh Truth! oh Liberty!...' One is not far distant from the sentimental novel here, though of course Berkeley is making fun of the atheist Alciphron.

Berkeley's argument in this much longer work gains in plausibility from his willingness to state contrasting views more cogently. He acknowledges that the atheistic position is both possible and honest and does not equate atheism with immorality, which many clerics did automatically. Views of doubtful morality are not attributed to freethinkers and atheists, though the dialogue form allows Berkeley to associate what he regards as reprehensible views with freethinking. In the second dialogue (the work is in seven dialogues), for example, the equation made by Bernard Mandeville (1670-1733) between private vice and public benefit is sympathetically discussed by Alciphron. Berkeley is willing to take seriously the manner of both the freethinker and the atheist; unless a convincing philosophical proof of the existence of God could be established, the atheist's case would be established by default. Basically, Berkeley's argument is from effect to cause: we see evidence of God's handiwork and therefore we infer his being. (Hume was later to demonstrate the tautological nature of this argument.) God exists because he has to; he is the only construct capable of explaining what is otherwise inexplicable.

In *Alciphron*, Berkeley refined the analogical argument to a high degree. In doing so, he prepared the way for the mater of the analogical argument, Bishop Joseph Butler (1692-1752). Butler first attracted attention with his *Fifteen Sermons Preached at the Chapel of the Rolls Court* (1726). These sermons contain the core of Butler's thoughts on morality, in which the emphasis is on man's psychology and not on a set of moral axioms. Butler is concerned to find a model of behaviour that comprehends the various passions and affections to which man is subject. Ideally, man is able to subordinate the antisocial impulses of irrational self-love to the benevolence which also exists in his character. Above all, he is guided by the voice of conscience.

Butler's ethic is humanitarian and pragmatic, but his claim to intellectual fame comes from his *Analogy of Religion* (1736). Like other writers, he was interested in the cogency of natural religion, positing that 'though natural Religion is the Foundation and principal Part of Christianity, it is not in any Sense the whole of it'. Butler's basic argument — that our experience of X leading to Y also leads us to expect that what we regard as X_1 will lead to Y_1 — is respectable enough. He insists throughout the *Analogy of Religion* that we must understand what constitutes evidence and probability. He links doubt and evidence in an arresting way: 'Doubting necessarily implies some Degree of Evidence for That, of which we doubt' (p.224). Like Berkeley, Butler concludes that the degree of evidence available obliges us to believe in Christianity.

Butler's treatise is as much methodological as anything. Suggesting that the analogical method has not been sufficiently appreciated, he proposes to see in what ways it can validate our intuition about the nature of the world and the existence of God. The first topic to consider is that of a future life, in which the analogy is applied as follows: man is born into the world as a helpless infant, develops, learns by trial and error and with the guidance of others, and lives to a ripe old age, wiser or at least more experienced than he was as a child. Childhood is thus a preparation for maturity. Equally, let us consider the similarity of our life on earth to that of a child and our maturity to that of a future life. Training, learning and habit educate the child and enable him to develop to adult maturity; otherwise, all the effort would be in vain. Since nothing is in vain, then, by analogy, life here must be a preparation for a future life, as the analogy of nature suggests: 'when we go out of this World, we may pass into new Scenes, and a new State of Life and Action, just as naturally as we can into the present.'

The discussion of a future state leads naturally into a discussion of the kind of society that one will find in the future state, with the emphasis on reward and punishment, on God as moral governor. Just as in this present state we can anticipate pleasure or pain as a result of actions we may take, so may we regard the whole of this life as one in which we may prepare ourselves for pleasure or pain beyond the threshold of death. Butler looks into the present arrangement of the world for evidence of a larger and more comprehensive moral government and finds that virtue in society promotes the public good, security and power. Looking at the 'invisible World' he affirms: 'there must be a like natural Tendency in the derived Power, throughout the Universe, under the Direction of Virtue, to prevail in general over That, which is not under its Direction; as there is in Reason, derived Reason in the Universe, to prevail over brute Force'.

In short, Butler takes the received perceptions of this world as something rather different from those in Berkeley's treatment of the issue. Butler regards them as a hint, a prolegomenon of a more perfect future state towards which man can move. The existence of God, if not the rightness of Christianity, is never in doubt. Berkeley, on the other hand, was concerned to find new arguments for the existence of God and then to infer principles of morality and government from them. Berkeley proceeds as if the establishment of primary metaphysical tenets is of the first order; Butler is more concerned with the practical consequences of religious thought.

Butler's argument has the attraction of novelty if not the cogency of originality. Today one finds greater interest in the deployment of the analogical method of arguing than in the actual arguments themselves. Argument by analogy was regarded in the eighteenth century as fruitful and accurate: Swift uses it in all his major writings — seriously in the *Drapier's Letters*, for satiric purposes in *Gulliver's Travels*. The opening lines of Dryden's *Religio Laici* are an earlier poetic manifestation of the method. Pope mocks the 'poor Indian' (*An Essay on Man*, I, 99) for reasoning analogically but simple-mindedly, but then constructs his Chain of Being with the aid of the analogical argument. Butler's use of it in the *Analogy of Religion* is representative of the age as well as the culmination of its logical and epistemological effectiveness.

While these impressive intellectual attainments were taking place within (or slightly without) the confines of the established church, a much more far-reaching development in terms of its social and historical consequences was taking place in villages, camp-grounds and disused breweries. John Wesley (1703-91), the fifteenth child of Samuel and Susanna Wesley, was bringing salvation out of the seminaries and into men's hearts, faith out from the pages of books and into everyday lives. Any short impression or summary of Wesley is likely to do him injustice. In quantitative terms, Wesley's enduring effects were greater than those of all the eighteenth-century theologians combined, probably even greater than the scientific accomplishments of Newton. A man of unbounded energy and zeal, Wesley could cheerfully preach two sermons a day, travel some hundred miles a week, read while riding a horse, sleep a maximum of six hours a night, and still have time to write and keep a journal.

The origins of the term 'Methodism' can be traced to Christ Church, Oxford, where John Wesley and his brother Charles formed a 'Holy Club' which met regularly for prayer, Bible study, and that most familiar byword of Methodist practice, 'fellowship'. John had gone to Christ Church in 1720 and rose to a fellowship at Lincoln in 1726, the same year that Charles entered Christ Church as an undergraduate. Sometime in 1729, Charles and John, and several other young scholars, began 'to observe the method of study prescribed by the statutes of the university' (Charles Wesley to Thomas Bradbury Chandler, letter of 28 April 1785). As they were methodical and regular in their devotions, the nickname Methodists was bestowed on them. Within the university they were more frequently the objects of ridicule than of emulation.

Beyond the university, however, they had a far greater effect in the years to come. The turning point in John Wesley's evangelical career can be precisely dated from his own journal. In the evening of 24 May 1738 he had attended a meeting at which Luther's preface to the *Epistle to the Romans* was being read. Wesley reports feeling his heart 'strangely warmed' and that he had found new trust in Christ 'for salvation, and an assurance was given me that he had taken away *my* sins, even *mine*, and saved me from the law of sin and death' (*Journal*, 1738). With his mission in life now clearly defined, Wesley set out to preach the gospel but found the doors of the established church (he had been ordained in 1725) closed to him. At this stage, another famous name in Methodism, George Whitefield (1714-70), probably the greatest preacher of the eighteenth century, suggested that he take the message of the gospel directly to the people. He did, and the rest is history.

Hellfire and damnation have never been so attractively presented. What Torquemada could not do for the Catholic church in the Inquisition Wesley managed triumphantly for his creed. Everyone who attended Wesley's meetings heard of the damnation in his or her soul, of the need for a spiritual reawakening, a 'new birth'. The devil had to be cast out of men's hearts so that Christ might enter. Most important of all, Wesley was preaching to people who had never been within the confines of an established church, to whom religion was still a 'them-and-us' proposition. Wesley found his congregation among the poor, the criminals, the outcasts; as rumours of his compassion and genuine interest in their welfare were transformed into facts, the congregations increased. Nor was he pandering to the taste of the mob. The morality of Methodism was extended to public and social life, and Wesley vehemently opposed smuggling, political bribery, press gangs and slavery.

From a reading of Wesley's sermons, one would be hard pressed to say what his attractions were. His sermons are closely reasoned, packed with information and interpretation; and most of them seem very long. But, having preached to the forgotten, he did not forget them. Methodist chapels were organized for the good work to continue. Men and women found that administration of the Christian life was left in their hands, that daily and weekly devotions were planned and expected, and that Wesley returned to make sure that the 'new birth' did not die an early death. A rigorous discipline was expected of Methodists, and a range of practices to cover one's entire life was prescribed, just as other activities, such as wife-beating, drunkenness and even idleness, were relentlessly proscribed. To the worship of God and the practice of Christianity Wesley brought an order and organization character-istic of the age, but radically different in form and effect from anything the church had ever known. Indeed, Wesley transformed the ideas of order and harmony from aesthetic abstractions into practical consequences.

As a preacher, however, Wesley was probably eclipsed by George Whitefield, an orator who earned David Garrick's approval. White-field's preaching brought emotional energy out of people; Wesley's genius lay in seeing that it was put to good and lasting use. To judge from contemporary reports, Whitefield must have been extraordinary. He preached as much as sixty hours a week, fre-quently with tears in his eyes from the fervour of his devotion, and with his congregation sobbing. His sermons have none of the logic or reasoning found in Wesley's and clearly depended more on their dramatic presentation than their content. Thus Whitefield and the Wesleys established a movement that, though considerably differ-ent in tone, nevertheless coincided with the new emphasis on man in literature during the century. Whereas the established church had started with God and worked downwards to the clergy, Wesley started with the potential Christian and worked inwards to the heart. The intellectual logistics of the life-to-come in Butler's *Analogy of Religion* were complemented by the energetic search for 'new light' and spiritual rebirth in this life before one could even think about the next. Berkeley's metaphysical doubts about the material world were of little consequence to a Methodist: the real world was there, full of satanic temptation, and it required extraordinary resolution and devotion to keep to the straight and narrow path.

The era of Hume

With Francis Hutcheson (1694-1746) one reaches both a transitional figure and a transition in the *style* of thinking. Born in Ireland, and educated there and in Glasgow, he seemed destined for a quiet career as a schoolmaster in Ireland, when he was elected to the chair of moral philosophy at Glasgow University at the age of thirty-five. Philosophically he could be said to derive more from Shaftesbury than Butler, as his adaptation of the idea of 'moral sense' indicates. But he might be best introduced as the author of a famous phrase and a synthesizer of a persistent concept. In his first published work in 1725, *An Inquiry into the Original of our Ideas of Beauty and Virtue*, he argued that our moral sense led us to judge what best promoted virtue, and he seems to have been the first to have quantified morality: '... *that Action* is *best*, which procures the *greatest Happiness* for the *greatest Numbers*; and *that, worst*, which, *in like manner*, occasions *Misery*' (3, viii). A century later Jeremy Bentham was to tie the idea of 'the greatest happiness for the greatest number' firmly to the idea of democratic government and, of course, to general utility.

It is easy to undervalue Hutcheson's formulation of this idea. While his moral philosophy is often couched in theological terms, it is nevertheless man-oriented rather than God-centred. Butler's ethic is dominated by psychology, Berkeley's by abstract metaphysics, Shaftesbury's by emotional indifference; yet Hutcheson not only gives the impression of caring, but starts with particular situations and problems and works forward from them to the above generalizations. Thus his moral philosophy is not only idealistic but practical: it postulates a goal as well as a means of achieving it.

However, by equating the public good with that approved by the moral sense, he is involved in a self-defeating tautology.

Hutcheson persisted with this notion throughout his career, though it appears with less epigrammatic force in his posthumous *System of Moral Philosophy* (1755), which consolidates his various ideas on the subject of morality. There he affirms that 'the *moral faculty* most approves and recommends such dispositions as tend to the general good, and at the same time such as may give the noblest enjoyments to the agent upon reflection.' Yet this still does not solve the problem of why that which the moral sense approves is coextensive with the public good; one is explained in terms of the other, and Hutcheson would not allow of the moral sense approving something that did not promote the general welfare. Fortunately there is always God, and Hutcheson introduces him into his system in order to save it from logical collapse, much in the same way that Berkeley resorted to God to prevent universal solipsism. For example, 'God declares by the constitution of nature, by the *moral faculty* he has given us, that he espouses the cause of virtue and of the universal happiness.' God had created an ordered and perfect universe, and it was unthinkable that he would so contrive things as to promote, say, the greatest good for the least number.

One of the attractive qualities of Hutcheson's thought is his willingness to risk failure; that is, he is willing to articulate ideas and theories without worrying too much whether they are logically consistent, empirically provable, or internally coherent. One of the most entertaining manifestations of this willingness to think laterally, as it were, lies in his mathematical formulation of moral actions. For example, 'The *moral Importance* of any *Agent*, or the *Quality* of *publick Good* produc'd by him, is in a *compound Ratio* of his *Benevolence* and *Abilitys*: or (by substituting the initial Letters for the Words, as M = *Moment* of *Good*, and μ = *Moment* of *Evil*) M = B × A.' The benevolence of the moral agent is in inverse proportion at the moment of good to his abilities: $B = \frac{M}{A}$. Two decades later, David Hartley (1705-57), in his *Observations on Man* (1749), used a similar quasi-mathematical formulation to discuss man's relationship to God. Hutcheson, however, has the unfortunate distinction of being the first modern moralist to employ the forms of Newton's theorems in order to convert the generalizations of ethics into analytical propositions.

Hutcheson's move from Ireland to Scotland has almost a symbolic significance, for in the 1740s the centre of philosophical and intellectual activity shifted decisively to Scotland. In 1739 Hutcheson received a series of letters and other manuscripts from a young Scot who had unerringly chosen both the pre-eminent philosopher of the day as well as a helpful and constructive critic to evaluate his first incursion into philosophy. David Hume (1711-76) had already published the first two volumes of his *Treatise of Human Nature* in January 1739, and had asked Hutcheson for his suggestions about the third volume, to be published on 30 October 1740.

Unfortunately for Hume, his first work — a major contribution to the history of philosophy — 'fell dead-born from the press', to quote him quoting Pope on its fate. Yet later works — essays, political discourses, a history of England and works on religion — were extremely successful and made Hume one of the best-paid authors of the century.

Hume brought to philosophical inquiry an analytical mind of astonishing power. Bertrand Russell once wrote, 'To refute him has been ... a favourite pastime among metaphysicians.... I find not one of their refutations convincing...'[4] The best example of Hume's powers can be found in what is probably his most notable contribution to philosophy, the analysis of induction (briefly, reasoning from a part to a whole, or from particulars to a generalization). Hume makes a basic distinction between probability and certainty: the latter is found in such things as the propositions of mathematics, while other kinds of knowledge are probable. We can, for example, see that X precedes Y on any number of occasions, or that X is contiguous to Y, or that X is larger than Y, and so forth; but it would be logically faulty to assume that these relationships were inviolable or irreversible. We may act on the supposition that the sun will rise tomorrow morning, that the flowers in the garden will bloom, or that the light will come on when we flip the switch. In the latter two instances, we have probably experienced disappointment, while none of us has ever been aware, even on the murkiest days, of the sun's not rising. Hume's point is that the rising of the sun belongs to the same class of activities as the other two (or would have been had the 'enlightenment' of Scotland in the eighteenth century included

4 Bertrand Russell, *A History of Western Philosophy* (New York, 1945), p.659.

electricity) and is not similar to such propositions as 2 + 2 = 4. Whatever is, Hume observes, may not be.

Hume's analyses of induction, and of cause and effect, are his most important contributions to philosophical thought, but they were largely unrecognized and unacknowledged in his own time. What excited the attention of his contemporaries was Hume's treatment of religion, particularly the section 'Of Miracles' in his *Enquiry concerning Human Understanding* (1748 — first published with the title *Philosophical Essays concerning Human Understanding*). In the eighteenth century, the number of tracts, pamphlets and dissertations devoted to miracles and the concept of the miraculous must run well into the hundreds and, if one includes published sermons, the thousands. Hume's discussion was the most controversial thing he ever wrote. A miracle he defines as a 'violation of the laws of nature' (p.114) and argues that the evidence advanced in support of a particular miracle is difficult to verify, especially when reports of miracles so frequently contradict each other. When one is told of a miraculous occurrence, say the restoring to life of a man dead and buried, one immediately begins to question, if not doubt, the veracity and reliability of the reporter.

Experience, Hume says, convinces us of the predictability of the laws of nature and 'gives authority to human testimony'. When our experience conflicts with the report of a miracle, it is wise to rely on what we know can happen rather than to give assent to that which has never before happened in our experience. The consequences for religion based upon miracles are pretty drastic: 'no human testimony can have such force as to prove a miracle, and make it a just foundation for any such system of religion'. Curiously enough, Hume's position was not radically different from that of several clerics. For example, in the same year that Hume's essay on miracles appeared, Conyers Middleton (1683-1750) published his *Free Inquiry into the Miraculous Powers*. Though ecclesiastically oriented, Middleton's argument casts doubt on the reliability of human testimony and posits that since we have no experience of miracles in our own age or recent past (with the possible, but theologically awkward, exception of witchcraft) we should not assume that human experience was any different in the time that miracles allegedly occurred. He attributes the reports of miracles to the credulity and stupidity of earlier ages. While Hume's attack on miracles was different only in degree, not in kind, from that made by Middleton (and other clerics and theologians), it was nevertheless more hotly contested: internal subversion could be subjected to the authority of bishops and archbishops, but challenges from the heterodox required the strongest possible response.

Hume's other contribution to intellectual inquiry (and by implication to methodology of argument) appears in his analyses of natural religion, most notably in the *Dialogues concerning Natural Religion* (published posthumously in 1779). The 'dialogue' is concerned with, initially, an exposition of the argument from design, and, ultimately, its destruction. The argument from design is basically analogical: we see a house and infer a builder; equally, we see the universe and infer a creator. One of the best statements of the argument comes from the protagonist, Cleanthes:

> Look round the World: Contemplate the Whole and every Part of it: You will find it to be nothing but one great Machine, subdivided into an infinite Number of lesser Machines, which again admit of Subdivisions, to a degree beyond what human Senses and Faculties can trace and explain. All these various Machines, and even their most minute Parts, are adjusted to each other with an Accuracy, which ravishes into Admiration all Men, who have ever contemplated them. The curious adapting of Means to Ends, throughout all Nature, resembles exactly, tho it much exceeds, the Productions of human Contrivance; of human Design, Thought, Wisdom, and Intelligence. Since therefore the Effects resemble each other, we are led to infer, by all the Rules of Analogy, that the Causes also resemble; and that the Author of Nature is somewhat similar to the Mind of Man; tho' possessed of much larger Faculties, proportion'd to the Grandeur of the Work, which he has executed.   (Part II)

His antagonist, Philo, demolishes this argument by saying that, while we have experience of the construction of houses, we have none of that of universes or worlds. He is devastatingly sceptical about the assumption that thought is the ordering principle of the universe: 'What peculiar Privilege has this little Agitation of the Brain which we call Thought, that we must thus make it the Model of the whole Universe? Our Partiality in our own Favour does indeed present it on all Occasions: But sound Philosophy ought carefully to guard against so natural an Illusion' (Part II). This basic argument is elaborated and subtilized in an astonishingly resourceful manner. Indeed, the sheer elegance of Hume's prose disguises the relentlessness, not to mention the ruthlessness, of his mind. There is a wry irony to be found in the fact that Hume gives not only one of the clearest and most cogent expositions of the argument from design but ultimately, and with equal clarity and cogency, demolishes it completely, leaving it utterly devoid of intellectual respectability.

Since many eighteenth-century writers and thinkers, modern in outlook and temperament, had congratulated themselves fulsomely on freeing religion of *a priori* propositions, recondite rationalisms and high metaphysics, and investing it with the authority of empirical evidence, it was a bit disconcerting to have Hume come along and say that they had gone about it in entirely the wrong way. Starting from 'truths' that they believed to be self-evident, they then sought evidence from science, mathematics, empirical experience and analogical reasoning to substantiate not only the existence of God but his moral attributes, an afterlife, salvation, punishment, etc. Hume disputed not only the authority of their empirical evidence but the manner in which they used it. In effect, Hume had said, leave science and scientific reasoning to subjects where it was appropriate and acknowledge that faith was the best, if not only, sure foundation of religion.

Hume's intellectual contemporaries did not, for the most part, share his views on religion, though the thinker who would have been most likely to was his kinsman, Henry Home, Lord Kames (1696-1782). Lord Kames was trained as a lawyer, admitted advocate in January 1723 and elevated to the bench in 1752. He indicated an early interest in philosophical thought in correspondence with Dr Samuel Clarke, the metaphysician, and Andrew Baxter (1680-1750), a philosophical opponent of Berkeley. His first excursion into philosophy, *Essays on the Principles of Morality and Natural Religion* (1751), was rather more hazardous than he anticipated, though it was published anonymously. Unlike Hume, he regarded the cause-and-effect relationship as inevitable, and accepted that design in the universe was proof of God's existence.

However, when he discussed final causes in his section 'Of Liberty and Necessity', and concluded that man was little more than a machine governed by the same immutable laws of morality as the laws of nature, he invited trouble. He argued that the 'feeling of liberty' that we thought we had in moral choices was an illusion, and that man ought to recognize that he was not a free agent. This was not a view likely to be appreciated by orthodox theologians.

One of the impressive qualities Lord Kames displays in this book (as well as others) is an impeccable sense of logic. Once he has proposed that moral laws can have the same force, efficacy and stature as natural laws, he pursues the implications of the proposition to the ultimate conclusion, however unorthodox it may be. It is a technique that David Hume also uses, with even more devastating results, and, as the two were good friends despite their disparity in age, early discussion by Hume with Lord Kames could have suggested to the former just how powerful an aid to a philosophic argument relentless logic could be. Describing a logical technique is itself rather illogical, but the logic of the two Humes (the names are pronounced the same) is characteristically Scottish and tough-minded, as distinct from, say, Jesuitical or casuistical. Lord Kames, for example, takes Berkeley's pronouncement on existence, *esse est percipi*, and describes it first as 'at best ... an ambiguous expression'. This is something of a red herring, for Kames soon shows us that Berkeley's dictum is not ambiguous but tautological: he has assumed what he is trying to prove. What else can we perceive, Kames asks, but what we perceive? No one would be so foolish as to say that that which does not exist we nevertheless perceive. He concludes this attack on Berkeley with a ringing asseveration of the 'common sense' approach to notions of reality: 'We have a thorough conviction of the reality of external objects; it rises to the highest certainty of belief; and we act, in consequence of it, with the greatest security of not being deceived. Nor are we in fact deceived.'

Lord Kames's writings are full of sturdy common sense though very few flashes of genius or exceptional insight. His *Elements of Criticism* (1762) went through at least ten editions (including one American and one Continental) before the end of the century and was probably the closest thing to a textbook of 'practical criticism' that one could find in the eighteenth century. His critical method has been variously described as Newtonian, anthropological or legalistic. Samuel Johnson grudgingly admired the book despite the fact that its author was a Scot, while Voltaire regarded it as one of the worst books ever written. It was an attempt to bring system and method to the study of literature, and, in so far as it supplanted moralistic praise-or-blame attitudes and autocratic impressionism, it well deserved the favourable reception it had. Yet it is not so much a book full of ideas as one about method.

The most significant book to come from Lord Kames's pen towards the end of his career was his *Sketches of the History of Man* (1774). In contrast to the *Elements of Criticism*, it is full of ideas, many of them ingenious and most of them wrong. But, in understanding a culture and its literature, wrong ideas passionately believed in can be as revealing as neglected truths. The work was written primarily for the rising middle classes, with the quotations from other languages translated into English 'chiefly with a view to the female sex ...' The result is an interesting hotchpotch of sociology, history, anthropology and speculation. He attributes the diversity of the human species and its languages to the Tower of Babel (Genesis 11), finds that as the population increases man learns to control his environment, and notes an inverse relationship between the value of a commodity and its availability. His comments on the role of women were advanced for his time. He doesn't find them as capable of handling abstract thought as men, regards them as subordinate to male society, but wishes to see the education of women increased, their civil rights improved, and their role in society expanded.

The importance of the book lies in its awareness of society as an organic unit. Just five years before, Adam Ferguson (1723-1816) had published his *Essay on the History of Civil Society*, in which he foresaw the emergence of the state as a powerful force in individual life as well as an increasing stratification of the social classes, and Lord Kames's book was an attempt to prescribe the values and conventions of a society likely to change much more rapidly than any in the past. Patriotism, which Dr Johnson had referred to as 'the last refuge of a scoundrel', becomes for Kames the great uniting value and virtue in society. Small states, for example, are preferred to large ones because of the high incidence of patriotism in the former. Moreover, he advocates taxing the rich to aid the poor, revision of the penal code, and something like free trade. Many of these ideas he tosses out without fully considering the implications, but he was intelligently aware of changes in the structure of society and of the need for more comprehensive understanding of man's social passions.

This awareness of the changes taking place in society was shared by a number of Lord Kames's fellow Scots, but perhaps by none so conspicuously as Adam Smith (1723-90). Smith can probably be granted the distinction (if it can be so called) of unwittingly providing the intellectual basis for the sentimentalist movement in the eighteenth century. This phenomenon was characterized by a taste for and an indulgence in any situation that could move the observer to tears. A sentimentalist exploited to the full the sympathetic identification that one might make with the misfortunes of another, so that the grief and misery of any person, whether literary or real, provided an opportunity for heightened feelings, sympathetic involvement and emotional catharsis. The best example in literature is probably Henry Mackenzie's novel, *The Man of Feeling* (1771), and survives into the nineteenth century in such novels as *The Old Curiosity Shop* (1841). When Smith published in 1759 his *Theory of Moral Sentiments*, developing and expanding some of the hints and ideas of Shaftesbury and Hutcheson, he constructed a theory of ethics based on the principle of sympathy. He argued that the actions of other people form the most obvious objects of our moral perceptions; when we make moral judgements, we should, then, apply to ourselves decisions we have made about the behaviour of others. Not only do we perceive that an act is right or wrong, but we assign merit or blame to the perpetrator of the act. When we sympathize with the plight of any person we confer moral approbation upon his activities. The important point here about Smith's theory of ethics is that, like Hume's moral theory, it is directed towards man, and derives its sanctions and approbations from human energy and activities. It is part and parcel of a democratic movement away from the moral authority invested in God or his earthly representatives and towards various principles embracing or implying universal consent.

Important as this work is, it is completely overshadowed by Smith's next publication seventeen years later, *An Enquiry into the Nature and Causes of the Wealth of Nations* (1776). The influence of the *Wealth of Nations* as an exposition of a *laissez-faire* attitude in economic theory is impossible to summarize briefly. Smith is often thought of as the most ambitious (and best) defender of free trade, arguing that governments do more harm than good by interfering in trade, and that even the most self-interested trader is likely to do the individual less harm than a government acting from the noblest of motives. Of the individual trying to invest his capital as productively and efficiently as possible, Smith writes, in a famous metaphor, 'he intends only his own gain, and he is in this, as in many other cases, led by an invisible hand to promote an end which was no part of his intention' (IV, 2). The pursuit of self-interest promotes public welfare.

Smith was also the first to formulate a theory of the division of labour, seeing in it a means by which productivity could be impressively increased (his example was of a pin-maker). One doesn't need a very sophisticated mind to see the application of this theory in the Industrial Revolution or in the assembly line. Ironically, Smith doesn't give man credit for the effects of a division of labour; instead, he argues that it emerged from a human propensity to barter. Man is at the centre of Smith's theories, particularly in his formulation of a labour theory of value to account for the origin of a pricing mechanism. Smith posits a kind of golden age, without money, with plenty of land for everyone. How were prices for commodities or goods to be determined? Smith's answer is with another of his famous examples, in this instance a deer killed in two hours of hunting compared with a beaver requiring four; the price ratio between the two is strictly comparative — two deer for one beaver. Even in the most primitive societies commodities will be priced by this kind of labour valuing. One assumes that there will, of course, be a demand for deer and beaver and someone unfortunate enough to spend 100 hours killing a porcupine might not find a market for it.

Smith's economic theory, like that of Hume, is very much based on a psychology of man, in this instance man as an ambitious, socially oriented, product-valuing creature. It is probably safe to say that no single book of the eighteenth century has had so far-reaching and profound an effect on European and American civilization. The historian Edward Gibbon (1737-94), writing to Adam Ferguson on 1 April 1776, remarked: 'What an excellent work ... with which ... Mr Adam Smith has enriched the public! — an extensive science in a single book, and the most profound ideas expressed in the most perspicuous language.'

Though Hume and Smith are the most remarkable thinkers of the latter part of the eighteenth century, they wrote in a milieu of considerable intellectual activity. Indeed, they prompted other Scots to authorship, mainly in efforts to refute Hume. Of these, Thomas Reid (1710-96) is perhaps the most notable. He is generally regarded as the most typical representative of the philosophical school of common sense. Reid was stirred to thought by reading Hume's *Treatise*, but it was not until 1764 that he published his *Inquiry into the Human Mind on the Principles of Common Sense*. Reid was particularly alarmed at the implications for morality and theology of Hume's scepticism and by the apparent inability of philosophers to justify in logical or scientific terms the continuity of certain phenomena in the external world.

Reid's announced purpose was to find or elaborate a means by which our belief that a tree does not disappear when we are not perceiving it, or that one event follows causally from another, can be validated. Interestingly, the line that he takes is not that of Hume or Smith, an inquiry into the kinds of evidence we might accept in support of the ordinary beliefs of mankind. Instead Reid proceeds by analysing and discussing the five senses and argues that if we cannot trust the evidence of our senses what can we trust? (Reid could not conceive of a philosopher saying that we couldn't trust our senses and therefore couldn't trust anything.) As others before him, Reid finds the argument by analogy convincing; it is the means by which we relate new experiences to old ones and which helps us to validate the reliability of our sense impressions. The consequence of Reid's inquiry is an affirmation of what he calls '*the common sense of mankind*'. When we experience pain, we experience not only the sensation but a belief in the existence of the pain. Consequently we are led by all the principles of order and organization that we have hitherto experienced to believe in the authority of our senses.

Reid spent the early part of his career at King's College, Aberdeen, before going to Glasgow as Professor of Moral Philosophy (in the chair vacated by Adam Smith). While at Aberdeen, he helped to found the Philosophical Society, consisting of men such as the physician John Gregory (1724-73), George Campbell (1719-96) and James Beattie (1735-1803), the Professor of Moral Philosophy and Logic at Marischal College. Of these men, Reid was probably the most able and Beattie the most prolific. Beattie's first book was a volume of poems; his long poem *The Minstrel* (1771) was very popular and went through innumerable editions. He made an equal impact on the public consciousness with *An Essay on the Nature and Immutability of Truth, in Opposition to Sophistry and Scepticism* (1770), a book that so impressed King George III that he conferred a pension of £200 per year on Beattie.

An Essay on Truth was written primarily to confute Hume and Berkeley. The argument against Hume is advanced in *ad hominem* terms; Hume is described as 'replete with inconsistency', the 'cause of just offence to all the friends of virtue and mankind'; Hume has 'failed so egregiously in explaining the operations of the mind', has 'adopted the most illiberal prejudices', and so forth. In a postscript to his work Beattie writes of the 'disagreeable task' of criticizing scepticism, of 'disgust' at 'wrangling with an unreasonable adversary' (though no one was compelling him to do so), and his rhetoric is dotted with 'subversions', 'poisons' and 'overthrows'. As one can see, Beattie's method is rhetorical rather than philosophical. This is not to diminish its effectiveness. The book was widely regarded as a proper answer to Hume or Berkeley, but more especially to Hume. Dr Johnson, to name only one, observed 'Beattie has confuted him in this essay.'

Beattie adopts the term 'common sense' as sufficient to cover what he regards as self-evident truths. But the weakness of both his logic and his epistemology can be inferred from the first sentence of the first chapter: 'On hearing these propositions, — I exist, Things equal to one and the same thing are equal to one another, The sun rose today, There is a God, Ingratitude ought to be blamed and punished, The three angles of a triangle are equal to two right angles, &c. — I am conscious, that my mind readily admits and acquiesces in them.' Little effort is made to distinguish between the different kinds of propositions that Beattie has jumbled together, and the statement is more autobiographical than philosophical. Beattie, however, would argue that mankind has always regarded the propositions as having equal force and cogency, so for all practical purposes they are as true as they need to be. Like virtually every other writer we have considered, he was profoundly impressed with the analogical method of arguing, and accepted without hesitation the conclusions it produced.

Nevertheless, Beattie's favourite weapon is ridicule, which he wields with all the subtlety of a rapist. For example, in 'refuting' Hume he asserts that according to Hume's 'astonishing theory of power and causation, we can form *no idea* of power, nor of any being endowed with any power, MUCH LESS of one endowed with infinite power. The inference is — what I do not chuse to commit to paper. But our elegant author is not so superstitious.' Ridicule is a dangerous weapon; it can easily turn against anyone using it. Had Beattie's percipience been equal to his fear and abhorrence of Hume, he would have realized that that last sentence ineluctably labels him as superstitious. Beattie is reluctant to commit to paper Hume's implication: Hume is not so superstitious; Beattie must therefore be superstitious. Not the best of all possible recommendations for a Defender of the Faith.

Beattie thus has the unfortunate distinction of being the last substantial thinker of the eighteenth century who tried to unite intellectual inquiry with theological rectitude; Locke, Berkeley and Butler did so with more success. Beattie, in defending attitudes, theories and dogmas which the work of those authors and Hume had rendered intellectually indefensible, only hastened the divorce between intellectual inquiry and theology. With a few exceptions, none of them major, the age of acute intellectual analysis ended well before the close of the eighteenth century. The ideas retained their force and made an appearance in such unlikely forms as Wordsworth's poetry and Jane Austen's novels, but British thought had to wait until the twentieth century and Bertrand Russell for a thinker with the stature of Locke or Hume. It is still waiting for its Berkeley or Butler.

Select bibliography

The books in this reading list are for the most part well-known and standard texts. The dates given are for the first publication, but many of them have been frequently reprinted and are often available in cheap versions.

Aaron, R. *John Locke*. London, 1937.

Barlow, R.B. *Citizenship and Conscience: A Study in the Theory and Practice of Religious Toleration in England during the Eighteenth Century.* Philadelphia, Pa., 1962.

Becker, C.L. *The Heavenly City of the Eighteenth-Century Philosophers.* New Haven, Conn., 1932.

Bennett, J. *Locke, Berkeley, Hume: Central Themes.* Oxford, 1971.

Blackstone, W.T. *Hutcheson and Contemporary Ethical Theory.* Atlanta, Georgia, 1965.

Bryson, G. *Man and Society: The Scottish Inquiry of the Eighteenth Century.* Princeton, NJ, 1945.

Cameron, R.M. *The Rise of Methodism: A Source Book.* New York, 1954.

Cassirer, E. *Die Philosophie der Aufklärung.* Tübingen, 1932. English trans. Princeton, NJ, 1951.

Cragg, G.R. *The Church and the Age of Reason 1648-1789.* London, 1960.

———— *Reason and Authority in the Eighteenth Century.* Cambridge, 1964.

Cranston, M. *John Locke: A Biography.* London, 1957.

Fay, C.R. *Adam Smith and the Scotland of his Day.* Cambridge, 1956.

Gay, P. *The Enlightenment: An Interpretation.* 2 vols. New York, 1966-9.

Graham, H.G. *Scottish Men of Letters in the Eighteenth Century.* London, 1908.

Grave, S.A. *The Scottish Philosophy of Common Sense.* Oxford, 1960.

Howell, W.S. *Eighteenth-Century British Logic and Rhetoric.* Princeton, NJ, 1971.

Humphreys, A.R. *The Augustan World.* London, 1954.

Leland, J. *A View of the Principal Deistical Writers.* 3 vols. London, 1754-6.

Luce, A.A. *The Life of Berkeley, Bishop of Cloyne.* Edinburgh, 1949.

McCosh, J. *The Scottish Philosophy from Hutcheson to Hamilton.* London, 1875.

Maclean, K. *John Locke and English Literature of the Eighteenth Century.* New Haven, Conn., 1936.

Manuel, F.E. *The Eighteenth Century Confronts the Gods.* Cambridge, Mass., 1959.

Mossner, E.C. *Bishop Butler and the Age of Reason.* New York, 1936.

———— *The Life of David Hume.* Edinburgh and Austin, Texas, 1954.

Raphael, D.D. *The Moral Sense.* Oxford, 1947.

Raven, C.E. *Natural Religion and Christian Theology.* Cambridge, 1953.

Ross, I.S. *Lord Kames and the Scotland of his Day.* Oxford, 1972.

Stephen, L. *History of English Thought in the Eighteenth Century.* London, 1876.

Warnock, G.J. *Berkeley.* London, 1953.

Willey, B. *The Eighteenth Century Background.* London, 1940.

Williams, K. (ed.) *Backgrounds to Eighteenth-Century Literature.* Scranton, Pa., 1971.

4 Science

G. S. ROUSSEAU

I think the most profound remark I have ever heard about eighteenth-century science was uttered by a Frenchman at an international congress of literary studies. A young woman had commented on one of the scholarly papers. She said that, while she recognized that Pope and Wordsworth obviously lived in vastly different worlds, she couldn't grasp the change precisely. Here was the Frenchman's cue, and to this day I am not sure who he was, though his erudition was considerable. He arose, pointed his finger at the entire audience — over 500 people — eyes sparkling and quivering with excitement. 'My dear girl,' he exclaimed, 'console yourself. You are the product of your times. Your teachers who have taught you very much about the texts of these writers, Swift, Pope, Johnson, Boswell, Sterne, how to read them closely, who have instructed you about the history of that enlightened century, its politics and several revolutions, its music, art and taste, even its various religions and sects, have taught you little about one realm. They rarely discuss its *science*, the single most unusual aspect of the progress of that age when compared with its predecessors and successors. And not merely the facts of this crucial science [this is the part that made me listen] but its *context* [how he stressed that word!], the effect science was having on the daily lives of those people, the way it caused them optimistically to hope that someday everything would eventually be known, that man might conquer over every aspect of the universe.'

The Frenchman's point was well taken. He had caught some of
the excitement of those people themselves. Nothing he expressed,
neither 'the medium nor the message', was academic or pedantic.
He was simply trying to make an important point — the *most*
important point — about science in that century, namely that it
ought to be viewed 'whole', not in part or pieces, and that someone
today looking back at it must try to see it from the point of view of
'those people' and without contemporary bias. And he had
managed to say all this briefly and emotionally.

He was, of course, absolutely right. Most 'world-picture' or
'background' books omit science altogether; and those that include
it cursorily focus on one or two main tendencies, hardly 'viewing it
whole'. Moreover, there is in these books usually a perverse
tendency 'to judge' the science, from our point of view today, as
'good' or 'bad' science. Least of all do 'those people' seem to
count: people surely no duller than or essentially different from you
or me. Finally, the Frenchman's brilliant reply to the young woman
was correct about the need to explain 'the great change' she had
worried about. Probably no single transition has been discussed
more often than the so-called shift from neoclassicism to Romantic-
ism: in schools, colleges and universities, all around the world, as
well as in countless books. If we are to credit the reply, any account
of this development is incomplete without the inclusion of science.
No, this is not going far enough: more urgently, science, the 'most
unusual aspect', permits us to make sense of the other factors —
politics, economics, philosophy, literature and the arts.

How can this have been true? How can science have played such
an extensive role? It was and it did by a curious paradox. The great
age of scientific discovery, as Alfred North Whitehead and others
have noted, was the seventeenth century; but it took time for its
impact to be felt. There is almost always a time-lag in large cultural
developments — one thinks of Freud's theories of the psychosexual
personality that are just beginning to be absorbed into our daily
lives today under the popular rubric about 'the sexual revolution'.
Eighteenth-century man was the beneficiary of seventeenth-century
scientific discovery; as such, he was also the first modern man
deeply to question the role of science and the effects of technology
on his normal everyday life. It is a baffling but veritable paradox
because the century that 'makes' the science doesn't enjoy its

effects; and, it turns out, the century that does enjoy its advances doesn't invent it. The practical effects of all sorts of previous discoveries would then seem to be the subject of eighteenth-century science. The inquiring among us will ask, what then were these effects in England?

The Royal Society: Ancients and Moderns

First and foremost must be considered the English government's sponsorship of the Royal Society (founded in 1662 by Charles II and supported by Royal Charter), the only national consortium dedicated to the advancement of scientific knowledge. Many students know about the history of its establishment in the Restoration and about its Baconian philosophy captured in its motto: *nullius in verba* ('on the word of no one'); also know that its early fellows included many prominent literary figures of the day — Evelyn, Pepys, Dryden, Isaac Barrow, Sir William Petty, Henry Oldenburg, Christopher Wren, John Locke, Pope's friend John Arbuthnot, and others. Its *Philosophical Transactions for the Advancement of Natural Learning* were read with delight and instruction by scientists and non-scientists as a multitude of comments in Restoration correspondences makes evident. Finally, its early experiments at 'Gresham College' which housed the young Royal Society in spacious rooms in the heart of the City, its experiments in chemistry, physics, hydrostatics, magnetism, microscopy and the transplant of animal organs, captured the popular as well as the scientific imagination.

But the society's development after the first two brilliant decades of its existence is not so well known. By 1680 a variety of administrative and financial difficulties had already beset it; it was not even certain that it would survive to the end of the century. Worst among these problems, surely, was the statistical fact that only a small percentage of the fellows were scientists (approximately 30 per cent in 1665, 20 per cent in 1690 and 15 per cent in 1700), as opposed to amateur 'virtuosi' and other types of 'projectors' elected to membership.[1] This chronological distribution may seem a

---

1 In Restoration and eighteenth-century parlance 'virtuoso' signified an amateur as opposed to a professional scientist, i.e. one who had studied the subject in

blessing to us today, living as we do in an age of specialization. It was not then; at that time knowledge had not as yet been departmentalized nor mercilessly fragmented, and there was little if any need to bring men of different 'disciplines' together. The presence of relatively few hard-core scientists in Britain's only national scientific society meant that serious research was dampened; it had imposed limitations. Other fellows included men (there were no women; women were legally not admitted until 1923) from different walks of life, especially wealthy aristocrats and finely educated dilettanti who liked to dabble in science as proof that they were well-bred 'gentlemen'. This segment of the membership — for example, such amateurs as Sir Joseph Williamson, Secretary of State and later a diplomat; the so-called 'lewd' Earl of Carbery; the absentee Earl of Pembroke, whose one-year presidency is remarkable inasmuch as he is said not to have attended a single meeting of the Royal Society during that year, 1689-90 — advanced its own needs rather than served the redoubtable advancement of science. It permitted virtuosi to remain in the vanguard of science, perhaps the most exciting topic of the day, while relieving them of the burden of making any serious contribution; and as a consequence, and as most historians of the Royal Society have recorded, these years in the final quarter of the seventeenth century were among the bleakest in the society's history.

Some of this situation changed after Newton succeeded as president in 1703, a year before the publication of his *Opticks* which caused so many poets, as Marjorie Hope Nicolson has noticed, 'to demand his Muse'. By 1703 Newton had already discovered the

school and university and who usually earned his living through it. 'Projectors' (remember Swift's attack on them in *A Tale of a Tub* and *A Modest Proposal*) could be either professional or amateur scientists; 'projects' in either case were their schemes or plans for improvement. 'Natural philosophy' was then the common term for our 'science' but with an important difference: it united concepts implicit in our science *and* philosophy, now commonly divorced. For example, the fourth meaning of 'philosophy' in Dr Johnson's *Dictionary* (1755) is 'the course of sciences read in the schools'. Thus Richard Helsham, a typical physician in the middle of the eighteenth century, could bring together *all* his learning under the title *A Course of Lectures in Natural Philosophy* (1743) in the same year that Pope published *The Dunciad in Four Books*. Further discussion of the term is found in Allan Ferguson's little book, *Natural Philosophy Through the Eighteenth Century* (1972).

calculus (then called 'fluxions') and had demonstrated the mathematical orderliness of an apparently infinite universe about which Joseph Addison the critic wrote in 1712 his 'Pleasures of the Imagination' (*The Spectator*, Nos 411-21). These contained five papers on the 'primary' pleasures, five on the 'secondary', and essay No. 421, a fitting and polished conclusion to both sets. In 1687 Newton had published his *Principia Mathematica* or, as it was known in Andrew Motte's eighteenth-century translation, *The Mathematical Principles of Natural Philosophy ... To which are added the Laws of the Moon's motion, according to gravity*. Newton's value to the Royal Society, however, was greatest in the prestige he afforded them: he was undoubtedly the most reputable scientist in England, perhaps in all Europe, and he had furthered scientific knowledge more than any other mortal. With Newton as its head, the Royal Society would necessarily project a distinguished image: it need not worry collectively about the growing ranks of its virtuosi. Reverence at once set in and, as one contemporary observed, 'Newton worshipped and revered, became the darling of the Society.' Later on (1730) Pope thought Newton had been 'worshipped too much' and expressed this belief, in two now famous couplets in *An Essay on Man*:

> Superior beings, when of late they saw
> A mortal Man unfold all Nature's law,
> Admir'd such wisdom in an earthly shape,
> And Shew'd a NEWTON as we shew an Ape.

Though Pope considered the Royal Society's ('Superior beings') adoration extravagant, there can be no doubt that Newton's presidency magisterially enhanced the status of the society until his death in 1727; nor had anyone been such a patron of science while possessing so much 'universal genius' himself. Newton's equal was not to be seen again in that century, not even in the remarkable presidency of Sir Joseph Banks (1743-1820), a distinguished naturalist who presided more democratically than Newton had.

Nevertheless the society, particularly certain of its fellows, continued to be criticized, even publicly ridiculed, after the death of Newton, although by a relatively small minority of the British intelligentsia. When Steele commented in *Tatler*, No. 236 (1709), about the 'dullness' of every FRS, he was not expressing the typical Englishman's view:

They seem to be in a confederacy against men of polite genius, noble thought and diffusive learning; and choose into their assemblies such as have no pretense to wisdom, but want of wit; or to natural knowledge but ignorance of everything else. I have made observations in this matter so long that when I meet a young fellow that is a humble admirer of science, but more dull than the rest of the company, I conclude him to be a FRS.

Steele then was thirty-seven and Commissioner of Stamps, and perhaps was not as venerable and formidable as he here gives out. But the view he expressed became more commonplace as the century wore on: certainly in the presidencies of Sir Hans Sloane (1727-41), Martin Folkes (1741-52), Lord Macclesfield (1752-64), Lord Morton (1764-8) and James West (1768-72). Again and again the arguments advanced were the same: that too many 'gentlemen', i.e. amateurs, had been elected to membership; that there ought to be more dedicated scientists and fewer antiquarians; that too many papers in the *Philosophical Transactions*, as John Hill (1714-75) was acidly to point out in the 1750s in several virulent satires, were not worth printing; that many of the 'projects' delineated at the society's meetings each Wednesday in Crane Court (1710-80) and after 1780 at Somerset House were foolish, useless and without practical application; that the society's finances, as Dr Hans Sloane bluntly put it, 'would needs be placed on a sounder footing' if permanent stability were to be achieved; and, perhaps most consequential for its destiny and role in the national life, that the scientific policies of the Royal Society were too conservative, its activities even more retrograde than scientific programmes at Oxford and Cambridge, which could hardly be classified as 'liberal'. These changes resounded throughout the century. True, Banks, the society's most illustrious president (1778-1820) after Newton and an influential figure with the government of George III, attempted to strengthen all the programmes. But he was, in part owing to his silly paternal attitude to the younger men, unsuccessful. All in all, then, the society from 1680 to 1780 fared ingloriously, except during Newton's presidency.

Jonathan Swift's concept of the Royal Society affords a further opportunity to measure its strengths and weaknesses, not because his view reflected that of the majority but rather because he himself understood it so well and commented so prolifically on its diverse aspects; also, because Swift was a complex, perhaps the most complex, intellectual figure of his age, virtually incapable of simpleminded comment. Swift (1667-1745) was old enough to have grown up with the Royal Society; he was indeed the first generation of Englishman to experience its effects. Unlike Pope, he was old enough to have personally witnessed the reinforcement of empirical philosophy (the 'New Science') and pious religious belief (Physico-Theology); and as a young man he saw them appear to support each other in the learned debates of the 1690s. He actually saw the harmonious wedding of science and religion in the much celebrated figure of Robert Boyle (1627-91),[2] a 'Christian Virtuoso' who published in 1690 (the same year that saw Locke's *Essay Concerning Human Understanding*) a book entitled *The Christian Virtuoso: Shewing that by Being Addicted to Experimental Philosophy a Man is Rather Assisted than Indisposed to Be a Good Christian*. Printed a year before Boyle's death, the book represented his last will and testament about science's support of religion. Swift also saw the two realms commingle in the life of John Norris (1657-1711), the pious Rector of Bemerton whose writings Swift had read in Sir William Temple's Library at Moor Park in Surrey. Norris lost no chance, especially in his philosophical magnum opus *An Essay towards the Theory of the Ideal or Intelligible World* (1701-4), to assert that science fosters religion rather than produces atheism. Elsewhere Swift witnessed the marriage in the establishment by a codicil in Boyle's will of the 'Boyle Lectures' for the purpose of stemming heresies in England. Many years later William Derham (1657-1735) commented on the Boyle Lectures in his *Physico-Theology; or, A Demonstration of the Being and Attributes of God, from the Works of His Creation, Being the Substance of Sixteen Sermons Preached in St Mary-le-Bow Church London, at the Honourable Mr Boyle's Lectures, in the Years 1711 and 1712*:

---

2 Boyle's printed works are found everywhere in the libraries of literary men of the period — Dryden, Swift, Fielding, Richardson, Johnson and others. Pope possessed at least one, Boyle's *Medical Experiments*, and, in view of Pope's terse affirmation that his life had been 'one long disease', it is not at all surprising that this should be the book by Boyle he wanted most.

'To be ready to satisfy real Scruples, and to answer such new Objections and Difficulties as might be stated, to which good Answers had not been made.'[3] Finally, the wedding of science and religion was evident in the life and work of Thomas Sprat (1635-1713), bishop of the Church of England, Doctor of Divinity, Fellow of the Royal Society, and author of the first *History of the Royal Society of London* (1667). In fact, many fellows were members in good standing with the Church of England.

Nevertheless, Swift savaged the Royal Society in Gulliver's third voyage. Here, as is well known, he ridiculed papers of the projectors printed in the *Philosophical Transactions*, not as a result of any innate hatred of modern science nor from annoyance at the society's mismanagement of its own affairs (about which he seems to have known more than scholars have guessed), but because of their substantive absurdity. Swift had to laugh at the scientific experimentation reported here, precisely one of the society's strongest self-criticisms. Like Bacon before him, Swift deemed science in comparison to politics the far more useful subject; scientists, in the words of the King of Brobdingnag, are men who 'do more essential Service to [the] Country, than the whole Race of Politicians put together'. Swift, no opponent of science, affirmed its positive ability to enhance man's daily material comforts; but when he saw

3 It is worth the space to print a chronological list of the lectures: Richard Bentley, *A Confutation of Atheism* (1691); Bishop Kidder, *Demonstration of the Messias* (1693); Bishop Williams, *The Certainty of Divine Revelation* (1694); Bishop Frances Gastrell, *Of Religion in General* (1695); John Harris, *Immorality and Pride, The Great Causes of Atheism* (1698); Samuel Bradford, *The Credibility of the Christian Revelation* (1699); Dr Blackall's *Eight Sermons* (1700); George Stanhope, *Christian Faith Compared* (1702); Samuel Clarke, *A Demonstration of the Being and Attributes of God* (1704); John Hancock, *Arguments to Prove the Being of God* (1706); William Whiston, *The Accomplishment of Scripture Prophesies* (1707); Dr Turner, *The Wisdom of God in the Redemption of Man* (1708); Dr Butler, *Religion No Matter of Shame* (1709); Josiah Woodward, *The Divine Original... of the Christian Religion* (1710); William Derham, *Physico-Theology; or A Demonstration of the Being and Attributes of God* (1712); Benjamin Ibbot, *The True Notion of Free Thinking* (1713-14); John Long, *Natural Obligations to Believe the Principles of Religion* (1718); John Clarke, *An Enquiry into the Cause and Origin of Evil* (1719); Brampton Gurdon, *The Pretended Difficulties in Natural or Revealed Religion No Excuse for Infidelity* (1721-2); Thomas Burnet, *The Demonstration of True Religion* (1724); William Berriman, *The Gradual Revelation of the Gospel From the Time of Man's Apostacy* (1730-2).

how absurdly the scientist plied his profession (as in the attempt 'to extract sunbeams from cucumbers' and other similar studies of Nehemiah Grew, Boyle, Hooke and Stephen Hales or in 'the blind man mixing colours by feeling and smelling', as in Dr Finch's report to Boyle), then Swift knew he must speak out plainly. For him a man is first a human being and then a scientist: the priorities can never sensibly be reversed. Therefore, when Lemuel Gulliver encounters 'astronomers and mathematicians' in the Grand Academy of projectors at Lagado 'who have so entirely dedicated their time to the planets, that they have been careless of their family and country, and have been chiefly anxious about the economy and welfare of the upper world', he, as Swift's mouthpiece, here attacks them unsparingly. Halley (1656-1742), Hans Sloane (1660-1753) and many other prominent fellows were understandably vexed; Flamsteed (1646-1719) and Wren must have turned in their graves. Newton, only a few months from his own death, was too old and infirm to care, but the younger members were offended and now considered Swift among the ranks of their severest critics. They especially took umbrage at the tone of his personal satire: they knew that Finch and Boyle, for example, were the originals of Swift's 'blind men', his genuine targets. These younger members of the Royal Society also responded negatively and passionately to Swift's lack of modesty: after all, he himself was a clergyman, not a scientist, and, though he was well read, his own scientific credentials were virtually nonexistent. They never paused to reflect that theirs was an age when intelligent men — Swift not excluded — believed themselves qualified to speak out on *all* technical subjects: economics, mathematics, music, medicine, hydrostatics. To readers willing to make hasty judgements *Gulliver's Travels* lent the impression in the late 1720s that Swift could be enlisted among the small but growing number of those men and women hostile to science, among those who preferred the 'Ancients' to the 'Moderns' precisely because of the 'modern' craze over absurd scientific effort.

I have already stated that I do not believe Swift was an opponent, even though it may then have seemed so. I have selected him precisely because his complex stance cannot be reduced to a simple 'yea' or 'nay': actually Swift's *disapproval* of the 'corruptions' involved in experimentation within his own *approval* of science was

patently rare. The author of the best prose of the century — perhaps
the best prose in the language — was not such a 'simple minded
swain' that he could not see what immense difficulties lay in the
way of making a pronouncement on science at large.

Swift's contemporaries were less complex; they viewed science
more straightforwardly than he had in *A Tale of a Tub* and
Gulliver's Travels. At first they viewed science almost directly in
relation to the activities of the Royal Society, but as the century
wore on they learned, sometimes by painful experience, that the
connection was increasingly less valid. Pope, though a professed
humanist, was amused by the pettiness of virtuosi; yet when in
1713 he heard William Whiston (1657-1752), the astronomer who
succeeded Newton as Lucasian Professor of Mathematics at the
University of Cambridge, explain Newton's 'system of astronomy'
in Button's coffee-house, Pope was transported:

> You can't wonder my thoughts are scarce consistent, when I
> tell you how they are distracted! Every hour of my life, my
> mind is strangely divided. This minute, perhaps, I am above
> the stars, with a thousand systems round about me, looking
> forward into the vast abyss of eternity, and losing my whole
> comprehension in the boundless spaces of the extended
> Creation, in dialogues with WHISTON ...
>
> (Pope to Caryll, 14 August 1713)

Unlike Pope, the novelists held to no single opinion. Defoe — of
the generation of Swift rather than Pope — was seemingly immune
from science except in commenting journalistically on its quasi-
magical and alchemical aspects. Richardson, as we shall see later,
was very much cognizant of contemporary psychological theories (to
assist his own theory of character, perhaps) but not of other
domains of science, and, curiously, he reveals in his novels no
interest in the creeping 'Newtonian revolution'. Fielding, on the
other hand, was profoundly concerned and took the time to
compose several satires on the Royal Society: for example *Some
Papers Proper to be read before the Royal Society concerning the
Terrestrial Chrysipus, Golden-Foot or Guinea, collected by Petrus
Gualterus, but not published till after his death* (1743). Smollett
and Sterne, in the next generation, referred to science in their
novels more often than their predecessors, Smollett by using the

type of 'the physician' to signify the worst elements of modern science and Sterne by referring outright or alluding coyly to all the sciences within a 'tradition of learned wit'. But the most profound use of science was made by mid-century poets. Thomson, like his predecessor Pope, was enraptured by Newton's *Opticks*, especially the poetic possibilities of Newton's theories of the prism and colourful rainbow, as his poem *The Seasons* (1726-30) abundantly demonstrates. Young's Lorenzo in *Night Thoughts* (1742), like Akenside's enthused narrator in *Pleasures of Imagination* (1744), is intrigued by the speed of light as proof of the validity of certain personal theological preferences: again a wedding of 'new science' and 'old theology'.

Perhaps the attitude of the century was best summed up in Dr Johnson's position. Like Swift (of whom Johnson was often critical), he was deeply involved with science, praising such 'universal geniuses' as Newton, and sceptical of its large cooperative 'projects' and often hasty results, not unlike those found in the works of the Royal Society. But, unlike Swift, he took pains to defend science in all its practised forms, especially by exalting its modern triumphs. He praised Galileo's works as a 'classic of Italian literature' and considered factual 'scientific learning' among the best types of knowledge a man could possess. Yet he most approved of science's utilitarian aspects, the possibility, as he said, of putting 'electricity, the great discovery of the present age', to good human use. When science trod on the toes of religion or morality, he was quick to reprove it, as he did on more than one occasion; but he possessed none of the open hostility of the Scriblerians, and certainly was never contemptuous of or opposed to science in principle.

Newton and Newtonianism

Two predominant attitudes seem to have been emerging as the century wore on. First, the widespread belief in the positive aspects of science — the notion that it was good, something here to stay; second, an increasingly milder strain of criticism when it failed to live up to its glorious promise and magisterial reputation. The first was abundantly evident, nowhere more so than in attitudes towards Newton, symbol of its best virtues. The second — mild criticism — appeared in response to the projects and petty squabbles of scientists such as those found in the Royal Society, but by no means limited to them. Among the best writers of the age far more were impressed, as we have seen, by the advantages of science than by its defects; for every Restoration satirist or Scriblerian wit who mocked science, there were two or three authors who seriously praised it. And by the decade (1727-37) following Newton's death, science was beginning to enjoy the public praise it was to witness down to the end of the century.

In a sense — but only that — Newton had been the deciding factor. A historian of science has noted that 'if Newton had lived in another epoch or achieved significantly less than he had, the whole course of English civilization would have been different.' This may be an overstatement; but it captures the quintessence of the progress of eighteenth-century science. Newton showed diverse Englishmen such as Swift and Dr Johnson, and astute women like Elizabeth Carter (1717-1806), the bluestocking who brought out *Sir Isaac Newton's Philosophy Explain'd for the Use of Ladies* (1739), that a great scientist could also be a pious and humble Christian. Again and again during his own lifetime, Newton had insisted that he who had demonstrated so much about the universe understood the eternal mysteries, as Marjorie Hope Nicolson has written, 'no better than the rudest swain'. Though he had discovered the laws of gravity and light, he could not, as Newton himself pleaded, 'dispense with God'. He continued to assert that, while he was capable of saying *what* gravity was, he could not tell *why* it was. From our historical perspective it is known that he often behaved eccentrically at Trinity College, Cambridge, or in his post as president of the Royal Society; yet he was the first to point out that he was not a 'perfect man'. He certainly never professed to be able to solve all human problems 'on this earth'. Miss Nicolson has captured again an aspect of his impact often overlooked by those focusing on the 'extreme' attitudes to eighteenth-century science:

> The respectful treatment which Pope — in common with his age — accorded Newton was probably not only the result of the fact that even those who opposed the extremes of science recognized Newton's pre-eminence, but also a tribute to Newton's own humility; the generation knew that Newton had never set himself up as an oracle, that he would have

resented the adulation his memory received, that he felt
himself only a child gathering pebbles upon the seashore of
knowledge.

The Blakean ring of her concluding remark is not without point.
Actually Newton and Blake would have had much more to say to
each other than is commonly thought. The Blake who scoffed at
'the Atoms of Democritus' and 'Newton's particles of Light' had
been coerced by the eighteenth century into viewing Newton as a
demigod *sans* human frailty, as well as an immortal who had
answered Job's last question about the construction of the heavens.
Newton's colleagues in the Royal Society — the so-called adulating
Newtonians of the early eighteenth century — were in part responsible for the start of this development; later on so too were moralists
and religious thinkers who dared to apply the laws of Newtonian
calculus to ethical and psychological problems, thereby giving
others the impression that Newtonian science was a 'universal
system' just as some quacks had claimed their elixirs a 'universal
cure'. Newton, having been deified as a model scientist, was an
easy target for those who believed he did not deserve the praise. But
adverse commentary was insignificant in comparison to the praise
and favourable interpretation he was given, especially the real man
and the legend about him that gradually hardened into myth. As
the century progressed, general enthusiasm understandably waned
and became more reasonable and cautious; but it would be
incorrect to state that the tide ever turned against Newton.

The reasons for this are rather clear and have less to do with the
great scientist's person than with aspects of his 'science'. Both the
Latin *Principia* and the English *Opticks* are basically mathematical
treatises. Their theories, it is true, are capable of verbal summary,
especially in the scholia to the *Opticks* — such as 'the concept of
gravity and centrifugal force' in the *Principia* and 'the science of
colour and light' in the *Opticks*. But *au fond* their dominant impulse
is quantification of physical phenomena and astronomical movements. 'He, whose rules the rapid Comet bind', Pope had
remarked in *An Essay on Man* in a passage celebrating Newton, had
uncovered the mathematical movements of the heavens, stars and
earth. Throughout the eighteenth century scientists other than
astronomers and mathematicians turned to Newton's two treatises

in an attempt to quantify — and this is the remarkable thing — their own unrelated disciplines. The 'mathematical craze' was spreading everywhere, one alarmed reactionary commentator noticed. Ever since 1690, the date of publication of the *Principia*, iatromechanists who sought to quantify the sciences of the body — anatomy, physiology, morphology, medicine — had been proliferating. Their numbers included Archibald Pitcairne (1652-1713), a Scottish physician who quickly applied Newton's laws of the heavens to the body, as well as Borelli (1659-1713), David Gregory (1661-1708), Lorenzo Bellini (1643-1704), Bedini (d. 1727), James Keill (1673-1719), Thomas Morgan (d. 1743), Charles Oliphant (1674-1736), Nicholas Robinson (1697-1775) and others. Still others later on tried to quantify geology, botany, chemistry and, in the 1720s, politics and operations of government. A few titles are sufficient to suggest the nature and range of Newtonian influence in areas Newton himself least expected. Early among these printed works (how many manuscripts were actually written will never be known) was *Apollo Mathematicus: Or the Art of curing Diseases by the Mathematicks, According to the Principles of Dr Archibald Pitcairne* (1695), directly inspired by a recent reading of Newton's *Principia* and Pitcairne's medical works. This work by Sir Edward Ezat (a *nom de plume*) satirized Pitcairne for applying Newton's calculus to the 'science' of medicine and stirred a controversy that endured for more than a decade. 'Apollo Mathematicus' did not understand Newton's 'fluxions' but considered it 'preposterous' to apply them to 'physick'. Nor did the matter die then. In the 1720s, when adulation of Newton by the Newtonians was at a peak, other attempts were made. In 1725 Nicholas Robinson, MD, brought out *A New Theory of Physick and Diseases, founded on the principles of the Newtonian Philosophy* and Thomas Morgan published *Philosophical Principles of Medicine, in three parts, containing I. A Demonstration of the General Laws of [Newtonian] gravity, with their effects upon Animal Bodies. II. The more particular [Newtonian] laws, which obtain in the motion and secretion of the vital fluids ... III. The primary ... intentions of medicine in the cure of diseases, problematically proposed and mechanically resolv'd* — works, with others, that once again raised questions about the extent of Newton's genius.

The crucial issue in all these works — space permits the mention of only a few — was the application of mathematics to other developing sciences. George Cheyne (1671-1743), Samuel Richardson's medical friend about whom more will be said, succinctly put the matter in the preface of his own book on iatromechanism: 'It is very hard to apply *Geometry* to *Physiology*, with such Accuracy and Niceness, as to exclude all possibility of Wrangling.' Perhaps so, but these scientists were willing to try, despite the reception they might receive. Trained in the 'sciences of the body', they had also studied the mathematical 'systems' of Euclid, Bartholinus and Newton, as well as the physico-theologies of Thomas Burnet (1635-1715) and John Keill (1671-1721, not to be confused with his brother mentioned earlier), and were brave enough to reach out. They could not have known what they would discover, but Newton's own originality had set a clear example of the 'ways of truth'. Dr Cheyne sounded a familiar note when he urged them to reap 'all the Advantages in Practice from Mechanick [Newtonian] Theories', lamenting at the same time that physiology was still 'too primitive'. Others commented that the attempt was premature, that not enough was as yet known about physiology. Still others — like the anonymous author of a satire in the British Museum merely entitled 'The Quack Doctors' — ridiculed iatromechanical jargon in low burlesque rhymes:

> His Origin we'll now describe;
> This Member of the Quacking Tribe,
> Him we shall find, like all the rest,
> But an Iatro Mechanic bred at best;
> And that too of the lowest class ...

As late as mid-century, satires were still flowing from the pens of paid hacks and outraged doctors, thereby indicating that interest in iatromechanical ideas had not been extinguished. One scribbler as much as admitted this in *A Gothic Oration, In Praise of a Bad, a Tedious, and a Puzzling Practice in Physick* ... bound together with a series of medical satires in the Wellcome Institute for the History of Medicine called *Ironic and Serious Discourses on the Subject of Physick* (1749).

In these and other 'sciences', Newton's 'fluxions' — though Leibniz claimed to have discovered them as well — were a prerequisite not to be bypassed. As the century progressed it appeared to many that Newton, rather than any one of his predecessors, had been the most important scientist in the history of Western civilization. Kepler's laws, Galileo's telescope, Hooke's microscope, Leeuwenhoek's discovery of the existence of male spermatozoa, and Harvey's discovery of the circulation of the blood were all significant imaginative leaps accompanied by solid scientific demonstrations. But Newton's precision in 'proving' his already remarkable theory seemed unparalleled. Regardless of our attitude towards the mixed blessing of quantification, Newton's contemporaries admired 'numbers' and equated them with validity. In one realm — poetry — Newton despite himself was already salient. In the words of Miss Nicolson, one of his shrewdest students in this century, 'Newton gave colour back to poetry from which it had almost fled during the period of Cartesianism.' This is true, but other realms were still untapped even by the poets. If the 'laws of the universe' could be mathematically pinned, so could the 'laws of mankind'. Thus the optimism that especially prevailed among certain of the Scottish philosophers about precise — i.e. mathematical — sciences of ethics, politics, psychology, aesthetics and (of course) art and architecture which, through Leonardo and others in the Renaissance, had originally been mathematically derived. Wren, one of the charter members of the Royal Society, had long ago put his mathematical expertise to use in his churches. But now in mid-century the discovery remained for application beyond the realms of architecture and medicine to the relatively new 'sciences of man'. What therefore began at the opening of the eighteenth century as a feat in astronomy ended in a near-revolution of all the sciences — 'near' because the nineteenth century would have to complete the task. And at the centre of all this activity was Newton and, as shall be seen later, John Locke too. Pope's sense of a progression from 'God' to 'Newton' to 'light' proved historically true. 'God said, "Let Newton be!" and all was Light'! The epitaph was perfect!

Yet the deity's will would have been enacted much more slowly if scientists other than Newton and societies other than the Royal Society had not also contributed. It is notable that most of these men and groups were located outside London, following the dissemination of knowledge into the provinces. One of the earliest was the Lunar Society, founded in 1766 at Birmingham by Matthew

Boulton (1728-1809), the manufacturer of light metal goods who later purchased the patents of James Watt's (1736-1819) steam engine. Joseph Priestley (1733-1804), one of the members of the Lunar Society, was to become the foremost chemist in Britain in the late eighteenth century, responsible in large part for the overthrow of the still prevalent phlogiston theory. Another important scientific society outside London established in the same period was the Manchester Literary and Philosophical Society. It boasted among its members Thomas Percival (1740-1804), the great 'charity physician' who revolutionized care for the poor. In Scotland the Philosophical Society of Edinburgh was founded in 1732, enlisting the names of members who now collectively read like a 'Who's Who' of the Scottish Enlightenment: David Hume the philosopher, Adam Smith the economist, Joseph Black (1728-97) the chemist, James Hutton (1726-97), sometimes called 'the father of modern geology', and so on. These and other societies were the 'Modern' counterparts of earlier societies devoted to study of the 'Ancients': for example, the Society of Antiquaries founded in 1717; the Spalding Gentlemen's Society founded in the same year by Maurice Johnson (1688-1755); and dozens of others in the provinces. Newton, Sloane, Folkes — all presidents of the Royal Society — were members of the Spalding Society; so too were Pope and Gay, the poets. Conversely, Joseph Banks (1714-61), father of the Banks who was to become president of the Royal Society, was also a member, though his main interests, like his son's, were scientific rather than antiquarian. In all these developments and details about the rise of scientific societies it must be borne in mind that it was an age when poets read scientists, scientists poets, and philosophy was a subject common to both. The presence of dozens of medical works in the libraries of Dr Johnson and Laurence Sterne was hardly accidental. They read them with delight and instruction. Similarly, so-called Ancients were interested in topics of the Moderns, notwithstanding the much discussed Ancients-Moderns controversy that had flared in the first decade of the century but which soon abated.

Scientific activity in the provinces cannot therefore be minimized. Furthermore, a pattern was developing in which London provided the theory of science while the provinces supplied the application. London, Johnson's 'neighb'ring town' with her numerous scientific clubs and societies for 'the advancement of learning', attracted men inclined to the philosophical aspects of the sciences; the provinces, especially the Midlands and the North, looked for practical solutions, perhaps as a result of geographical necessity. Newton's friend, J.T. Desaguliers (1686-1744), achieved this distinction rather early in the century. He had been among Newton's most ardent admirers and had distinguished himself by a long poem on the *Newtonian System of the World, the Best Model of Government* (1728), insisting that the mathematical discoveries of the *Principia* should be applied to every branch of human activity. By attempting to quantify politics and give it a scientific aura, his effort resembled that of the iatromechanists already discussed. But after Newton's death he grew interested in the technological aspects of science, most notably in his own inventions for the application of steam. Therefore, when he later wrote *A Course of Experimental Philosophy* (1734), he had occasion to discuss Thomas Newcomen's (1663-1729) steam engine. Desaguliers actually misreported many of the details of Newcomen's attempts to find an effective machine to convert heat into mechanical energy. But in one area Desaguliers commented in a useful way. This relates to Newcomen's largely empirical skill. 'After a great many laborious attempts,' Desaguliers wrote at the end of his lengthy treatment of Newcomen's career, 'they [Newcomen and his collaborators] did make the engine work; but not being either philosophers to understand the reasons, or mathematicians enough to calculate the powers and to proportion the parts, very luckily by accident found what they sought for.' Newcomen, a blacksmith of Dartmouth in the West country, seemed incapable to Desaguliers of possessing more than 'empirical skill' to put into practice the suggestions of 'real scientists'.

A similar case existed in John Harrison (1693-1776), the Yorkshire watchmaker who had come closer than any other man in the eighteenth century to solving the problem of ascertaining the longitude of a ship at sea. In view of British military and naval power, this had long been the superlative priority with the government. Almost every early FRS in the Restoration turned to this problem at one time or another; none was successful. In July 1714 the government established a Board of the Longitude offering prizes up to the amount of £20,000 for successful methods of finding the longitude within a stated number of degrees of accuracy. Although Tobias Meyer (1723-63), the director of the university observatory at Göttingen, was given the board's first award, his method was far from successful. At best it required about two hours of mathematical calculations and was only accurate to within twenty miles. Needed instead were accurate mechanical clocks, small enough not to be too costly to manufacture. Harrison invented these and, in the words of one marine historian, 'gradually minimized their inherent defects by sheer mechanical skill'. Once again, the Yorkshireman's 'empirical skill' as compared to potential 'theoretical knowledge' was the subject of discussion, as in the previous case of Newcomen. This time, though, there was a difference. Ever since the early eighteenth century — as Miss Nicolson and I have written elsewhere — 'this matter of the longitude was the most urgent scientific problem to the government, far more important in the minds of monarchs and Parliaments than remote astronomical theories'. Moreover, almost everyone, it seems, had given his opinion on the matter, laymen especially. The Scriblerians — Pope, Gay, Swift, Arbuthnot, joint authors of *The Memoirs of Martinus Scriblerus* — had written at length about it; and Newton, Halley, Flamsteed, Samuel Clarke, the English divine who defended Newton against Leibniz, Roger Cotes (1682-1716), the mathematical genius and Professor of Astronomy at Trinity College, Cambridge, who tragically died at the age of thirty-four, discussed it constantly. Whiston, about whom we have already heard, and Humphry Ditton (1675-1715), a minor mathematician who had been one of the early popularizers of Newton's *Principia*, set it as their primary task after 1714 and eventually, but wrongly, thought they had discovered it. Swift or one of the other Scriblerians wrote an 'Ode for Musick, on the Longitude', and Prior was sure to nod at it, however playfully, in *Alma*:

> Circles to square, and Cubes to double,
> Would give a Man excessive Trouble;
> The Longitude uncertain roams,
> In spight of Wh____n and his Bombs.

'Whiston's bombs', like many other abortive attempts, were ridiculed for their absurdity and until the 1730s the longitude seemed an insoluble riddle. Thus when Harrison's chronometer finally proved the premiss wrong, there was not so much said about his own origins and abilities as otherwise would have been the case with a lesser problem.

Harrison's chronometer, Newcomen's steam engine, Watt's better engine: these practical instruments necessary for England's pre-eminence as a maritime power whose greatest wealth was shipping were far removed from Newton's abstract hypotheses. Yet in the progress from the theoretical vein to the practical application, one kaleidoscopically views the march of science from about 1680 to 1780. Theories everywhere in the country were quickly being absorbed into daily 'practical science'. And men barely trained in mathematics nevertheless persisted until repetition produced 'empirical perfection'. Thus the movement from science to technology and their intrinsic relation of *concordia discors* was then firmly established. By 1774, when John Wilkinson (1728-1808) patented his precision cannon borer that made possible the commercial development of Watt's improved steam engine, it was a different world from the one ridiculed by the Scriblerians in 1714. Everyone, rich and poor, native and foreign, could directly or indirectly witness the advantages attributed to science — in particular to the now indispensable laws about the nature of gravity. Though Swift, Pope and all of 'their tribe' sometimes bitterly complained about the 'adoration of Newton' — Christ the Second — it may well be that Desaguliers was right after all. At least history had proved him right when he contended that Newton had transformed the world from 'ancient' to 'modern', or in less superlative terms, Newton had etched out modernity itself:

> Newton the unparallel'd, whose Name
> No Time will wear out the Book of Fame,
> Coelestiall Science has promoted more,
> Than all the Sages that have shone before.
> Nature compell'd his piercing Mind obeys,
> And gladly shows him all her secret Ways;
> 'Gainst Mathematics she has no Defence,
> And yields t' experimental Consequence;
> His Tow'ring Genius, from its certain Cause
> Ev'ry Appearance *a priori* draws,
> And shews th' Almighty Architect's unalter'd Laws.

Medicine

Medicine was the other 'science' at that time that rivalled mathematics in its forward strides. Although it boasted no 'universal genius' like Newton, it claimed Albrecht von Haller (1708-77), the great Swiss physiologist in Göttingen who also wrote poetry and novels, and his teacher Hermann Boerhaave (1668-1738), a Dutch professor of medicine at Leyden who instructed more leading physicians than anyone else in the eighteenth century. Boerhaave's fame was spread so far and wide that a letter merely addressed 'to Boerhaave of Europe' allegedly reached him. Both these influential medical scientists stressed one thing: the urgent necessity of all medical men to integrate the findings of other sciences. The integration of medicine and mathematics in the work of various iatromechanists has already been discussed. But this was accommodation of one other 'science' only, and thinkers like Boerhaave and Haller were emphasizing integration with *all* the sciences. They asked not only for the allied areas of physiology and anatomy, but less evident ones ranging from botany and microscopy to economics (for living conditions of the poor) and arithmetic (for vital statistics and personal case histories).

Although Boerhaave and Haller were not 'Englishmen', this fact alone did not detract from their justly deserved reputation in the British Isles. Dr Johnson idolized the former — 'May those who study his Writings, imitate his Life' — perhaps more than any other scientist and certainly more than Newton. 'There was in his Air and Motion', Johnson wrote in his *Life of Boerhaave* published in Robert James's *Medicinal Dictionary* (1743), 'something rough and artless, but so majestic and great at the same time, that no Man ever looked upon him without Veneration, and a kind of tacit Submission to the Superiority of his Genius.' The physical similarity of the two men was apparent enough. For Johnson, Boerhaave's greatest 'genius', like Dr Thomas Sydenham's (1624-89) before him, was 'piety', not chemistry or medicine or any of Boerhaave's books. Unlike Swift's 'fools' in the Academy of Lagado, Boerhaave, according to Johnson's biography, never permitted his 'pride' to guide him: 'so far was this Man from being made impious by Philosophy, or vain by Knowledge, or by Virtue, that he ascribed all his Abilities to the Bounty, and all his Goodness to the Grace of

God.' This is indeed a very different picture from Smollett's 'wrangling physicians' in *Humphry Clinker* or Hogarth's in 'A Consultation of Doctors'. But it provides the necessary corrective to a jaded Georgian age that had lost its confidence in any type of practising physician, 'Sons of Mammon' as one satirist called them, and 'filthy children of Lucre', as did another.

Britain had her distinguished medical men too, though none on a parity with these two extraordinary models. For rather clear reasons, Britain's leading medical men were primarily Scotsmen trained in Leyden by Boerhaave himself; later they returned to their native country and put into practice the new techniques they had learned. There were Alexander Monro (1697-1767), known as Monro *primus*, and his son Alexander (1733-1817), Monro *secundus*, both distinguished teachers of medicine and anatomists immortalized by Pope in the *Dunciad* and *Imitations of Horace*; William Cullen (1710-90), after Boerhaave probably the leading European physiologist in a chair of medicine, and Cullen's student John Brown (1735-88); Robert Whytt (1714-66), the 'philosopher of medicine' who probed deeply into questions about medicine and man; the obstetricians William Smellie (1697-1763) and William Hunter (1718-83), and William Hunter's brother John (1728-93), whose 'smalle Latine and lesse Greek' did not prevent him from becoming the 'first modern surgeon'.

These and many other British physicians are noteworthy, but their achievements cannot be compared to those of the great Continental physicians. In part this resulted from the conservatism of the British, especially the English, universities — they turned out a 'product' seemingly incapable of imaginative vision and genuine love for medical research — and in part from the different conception of physicians in England. *Ferdinand Count Fathom*, the third novel of Smollett (1721-71), provides one of the best examples of these differences. Smollett himself was a practising physician and had observed medical men all his life; he personally knew many of the celebrated doctors just mentioned, especially the Hunters; he was pre-eminently qualified to comment on every aspect of their activity and he did so. Collectively Smollett's doctors represent the first extended use of a professional group for fictional purposes, at least by a novelist of stature. In his customary satiric vein he depicts the foibles and follies of particular doctors, and attacks the profession generally. Yet the analysis is not without subtlety: by the use of various literary techniques — and this is why Smollett is of unusual interest both to the scientific and literary world — he makes the medical profession a symbol of the disruptions, corruptions and irrationality of the whole social order. He met the prejudices of contemporary readers — that is to say the common English man — in making the physician an emblem of pedantry, oddities, professional jealousy, hypocrisy and venality. His physicians are distrusted by their own colleagues and despised by the general public. For every 'good' physician — the young Dr Morgan in *Roderick Random* — there are five 'evil' ones; their grotesque names alone indicate their salient qualities: 'Dr Crab', 'Dr Grubble', 'Dr Lavement', 'Dr Snarler', 'Dr Simper', 'Dr Buffalo', 'Dr Crabclaw', and dozens of others. The preponderance of bad ones to good ones is so great that there can be no question where Smollett himself stood. In Chapter 52 of *Count Fathom* the antihero, Ferdinand Fathom, having become a doctor — in the words of the title of the chapter — 'Repairs to the Metropolis [London], and enrols himself among the sons of Paean'. No sooner has he done so than 'Dr Fathom' discovers the greed, indecency and inhumanity of the London medical profession. Smollett's description is so vivid that part of it is worth quoting in full:

> In his researches, he [Fathom] found that the great world was wholly engrossed by a few practitioners who had arrived at the summit of reputation, consequently, were no longer obliged to cultivate those arts by which they rose; and that the rest of the business was parcelled out into small enclosures, occupied by different groupes of personages, male and female, who stood in rings, and tossed the ball from one to another, there being in each department two sets, the individuals of which relieved one another occasionally. Every knot was composed of a waiting-woman, nurse, apothecary, surgeon and physician, and, sometimes, a midwife was admitted into the partie; and in this manner the farce was commonly performed.
>
> A fine lady, fatigued with idleness, complains of the vapours, is deprived of her rest, tho' not so sick as to have recourse to medicine: her favourite maid, tired with giving

her attendance in the night, thinks proper, for the benefit of her own repose, to complain of a violent head-ach, and recommends to her mistress a nurse of approved tenderness and discretion; at whose house (in all likelihood) the said chamber-maid hath oft given the rendezvous to a male friend. The nurse, well skilled in the mysteries of her occupation, persuades the patient, that her malady, far from being slight or chimerical, may proceed to a very dangerous degree of the hysterical affection, unless it be nipt in the bud by some very effectual remedy: then she recounts a surprising cure performed by a certain apothecary, and appeals to the testimony of the waiting woman, who being the gossip of his wife, confirms the evidence and corroborates the proposal. The apothecary being summoned, finds her ladyship in such a delicate situation, that he declines prescribing, and advises her to send for a physician without delay. The nomination, of course, falls to him, and the doctor being called, declares the necessity of immediate venaesection, which is accordingly performed by the surgeon of the association.

This is one way of beginning the game: tho' the commencement often varies, and sometimes the apothecary, and sometimes the physician opens the scene; but, be that as it will, they always appear in a string, like a flight of wild geese, and each confederacy maintains a correspondence with one particular undertaker.

It is hard to reconcile Smollett's 'knot' and 'confederacy' with the rest of the eighteenth-century medical world, certainly with the achievements of a Boerhaave, Haller or Cullen or, more locally, with the Scottish physicians in Glasgow and Edinburgh. There is some truth in the argument that Smollett was vindictive. Although he had studied medicine at Glasgow, his own MD degree was awarded by Aberdeen, and it commanded little respect in London where 'every physician or surgeon boasted' — in the words of 'Dr Lobby' in *Count Fathom* — that he is 'resolved never to consult with any physician who has not taken his degrees at either of the English universities'. But revenge alone cannot account for Smollett's fierce exposure of 'his brethren'. There is enough medical satire in eighteenth-century English literature to suggest that medical men, in the large cities far more than in the country, were perpetual targets with good justification. In London, Bath, Tunbridge, Bristol, York, Harrogate, Scarborough and other fashionable places they cheated the rich and milked the poor. They fought so extensively among themselves — surgeons versus barbers, physicians versus apothecaries, etc. — that parliament was periodically compelled to step in to mediate. Moreover, the greatest number of them were incompetents without a valid medical certificate. Like the crooked physician and apothecary who nearly 'kill' Timothy Crabshaw in *Sir Launcelot Greaves*, many so-called 'medical men' could no more accurately diagnose illness than they could read Hebrew or Sanskrit. *A la fin* Smollett's harsh satire of the medical profession had some beneficial effects in the 1760s and 1770s, but not enough to be evident to the man in the street. Reform of the profession, especially its incompetence and love of Mammon, was slow. (It is still far from completion today.) Yet Smollett believed, as did some of his contemporaries, that conditions in the medical world were actually getting worse.

If these were in the social aspects of medicine — in certain limited areas of the physician-patient relation — they were certainly not in physician-patient relations at large, nor in available medical facilities, nor in advances in theoretical knowledge. While the 'market' appeared glutted with dozens of 'universal elixirs', their number was actually smaller than previously, although they may have seemed larger owing to improved manufacturing processes. Horace Walpole, the famous memoirist, acidly carped about such 'cure-alls' as tar water, hungary water, Arbuthnot's diet of asses' milk, Ward's pill and drop, Dover's powder, James's fever powder, John Wesley's concoctions, and a dozen other tinctures, oils and potions, but in comparison to the remedies of 1650 or 1550 they saved more people than they killed. Even household manuals such as John Wesley's *Primitive Physic* (1747; it underwent at least twenty-four editions by 1792) and *Domestic Medicine or the Family Physician* (1769) by William Buchan (1729-1805) had greatly improved over the previous century's handbooks. Medical statistics were more complete than they had ever been, partly as a result of the need to maintain a healthy and large British navy and army. Techniques of 'vomition' (about which Pope had bitterly complained) were being improved, and after 1723 inoculation against smallpox was introduced partly through the efforts of Lady Mary Wortley Montagu (1689-1762), first the friend and then the enemy of Pope, and Richard Mead (1673-1754), one of England's leading scientists and Pope's own physician for a time. The unrelenting great plagues of the seventeenth century had taught Englishmen fear: thus, when epidemics struck in the early eighteenth century, they were much more receptive to new methods of treating them than they otherwise would have been.

If vital statistics were now being kept and preventive medicine was improving, 'pest houses' and public hospitals were also being built at a much greater rate than ever. A knowledgeable historian of medicine has written that 'The eighteenth century was the most important century in the history of English hospitals, for it saw the beginning of the great voluntary hospital movement which served this country so well for nearly 250 years.' A list of the hospitals established then is striking and reveals the dissemination of medical care, once again, from London to the provinces.[4] This was also the period when charitable hospitals and establishments for the sick poor in the city were founded. In 1708 a French Huguenot refugee left a sum of money for the erection and maintenance of a hospital for his poorer fellow refugees. Thus the French Protestant Hospital in London was founded, leading in turn to the establishment of many such hospitals. Likewise, other charitable hospitals with similar rules were established. Swift, it will be remembered, made provision in his will for the founding of a hospital for the treatment of mental

4 A chronological list of British hospitals founded in the eighteenth century: the important London hospitals were the Westminster (1720), Guy's (1725), St George's (1733), the first Lying-In Hospital in St James's Infirmary (1739), the London (1740), the Foundling Hospital (1741) — whose walls Hogarth painted and for whose benefit Handel composed the *Messiah* — Middlesex (1745), the Small-Pox Hospital (1746), the Dispensary for the Sick Poor in Holborn (1769) — the first children's dispensary in Europe. Scotland founded the Edinburgh Royal Infirmary (1729), Aberdeen (1739), Dumfries (1775), Montrose (1780), Glasgow (1794) and Dundee (1795); and Ireland established hospitals in Dublin, the Jervis Street (1726), Dr Steevans' (1733), Mercer's (1733), the Meath (1756), and the North Infirmary in Cork (1721), Limerick (1759) and Belfast (1797). There were provincial hospitals at York (1710), Salisbury (1716), Cambridge (1719), Bristol (1735), Windsor (1736), Northampton (1743), Exeter (1745), Worcester (1745), Newcastle (1751), Manchester (1753), Chester (1755), Leeds (1767), Stafford (1769), Oxford (1770), Leicester (1771), Norwich (1771), Birmingham (1778), Nottingham (1782), the Wakefield Infirmary (1787), Canterbury (1793) and Stafford (1797).

illnesses — his greatest charitable act — and referred to it in the concluding stanza of his *Verses on the Death of Dr Swift, DSPD*:

> He gave the little Wealth he had,
> To build a House for Fools and Mad:
> And shew'd by one satyric Touch,
> No nation [Ireland] wanted it so much:
> That Kingdom he hath left his Debtor,
> I wish it soon may have a Better.

This hospital is still flourishing in Dublin today, but some other charity hospitals founded then have not fared so well because of a financial pinch. At first all these charity hospitals were free; but as time passed some form of contribution was necessary. At the charity hospital for the poor of the parish of St Margaret's, Westminster, those who could not give money were requested 'to give what they have to spare, as broken victuals, old clothes, linen, beds, bedding, chairs, stools, pots, dishes, glasses, etc.'. The establishment of hospitals was undoubtedly the most beneficial outcome of the 'Charitable Proposals' of 1715, this despite the original aim of the proposal to found a society to provide food, medicine, medical advice, nursing care and visitors to the 'poor sick'. Fielding H. Garrison, MD, the great American historian of medicine, has commented that 'Many new hospitals were built in the eighteenth century, but, in respect of cleanliness and administration, these institutions sank to the lowest level known in the history of medicine.' This is probably true; it would indeed be surprising if it were not. For this was the first century to imagine medical care on a grand scale, for the rich as well as for the poor, and it would have been miraculous if hospitals had learned at once to resolve all their hygienic or sanitary problems. Comparison, therefore, between Chaucer's small fourteenth-century hospital of about twenty beds in Canterbury and a large London eighteenth-century charity hospital, like St Margaret's, containing over 100 beds, or even a principal London hospital such as St George's, makes little sense even though it cannot invalidate the factual authority of Garrison's comment. Not until the epoch of Florence Nightingale in the 1840s and 1850s did cleanliness attain to any of its modern proportions. But by then most of the hospitals in this country were established and on their way to providing improved care for the sick.

The English malady: madness and suicide

'Lunatic hospitals for the insane' were another matter altogether. Until 1751 there was only one public asylum, 'Bethlehem Hospital Founded in the Year 1247 as the Priory of St Mary of Bethlehem, but from 1547 designated by His Majesty Henry VIII a Lunatic Asylum'. There were 'private madhouses', too, but only the affluent could be deposited there and conditions were as bad, if not worse, than in 'Bedlam'. By 1700 the situation at Bedlam (or Bethlem), which had been moved during the Restoration from Bishopsgate Without to Moorfields, was intolerable. 'Patients' were chained to iron bars in dark cells, slept nude in insanitary straw, and were encouraged to decay and die. The food was no better than that given to animals, nor was any attempt made to wash them. Even more ghastly, they were 'displayed' to the public, especially on Sundays, for 'two-pence-a-visit', the price of admission having doubled in a few years. Ned Ward described the activity in Part Three of the *London Spy*, commenting that 'visits to the lunatics' were as popular a sport as bear-baiting had been in the previous century, and Pierre-Jean Grosley, a French tourist who wrote books about his visits to London, went straight to Bedlam to see the 'madmen and lunatics'. Hogarth's eighth and last plate of *A Rake's Progress* suggests that the treatment of patients in 1732 — when he painted it — was no better than it had been a century earlier. Edward Moore (1712-57), a dramatist and journalist who wrote under the *nom de guerre* of Adam FitzAdam, described Bedlam vividly on 7 June 1753 in *The World*, a periodical catering to the upper class:

> In one cell sat a wretch upon his straw, looking stedfastly upon the ground in silent despair. In another the spirit of ambition flashed from the eyes of an emperor, who strutted the happy lord of the creation. Here a faithful miser, having in fancy converted his rags to gold, sat counting out his wealth, and trembling at all who saw him. There the prodigal was hurrying up and down his ward, and giving fortunes to thousands. On one side a straw-crowned King was delivering laws to his people, and other a husband, mad indeed, was dictating to a wife that had undone him. Sudden fits of raving interrupted

the solemn walk of the melancholy musician, and settled despair upon the pallid countenance of the love-sick maid.

Moore's readers were known to be snobbish and expected a description implicitly condoning conditions in the hospital. Even so, he had to speak out:

> But I am sorry to say it, curiosity and wantonness, more than a desire of instruction carry the majority of the spectators to this dismal place. It was in the Easter-week [of 1753] that I attended my friend there; when, to my great surprise I found a hundred people at least, who having paid their two-pence a-piece, were suffered unattended to run rioting up and down the wards, making sport and diversion of the miserable inhabitants; a cruelty which one would hardly think human nature capable of! Surely if the utmost misery of mankind is to be made a sight for gain, those who are the governors of the hospital should take care, that proper persons are appointed to attend the spectators, and not suffer indecencies to be committed, which would shock the humanity of the savage Indians. I saw some of the poor wretches provoked by the insults of this holiday mob into furies of rage; and I saw the poor wretches, the spectators, in a loud laugh of triumph at the ravings they had occasioned.

Moore's sympathetic response was outweighed by all types of British and foreign 'savage Indians', real and fictional. A young lady in Samuel Richardson's *Familiar Letters* complained that, during her visit to the hospital in Moorfields, her 'own sex' was so rude 'as to endeavour to provoke the patients into rage and make them sport'. Fifty years earlier, at the turn of the century, Tom Brown, author of *London Amusements*, considered a visit to Bedlam a prerequisite for 'any gentleman, disposed for a *touch* of the times'. Both women and men took advantage of the invitation to taunt the inmates. Yet Harley, the sentimental hero of Henry Mackenzie's *Man of Feeling*, agreed with Edward Moore that 'it is an inhuman practice to expose the greatest misery with which our nature is afflicted to every idle visitant'. William Cowper the poet knew 'the greatest misery' as well as anyone: he himself had been confined in Bedlam as 'a deranged person' and wrote passionately to his long-time correspondent John Newton about the cruelty of visitors.

In 1769 Dr John Monro (1715-91), then physician to Bedlam, finally succeeded in barring 'holiday' visitors from the hospital. The keepers were also instructed to examine chained patients. But by this time much had transpired in the 'madness business'. First of all William Battie (1703-76), the distinguished FRS and President of the Royal College of Physicians, had succeeded in founding St Luke's Hospital for Lunaticks. Situated opposite Bedlam in Upper Moorfields on the north side of what is today Finsbury Square, it opened in 1751 with Battie as its first physician. Battie's approach was diametrically opposed to Monro's at Bedlam. Unlike Monro, he never permitted 'penny sightseers' to visit, nor did he consider 'lunatics incurable'; also he took medical students, taught them — in his own words — the 'mad business' and wrote books containing case histories of the deranged and theories about their cure. *A Treatise on Madness* appeared in 1758, the first book in Europe to define madness scientifically and provide clues about psychiatric treatment by an experienced psychiatrist. Battie's treatise purported to lay to rest such old wives' tales as the possibility of 'lunar influence' and the notion — as the *Gentleman's Magazine* reported it in 1748 — that 'eating berries could make a man mad'. Understandably Monro across the road was vexed at the 'revolution in madness', and controversies between the two men continued for over a decade. But these personal considerations are minor: what is significant is the initiation of a whole new era in psychiatry, one that would culminate in the reforms of Philippe Pinel (1745-1826), the great psychiatrist at the Salpétrière Hospital in France at the very end of the eighteenth century. Dr Battie — from whose name the colloquialism 'batty' derives — also anticipated the movement towards neurophysiology by applying Albrecht von Haller's theory of 'irritability' to explain the phenomenon of mental illness. Battie, unlike the deeply conservative Monro, believed that insanity was usually caused by 'deluded sensation' and 'diseased imagination' rather than by impaired intellectual faculties. He therefore conceived of mental illness as a physiological instead of a purely psychological condition, and time, as we know, has confirmed his intuition. The speed with which he made 'converts to his theory' is also noteworthy. As early as 1755 Lady Mary Wortley Montagu wrote to her daughter Lady Bute about Samuel Richardson's 'ignorance in Morality' apropos *Sir Charles Grandison* which she was then reading:

> ... Sir Charles had no thoughts of marrying Clementina till she had lost her Wits, and the Divine Clarissa never acted prudently till she was in the same Condition, and then very wisely desir'd to be carry'd to Bedlam, which is realy all that is to be done in that Case. Madness is as much a *corporal* Distemper as the Gout or Asthma, *never* occasion'd by afflic- tion, or to be cur'd by the Enjoyment of their extravagant wishes. Passion may indeed bring on a Fit, but the Disease is lodg'd in the Blood ...   (my italics)

If Lady Mary had not actually *read* Battie, she had heard about his theories and adopted some of his language, and in this respect Lady Mary was not the only one. Gradually an analysis of mental disorder in neuropsychiatric terms became evident in daily conversation among educated people. Had Battie lived until the turn of the century, he would have witnessed some proof of his surmises among the neuropsychiatric theories in existence around 1800.

The public's attitude was also significant in the progress signalled by Dr Battie and St Luke's Hospital. Battie sounded a true note when he wrote at the start of his *Treatise on Madness* that 'Madness, though a terrible and at present a very frequent calamity, is perhaps as little understood as any that ever afflicted mankind.' Though 'little understood', more than a glimmer of light now shone on the incurables after the opening of St Luke's. For centuries lunacy had been thought to be 'devil sent'; as a result of its 'demonic nature' the idea of its curability did not even occur to scientists, much less to laymen, until the seculariza- tion of the eighteenth century. Michel Foucault, the contemporary French philosopher, has traced popular conceptions of madmen from the Middle Ages — when they were sent out on 'Ships of Fools' — to the end of the eighteenth century, by which time 'society decided that its madmen had to be confined to certain spaces known as clinics'. Part of the shift, at least in England, was accompanied by a new understanding and decency of the public. By the 1750s a movement was growing, as we have seen, to prevent acts of torture to the hospitalized insane. Only one decade later, and principally owing to the revolutionary ideas of Dr Battie, theories of cure began to emerge. By 1771 John Aikin, the Warrington physician already mentioned, advocated the construction of provincial lunatic hospitals in his important treatise entitled *Thoughts on Hospitals*. And in 1774 the Act for Regulating Madhouses was finally passed (14 Geo. III, c. 49) after fifteen years' discussion, safeguarding the welfare of patients in private and public madhouses. By the time King George III suffered his second bout of 'nervous insanity' in October 1788, the British world had learned to view mental disorder in a wholly new light, more tolerant, accepting and hopeful. More progress had been made since the middle of the eighteenth century through the efforts of St Luke's, Battie and his students (who themselves became distinguished 'mad doctors'), than throughout the rest of British civilization. 'Unreason' in all its forms, especially medical, was then a topic of universal concern, and rational methods of approaching the 'mad business' were beginning to develop. Thus James Adair (1728-1802), the fashionable Bath doctor who specialized in 'women's nerves', could write in his medical works: 'The metaphysical disquisitions of philosophers would certainly be very much assisted by a more frequent dissection of persons who die mad'!

Writers and artists no less than other sectors of the population responded too. It is well known that both Swift and Pope were very much alive to the wave of interest in lunacy and elevated their reactions to a genuinely imaginative degree: Swift especially in 'A Digression Concerning Madness' in *A Tale of a Tub*, and Pope by the use of madness as a leitmotif in the various versions of *The Dunciad*. Other writers presented information to their readers in a more didactic fashion. Christopher Smart, who had been a patient in St Luke's from May 1757 to May 1758 when he was discharged by Battie as 'cured', wrote extensively about his earlier visits there in his periodical *The Midwife*. Smollett read Battie's *Treatise on Madness* and Dr Monro's *Remarks on Dr Battie's Treatise* and plagiarized whole passages from them in his novel *Sir Launcelot Greaves* — a fact that need cause little alarm today since Smollett's readers in the 1760s were fascinated by the subject of madness and were eager to obtain information about it in any form. More important than the plagiarism, though, is Smollett's imaginative use of Battie's theories in the scenes in Smollett's private and public madhouses. Johnson commented incisively on the dangers of 'the uncertain continuance of reason' and on the 'disorders of intellect' in *Rasselas*. The poets, too, had much to say — not only Pope but those who followed him. Battie was the target of a considerable number of poetic satires in 1750-1 while he was busy searching for support to establish St Luke's. Perhaps the most notorious of these was a mock-epic poem named the *Battiad* (after *The Dunciad*), probably a joint effort of three minor writers, Moses Mendez, Paul Whitehead and Dr Isaac Schomberg (1714-80). The last was as 'medically conservative' as Monro and had been deprived by Battie of gaining membership of the College of Physicians — the most important licensing body in England. Sir John Hill, himself a most controversial figure, reviewed the *Battiad* in the *Monthly Review* and found it a product of the crisis in the 'mad business' that Battie had 'singlehandedly caused'. Schomberg's brother Ralph (1714-92), also a physician and author, selected Battie as his protagonist in another satirical poem with a Greek title, *Iatrorhapsodia* ('Physical Rhapsody'), published a few weeks after St Luke's opened. In those weeks in 1751 Battie was such a controversial public figure that Ralph Schomberg could ask in his poem

'Is N[-----][5] solid, B[-----] pure of Heart?
Loquacious B----- acts a double Part —'

and expect his readers to catch the allusion. These minor scribblings and dozens of others attest to the impact of the 'mad craze' at mid-century.

> There are more metaphors of the mind and references to mental institutions in the literature of this [eighteenth] century than literary critics have noticed — indeed the artist's personal struggle to define himself in relation to the world of sanity or insanity is so pervasive that it may be a leitmotif.... It is an ironic contrast that the supposed 'Age of Reason' should have produced so many cases of insanity among its writers, in England William Cowper, Christopher Smart, and others.

5 Robert Nesbit, MD (d. 1761), was a licentiate, together with Battie, of the College of Physicians.

I did not realize in 1969 (when I wrote this passage) how *many* references and how *very* ironic: if anything, the comment is an understatement. The attitudes towards madness held by leading physicians of the day and their opponents is but a part of the story. There were also the unrecorded views of the common man. All these, as well as those of the mad inmates themselves — views even less well known except for the statements of a few 'lunatics' such as Smart and Cowper who also were patients — comprise an exceedingly disparate conglomerate. Certainly there was no such thing then as a uniform attitude towards lunacy.

The development of psychological and neurological theory

At the close of the eighteenth century Charles Moore, an obscure vicar in Kent who had written *A Full Inquiry into the Subject of Suicide* (1790) in two thick volumes, asked the key question: 'As the conclusion drawn from these premises is logical and important, it behoves us thoroughly to examine into their pretensions to truth: or in other words to inquire, whether suicide necessarily implies madness? and whether madness necessarily excludes all guilt?' Again and again, that was the question being asked. It could not be answered until attitudes towards suicide itself were less vague than they had been at mid-century.

Chief among these attitudes was the notion that suicide was Britain's native form of madness. Her *vice anglais* was something universally acknowledged, even if no one could scientifically account for its appearance in England and nowhere else. Ever since Tudor days the suicide rate in England had been climbing at an alarming rate. By 1698 John Dennis, the literary critic, had proclaimed (in a theatrical work!) that there were 'more self-murders and melancholic lunatics in England, heard of in one year, than in a great part of Europe besides'. The South Sea Bubble of 1720 produced another great wave of suicides; and a foreign traveller, probably the Abbé Le Blanc, wrote of his visit to Britain during the 1730s that he could not 'master the astonishment it gave me to hear of such frequent self-murthers as happens here almost daily'. Then in 1755, as Thomas Gray noted in his correspondence, a peak of 'epidemical Self-Murther' seems to have been reached, especially after 'Lady M. Capel (ld Essex's Sister) a young Person, had just cut the veins of both arms across'. She was in her twenties and sixth in a succession of suicides occurring within a month. Edward Young, the poet and fellow of All Souls College in Oxford, was not exaggerating when he had written thirteen years earlier (in 1742) in *The Complaint: Or, Night Thoughts*:

> O Britain, infamous for suicide!
> An island in thy manners! far disjoin'd
> From the whole world of rationals beside!
> In ambient waves plunge thy polluted head,
> Wash the dire strain nor shock the Continent ...

followed a few months later by Blair's indictment in *The Grave*:

> Self-murder! — name it not: Our island's shame,
> That makes her the reproach of neighbouring states.

Cecil A. Moore, the American literary historian, has scrupulously surveyed the phenomenon of eighteenth-century English suicide and has demonstrated how a constellation of factors — ranging from climate and the six 'non naturals' (the eighteenth-century term for (1) air, (2) diet, (3) sleep, (4) exercise, (5) evacuation and (6) passions of the mind) to the ideas of deists who justified suicide — accounts for its pervasiveness among the British. Moore, having brought the 'English malady' under such a fine microscope and having charted its year-by-year course in the eighteenth century, connects the 'real' and 'literary' worlds of that time in a generalization that must be regarded as authoritative:

> No characteristic of English poetry in the mid-eighteenth century is more familiar to students of the period than the perpetual reference to melancholy. Though present in some degree in all periods of English literature, even from the time of the Anglo-Saxons, this strain had all but disappeared from polite literature after the Restoration; but now, in spite of the strenuous protests of Akenside and the other Shaftesburian optimists, it again came into fashion and indeed a greater vogue than it had ever had before. Whatever one's opinion of the intrinsic merit of this versified melancholy or of its genuineness as an expression of personal feeling, there can be no dispute over the quantity. Statistically, this deserves to be called the Age of Melancholy.

Melancholy and suicide were everywhere: in daily life, in poetry, even in Thomas Gray's mock-Horatian 'Ode on the Death of a Favourite Cat, Drowned in a Tub of Gold Fishes', an unhappy trifle of a poem that flirts with suicide in several of its stanzas. The 'English malady' — suicide, hypochondria, hysteria, the spleen, nerves, or any of the other names it went under — undoubtedly flourished in Moore's 'Age of Melancholy'. Yet Moore's subsequent comment is perhaps even more enlightening than the statistical observation about its pervasiveness: 'Some historians dismiss the entire phenomenon as nothing more than a *literary fad* and therefore of no significance whatsoever as an index of contemporary psychology.' This is a rather startling admission. Whatever melancholy in all its diverse forms might have been, it was never simply a 'literary fad'. The literati, to be sure, as Moore and others have suggested, dwelt on it; but they hardly invented it. It was a national 'condition' that proved to be — contrary to those historians Moore had in mind — a significant 'index of contemporary psychology', perhaps the most significant. The psychology of an epoch, after all, is formed by more than one factor in any case: fad or fashion alone could not have swayed a whole epoch unless these terms denote something most bizarre. Nor could mere fad alone have caused Dr George Cheyne to call melancholy '*the* English Malady *par excellence*', or Michel Foucault to write in *Madness and Civilization* that 'hysteria is the true eighteenth-century disease, far more typical of the age than gout, dropsy, or ague', as well as to insist that 'hysteria was the most real and the most deceptive of diseases; real because it is based upon a movement of the animal spirits, illusory as well, because it generates symptoms that seem provoked by a disorder inherent in the organs, whereas they [the symptoms]are only the formation, at the level of these organs, of a central or rather general disorder'. That is, hysteria or hypochondria (the terms were used interchangeably along with melancholy) is a bodily as well as a mental disorder. It was this set of mind-body relations that prompted thinker upon thinker, not merely medical men, to write books in the eighteenth century about hypochondriacal disorders. And even by 1760 or 1770 — randomly chosen dates — it seemed to many Britons that there was more to say, indeed that the subject itself was inexhaustible.

Another consideration is that everyone, it then seemed, had at one time or another written about the subject; and as a consequence it was more difficult to appear original. If Burton's gargantuan treatise, *Anatomy of Melancholy* (1621-38), lent an impression of having said the last word about 'white and black bile' and 'green and yellow melancholy', this fact in itself did not hinder Marston as well as other playwrights in the seventeenth century from treating the subject of Hamlet's therapy — melancholy; nor, later on, Bernard Mandeville (1670-1733), a physician by education and the author of the much discussed *Fable of the Bees*. Mandeville's *Treatise of Hypochondriack and Hysteric Passions* (1711) is the most comprehensive and authoritative after Burton's, but its medical authority alone should not obscure other works possibly more widely read by a lay audience. Such were John Archer's *Treatise of Melancholy and Distraction* (1673) in the Restoration, and Dr John Hill's *Hypochondriasis: A Practical Treatise* (1766), almost a hundred years later. These books, together with Cheyne's *English Malady* (1733) and many other similar treatises, confirmed the widely felt suspicion that nothing was of greater interest to the popular imagination than 'the state of the nerves'. Later on, Smollett had been able to construct an archetypal figure for the age — Matthew Bramble in *Humphry Clinker* — out of its substance, and the entire class of weepy eighteenth-century heroines such as Pamela and Clarissa basically owed their origins to the same *vice anglais*: in the words of Pope's physician William Cheselden (1688-1752) to the 'exquisite state of the nerves that leads to melancholy, to madness, and finally of necessity to suicide'. At the base of melancholy, as Burton had prudently commented long ago, was 'physiology'. Others, too, saw the connection, but no scientific discovery had as yet given evidence that it was true. Boyle, the great chemist, was not exercising his imagination in rhetoric or hyperbole when he commented in his greatest 'Baconian' work of a general scientific nature, *The Usefulnesse of Experimental Naturall Philosophy* (1663), that 'those great transactions which make such a noise in the World, and establish Monarchies or ruin Empires, reach not so many Persons with their Influence as do the Theories of Physiology'.

True as this may have been, it was nevertheless hard to spot a great 'physiologist' among the dozens who professed expertise in the new science soon to be called neurology. John Locke, the physician and philosopher, recognized Thomas Willis (1621-75), his teacher at Oxford, as the most important physiologist of the day; and more recently historians of science have agreed that Willis alone must be called the father of neurology. While still a student, Locke had heard Willis's lectures on anatomy at Christ Church and read his *Cerebri Anatome* (1665). In this neurological landmark Willis set forth a method for the removal and dissection of the brain; a new numbering and grouping according to function of the cranial nerves greatly improving on the old Galenical system; extensive descriptions of the basal ganglia, brain stem and cerebellum; and detailed schemes of the vagal and sympathetic nerves supplying the viscera. George Prochaska, the noted Czech physiologist of the eighteenth century, understood Willis's contributions to brain theory better than most scientists of the period studied by this volume and commented on his achievement in his *Dissertation on The Functions of the Nervous System* (1784):

> Thomas Willis, a celebrated member of the chemical sect, advanced, with some ingenuity, many new hypotheses as to the uses of the nervous system.... His own peculiar doctrines chiefly are: that the cerebrum subserves to the animal functions and the voluntary motions, the cerebellum to the involuntary; that a perception of all the sensations takes place in the ascending fibres of the corpora striata, and that though the descending voluntary movements are excited; that the understanding is seated in the corpus callosum, and memory in the convolutions, which are its storehouses; that the animal spirits are generated in the cortex of the cerebrum and cerebellum from the arterial blood; that they collect in the medulla, are variously distributed and arranged to excite the animal actions, and distil through the fornix as through a pelican; that the animal spirits secreted in the cerebellum are ever flowing, equably and continuously, into the nerves which regulate involuntary movements.... He maintains, that there are two souls in man, one rational, the other corporeal; the latter is alone given to brutes.

A more modern student of physiology has described Willis's great contributions in this way:

Willis believed that the imagination was seated in the *corpus callosum*. The soul (the 'lucid', the higher of the two souls) itself, of which imagination was a function, was diffused, 'radiant and beamy' through the whole head and its 'nervous dependencies' and the animal spirits were its fountain. The imagination was conscious perception, and was behind the *sensorium commune* (in the *corpus striatum*) in the sequence of perception. Only if an impression reached the *corpus callosum* from the 'common sensory' did a conscious sensation arise: perception involved contraction of the soul, motion its expansion.

It is therefore clear that Willis believed, for the first time, that the functions of specific nerves relate to localized areas of the brain. Before this time there had been no clear parameters to the brain's functions, and only the vaguest notion of the interaction of brain and nerves. After Willis's brilliant set of discoveries, the nerves were naturally elevated to new importance. This did not occur at once, but by the first decade of the eighteenth century the effects of Willis's discoveries were starting to be felt, especially in non-physiological subjects. Willis himself reaped all possible honours: he became Sedley Professor of Natural Philosophy at Oxford, had his books adorned by Sir Christopher Wren's anatomical figures, was described by his publishers as 'Dr Thomas Willis, that Famous and Renowned Physician', and found himself at the centre of a circle of brilliant scientific friends which included Richard Lower (1631-91), Sir William Petty (1623-87) and others. In the next two generations — respectively those of Boerhaave and Haller — diverse scientists were persuaded that Willis had been the founder of a new province of science: 'neurology'. What appeared difficult to estimate at first, triumphantly emerged as the new physiology of nerves.

Locke incorporated the new 'nerve physiology' into his theory of perception in the *Essay Concerning Human Understanding* (1690), a paradigmatic book now thought to have been among the two or three most influential — along with Newton's *Opticks* (1704), Shaftesbury's *Characteristics* (1711) and Burke's treatise on *The Sublime* (1756) — on the thinking of the next century. Locke's

application of crucial aspects of the 'new physiology' to a realm —
ethics and politics — not previously imagined to yield to scientific
types of explanation opened the door to the eighteenth-century
'sciences of man'. His imaginative leap was twofold: first his act of
'integration' itself, second his 'intuitive' sense that the whole
argument about knowledge pivots upon the concept of 'sensation'.
Both points depended on a broad knowledge of the best theories of
perception — precisely what Willis's discoveries about the brain
had made possible. For, once the soul was limited to the brain, as
Willis had successfully argued, scientists could debate precisely how
the nerves carried out its voluntary and involuntary intentions, and
what was the relation between nerves and other systems, especially
blood and lymph. The history of science reveals that they did just
this: no topic in physiology between the Restoration and the turn of
the nineteenth century was more important than the precise
workings of the nerves, their intricate morphology and histological
arrangement, and their anatomic function. On them depended all
the senses, not least that of sight — to which Newton's *Opticks*
addressed itself. Berkeley's 'solipsism' and Burke's 'sublime'
(about which more will be said) eventually turned to the nerves as
well; for the eighteenth-century philosophers increasingly came to
see that at the bottom of every psychological theory was a physiological one, thus confirming Boyle's suspicion a century earlier. In
the eighteenth century only Kant's metaphysical theory of a
'transcendental imagination' discarded the new physiology, a
development that need not concern us here since its effect in
England was not felt until about 1798. It is true that this
cumulative scientific development from physiology to psychology
could not have been undertaken without Harvey's discovery in the
1620s of the circulation of the blood, expounded in *De Motu
Cordis*. But to a greater degree it would not have been possible
without Willis's revolutionary theory of the brain.

The pre-eighteenth-century lineage of psychology is thus clear:
anatomy and physiology are its parents and neurology, or 'nerve
science', its tutor. Continuous generations of thought are clear to
those who can view them from a distance: Harvey, Willis, Locke;
Newton, Shaftesbury, Burke; Haller, Whytt, the Scottish psychologists (especially Kames). At the base of every wave-like continuum
is a great anatomist such as Harvey, or a physiologist like Haller,

who innovates and thereby causes contemporary psychologists to revise their best theories. Stated in paradigmatic abstract forms *sans* names, the 'waves' of thought in this epoch are equally apparent: for example, circulation of the blood in organic movement (Harvey); the organicism of the nerves regulated by the brain as a kind of 'heart' (Willis); perception, 'primary' and 'secondary' association, the basis of every epistemology or theory of knowledge (Locke).

But it was not long before the more general educated world registered its own fascinated response to this new universe of human physiology: philosophers, clergymen, rationalists, even poets. It is significant, for instance, that Richard Burthogge (1638-94), one of Locke's earliest and staunchest critics, thought the most proficient way to demolish his theories was by attacking his physiology. Thus the reason for Burthogge's 'balanced title' in his longest work *contra* Locke: *An Essay upon Reason, and the Nature of [Animal] Spirits* (1694). Conversely, John Sergeant (1622-1707), one of Locke's earliest supporters who defended him against the censures of Bishop Stillingfleet, commended Locke's knowledge of physiology in *The Method of Science* (1696). Locke's physiology 'absolutely' viewed in hindsight from the contemporary perspective of the 1970s is not in question; what counts is rather the sense in these and other rationalists that physiology somehow ultimately lay at the base of the deepest ontological and epistemo-logical questions of the day. In that epoch — think of the French-man cited at the beginning — science and philosophy were not far apart. Addison implied as much in his 'anatomical paper' (*The Spectator*, No. 281) and, much more brilliantly if less directly, in 'Pleasures of Imagination'. The former, on 'the nerves in the heart', perhaps unknowingly made the necessary connection for 'sensibility' which Richardson and his school found so important. It is impossible to imagine a *Clarissa Harlowe*, whatever else that book may be, without a blow-by-blow description of the 'exquisite state' of the heroine's nerves. Poets such as Richard Blackmore in *The Creation* (1712) also found a storehouse of opulent poetic images in the physiological terminology of the scientific controversies over the definition of imagination — images directly grasped from the language of 'the learned', who 'with anatomic art / Dissect the mind, and thinking substance part'. Involved with these questions were related ones about the 'flow of animal spirits', the brain's role in memory, and, of course, the role of memory in forming imagination. It was this heritage that ultimately shaped Wordsworth's greatest legacy: imagination, as opposed to mere fancy, begins in a 'spontaneous and powerful overflow of emotion'. Sixty years earlier Henry Brooke, a contemporary of Gray and Blair, had intimated as much in the enraptured tones in which he described the 'animal spirits' in *Universal Beauty* (1735):

> Quick, from the Mind's imperial Mansion shed
> With *lively Tension* spins the nervous Thread
> With Flux of animate Effluvia stor'd,
> And Tubes of nicest Perforation bor'd,
> Whose branching Maze thro' ev'ry Organ tends,
> And Unity of conscious Action lends;
> While [Animal] Spirits thro' the wandring Channels wind,
> And wing the Message of informing Mind;
> Or Objects to th' ideal Seat convey;
> Or dictate Motion with internal Sway.

'Animal spirits' winding through the empty 'Channels' of the nerves were by now (1730 or 1740) as valid a *topos* for the didactic or satiric poet as 'memory' and 'imagination' — the 'secondary stage' of nervous physiology in Locke's system — were to become later in the century. Dr Malcolm Flemyng (d. 1764) could write a Lucretian epic in Latin hexameter in 1740 entitled *Neuropathia*, a poem about the condition of the nerves in 'hysterics' and hypochondriacs; in another vein altogether David Hartley, the philosopher, announced in the *Observations on Man* (1749) that in questions related to memory 'discussion of the nerves must not be overlooked'. At the same time Edward Synge (1659-1741), author of *Sober Thoughts for the Cure of Melancholy* (1742), taught that the 'exquisite state of the nerves' is the surest clue to cure; and Akenside the poet, two years later, could not bring himself to disregard matters of 'nervous physiology' in *Pleasures of Imagination*.

If the forties were the great heyday for literature of all types concerning the nerves, the next few decades did not lag far behind. But now in a new tone: sceptical, weary and sometimes even rudely bumptious. Sterne and Smollett had read many of the physiological debates of the forties and fifties in England, especially those centring around Haller's theory of 'sensibility' and 'irritability'; when they wrote novels they expected their audiences to be familiar with them. Thus Tristram Shandy and Matt Bramble, both protagonists, learn about their own identity by taking cues from the world of physiology. Tristram himself is something of a modern anatomist, though he never gets any physiological theory correct. 'Now you must understand that not one of these was the true cause of the confusion in my uncle *Toby's* discourse; and it is for that very reason I enlarge upon them so long, after the manner of great physiologists, — to shew the world what it did not arise from.' Bramble, far more hypochondriacal than Tristram (with all the 'morbid nervousness' that implies), has 'had an hospital these fourteen years within myself, and studied my own case with the most painful attention; consequently may be supposed to know something of the matter, although I have not taken regular courses of physiology'.

'Melancholy Reflections' had also caused Gulliver to reflect in Laputa on the state of 'the Nerves ... Sinews and Muscles'. Earlier his maker Swift had parodied theories of 'vapours of the brain' in *A Tale of a Tub*. Throughout these decades of the eighteenth century, from 1700 at least until 1780, a glance at the nerves revealed much more than morbid disease or health: they even designated social class and economic custom. No one, certainly not Sterne or Smollett, had forgotten Mrs Sullen's casual remark in *The Beaux' Stratagem* (1707) to the effect that the all-mysterious 'spleen' — melancholy — 'had been only proper to people of quality'. Spleen, like related, if considerably more cerebral, activities such as memory and imagination, also depended exclusively on the nerves; and the fact that eighteenth-century Englishmen could believe in 'high-class' as opposed to 'low-class' nerves is itself a penetrating insight into its culture. The common man in the street, *à la* Mrs Sullen, probably knew little about neurology, and even most practising physicians did not usually keep abreast of the best in neurology. But competence and learning notwithstanding, there is no doubt that everyone — highborn and lowborn — knew a certain amount about the 'nerve business', as one commentator referred to the new subject. This is why Dr James Makittrick Adair, with whom the poet Burns took walking tours, writing late in the century, could declare, ironically, that people of quality did 'not know they had nerves' before the publication of Whytt's *Observations on ... Disorders commonly called Nervous, Hypochondriacal, or Hysteric* (1764). Just the opposite, in fact, had been true. Everyone — whether Mrs Sullen, Lemuel in Lagado, the distressed Clarissa, Mackenzie's sentimental Harley, Caleb Williams, or the local orange woman loitering about the Palace of St James — everyone knew something about the condition of his or her nerves. What differentiated their explanations depended upon their degree of literacy and education. But by now (1780 or 1790) the 'myth' or 'truth' about nerves was national, even European or universal, common knowledge. One could certainly not say the same for the previous hundred years before 1680, as even a cursory perusal of Burton's *Anatomy of Melancholy* proves.

A new theory of vision

Yet the spread of physiology was not limited to newfangled medical theories. Physiological inquiry was imported, sometimes wholesale, into discussions of metaphysics and aesthetics; more accurately, metaphysicians and aestheticians combed the best theories of physiology to see what assumptions they could 'read into' them. By 'reading in' they could 'scientize', as it were, or validate their own premises all the better; they could also, they thought, add vitality to subjects — metaphysics and aesthetics — in which originality was highly prized. No one imported from the new territory more carefully than Edmund Burke in his *Philosophical Enquiry into the ... Sublime* (1757), a treatise attempting to relate pre-existing aesthetic theories of the 'beautiful' to the 'sublime' in cautious, scientific manner.

Burke had scrupulously read Newton's *Opticks* before he drafted the *Enquiry* in 1748 while still a student at Trinity College, Dublin, and only nineteen — so scrupulously that most references in this work are, after Locke, to Newton. Burke also remembered in the treatise how the generation or two before his own had been intrigued by theories of sight and vision:

Mr Cheselden[6] has given us a very curious story of a boy, who had been born blind, and continued so until he was thirteen or fourteen years old; he was then couched for a cataract, by which operation he received his sight. Among many remarkable particulars that attended his first perceptions, and judgments on visual objects, Cheselden tells us, that the first time the boy saw a black object, it gave him great uneasiness; and that some time after, upon accidentally seeing a negro woman, he was struck with great horror at the sight.

After retelling this story Burke took pains to demonstrate that the 'horror' did not arise from any 'primary or secondary association' — how could it? — but from 'the natural operation' of the colour black. This development suggested to Burke 'an association of a more general nature [than Lockean association], an association which takes in all mankind'. Hence a universal law relating colours, or bright light and darkness, to specific emotions. Fear of darkness, Burke argued, was as common to a Voltaire in France or Linnaeus in Sweden as to Pope's 'savage Indian' or the exotic eastern creatures in Oriental tales. And Cheselden's blind boy was only one example in a long series in the early part of the eighteenth century: Newton's claim in the *Opticks* to have coordinated the primary colours with the notes of the octave; Locke's narrative, repeated in *Tom Jones*, of a blind man who compared the colour scarlet to the sound of a trumpet; Hume's further example of the blind man who tried to describe the taste of an *anana* (pineapple); and in 1757, while Burke was publishing the *Enquiry*, Père Louis Bertrand Castel's 'colour organ', exhibited in London and discussed everywhere, by which the deaf might 'see the music of the ears', the blind hear 'the music of the eyes', and normal people might 'enjoy music and colours better by enjoying them both at the same time'. By this means Burke linked 'intense light' with the 'aesthetic sublime' in a kind of post-Newtonian optical psychology, one that

6 William Cheselden, MD (1688-1752), the great surgeon and Pope's personal physician. Pope wrote to Swift: 'I wondered at your quaere, who Cheselden was? it shews that the truest merit does not travel so far any way as on the wings of poetry; he is the most noted, and most deserving man, in the whole profession of Chirurgery; and has sav'd the lives of thousands by his manner of cutting for the stone.'

would have far-reaching effects on the relation of painting and perception, but not without mildly chastising Newton and Locke for a 'blemish' here and there. Most important, though, for the new theory of vision was Burke's insistence on an understanding of the physiological processes of sight. This, he argued, had to precede a real grasp of its psychological effects. Consequently Part Four of the *Enquiry* begins with a careful analysis of Newton's *Principia* in so far as it accounts for emotions of pleasure and pain; and symmetrically closes with a section called 'Of Colour' also drawing its illustrations from Newton's *Opticks*.

The pervasiveness of Newtonian optics in Burke's aesthetics is not surprising. Most theories about 'vision' at mid-century, whether scientific, aesthetic or metaphysical, assumed they would have to start at least by wedding Locke's theory of mind to Newton's physiology of perception. As late as 1767 Duff was 'celebrating' Newton's optical discoveries — the rainbow, prism, light waves — in his *Essay on Genius* by describing Newton as 'an original Genius of the first rank'. This anatomy of 'light rays' Duff called one of the 'most astonishing efforts of the human mind'. Burke would have wholeheartedly agreed: in his own mind Burke thought he was but 'applying' Newton's analysis to another area, the psychology of terror. Vision, then, for all these thinkers essentially implied sight: the sight of the real grasped in the physiological act of seeing. Dr Johnson's definition of *vision* in the *Dictionary* (1755) tallies with these views by proffering a fourfold definition essentially concerning the faculty of sight:

1　Sight; the faculty of seeing.
2　The act of seeing.
3　A supernatural appearance; a spectre; a phantom.
4　A dream; something shown in a dream. A dream happens to a sleeping, a vision may happen to a waking man. A dream is supposed natural, a vision miraculous; but they are confounded.

Johnson's four categories divide themselves in half: two types of vision related to perception of the *visible*, two the invisible. Locke, Newton, Burke, Johnson: all dismissed perception of the invisible (spectres, phantoms, supernatural ghosts, miracles, dreams) as the product of a 'diseased imagination'. Nor would any have entertained the possibility that Johnson's third and fourth categories imply a radically different physiology from the first two, involving sight of the real. That was to come later, in the mid-nineteenth century. When Collins, Smart and Cowper (all allegedly mad and 'confined' to madhouses) wrote poetry replete with images drawn from the world of dream and vision, or from religious epiphanies revealed only to themselves, they were not, according to rational system-builders like Locke, Newton and Burke, or for that matter lexicographers like Johnson, 'seeing' anything except new appearances and images not grounded in reality.

Enthusiasm, as Warton's poem by that name suggested, was the least liked of almost any type of private experience. Ever since the opening of the eighteenth century there was little sympathy for 'vision of the ordinarily invisible', as one Anglican sermonist put it. Religious 'enthusiasts' were distrusted and worshippers of the supernatural were branded as atheists, witches or freaks. The poets — Pope, Gay, Hughes, Thomson — were no more tolerant than the philosophers. Locke, as is well known, had come down hard on 'visionaries': in the celebrated passages on wit and judgement in the *Essay*, he even mistrusted men who make allowances for too many 'pleasant pictures and agreeable visions in the fancy'. Berkeley, challenging Locke's position, nevertheless strengthened the case against visionaries who 'see the unseen'. Berkeley's best ideas about perception were set forward in *A New Theory of Vision* (1709; 1733) in which he argued for the doctrine '*esse* is *percipi*': to be is to be percipient. Here he denied material validity (in the sense of Aristotelian matter) to all essences except 'ideas' and 'sensations'. But his writings (except for *Siris*, a treatise about tar water as a universal panacea) were immensely difficult for the untrained, and hardly penetrated far enough to influence English literary men and women. Less appealing than Locke's, they addressed themselves almost exclusively to questions about percipience, and hence considered vision solely as the mental perceiving act. While exalting ideas as the only true material sensations, they diminished the whole aspect of physiological vision of those supposed Platonic 'forms' located far away in the skies, and instead paved the way to Blake's visionary universe. Hume, no less than Berkeley though differently, discredited 'expanded vision'; if anything, he attempted to bridge the gulf between the 'seen' and 'knowledge about it' by doubting that man could ever genuinely know what the connection was. Regardless of the influence of Berkeley and Hume on men of letters, there is no question that they abetted Locke's anti-visionary campaign. The effect of their collected writings and teachings was a theory of vision that appeared mechanical, materialistic and almost corporeal to many. While it was not absolutely so, the common man, when he knew about it, rather agreed with its tenets.

Psychology, neurology and perception, then, were consequently profoundly connected. It is as if the Frenchman's pious strictures about 'interrelatedness' were even more entangled in their native element in the eighteenth century than he intimated. Berkeley and Hume, two of the most piercing intellects of the century, may have superficially seemed unaffected by the new physiology of perception owing to their greater calling in 'rational philosophy'. And here, to be sure, in the fact that they could *seem* to avoid the new physiology, was a significant difference between their 'moral philosophy' and Burke's 'aesthetics'. But even they knew, all too well, that ultimately the physiological processes of Burke's 'darkness' would eventually provide clues to problems in the philosophy of solipsism and scepticism — so ingrained had the new science of the body's nervous system become by mid-century.

Willis's brain and nerve theory, Locke's psychology, Newton's optical ideas: all seemed isolated terrains until they converged early in the eighteenth century and produced a revolution in knowledge. No single label or phrase could ever capture the change or do justice to its substance; but if one phrase had to be selected, probably 'the *science* of man' would do best. Humanism around 1750, conceived as it had been for two centuries, was far from dead or even moribund. Yet the possibility that every subject related to man — his 'being', as Pope would have called it, his anatomy, his private and public behaviour, his economic activity, the physiology of the states of his mind — would soon be known, gripped the popular imagination much more so than traditional humanistic platitudes already evident in Tudor England. 'The *science* of man' — and as time progressed, from the 1750s to the 1780s, the scientific portion grew more significant than the humanistic — was ultimately the totally new product of a hitherto unprecedented coalescence. Astronomy and mathematics were 'old sciences' when Chaucer and

Shakespeare wrote; the names and ideas of Bacon, Boyle, Newton and Locke were familiar, even household, words to Dryden and company. But neither Chaucer nor Dryden, wise as they were, could have surmised what men of the generations from Anne to George III would accomplish. Suddenly — so it must have seemed to a Burke writing in the *Enquiry* — suddenly all the sciences were converging into a radically new synthesis, not 'expiring' and causing the return of Chaos and Night, as Pope prophesied in the *New Dunciad* of 1743. So too would it later seem to Blake when, in *Jerusalem*, he imagined the whole history of science as converging in the arch-demon Newton's philosophy. Nameless and still without an identity of its own, Burke called the new inquiry 'a science of the sublime and beautiful'. Still others — Gerard, Duff, Beattie, Kames, Stewart, Priestley — endowed it with different names. Yet all knew that the new way of thinking, spurred on by Newton and Locke, was here to stay. Now analysis of the mere prismatic hue of Newton's wave of light, or the tiny wonders of the insect world, were not enough. A certain irrevocable act of integration had occurred. While practical science, as Cowper noted, was 'building factories with blood', another integrated science, this one more tentative but none the less felt, was changing the way men would for ever 'know'.

Select bibliography

Books

Allen, D.E. *The Naturalist in Britain: A Social History*. London, 1976. (The first scholarly account of the rise of naturalism in England written by a historian and batologist; brief but incisive for the eighteenth century.)

Birch, T. *The History of the Royal Society*. 4 vols. London, 1756-7. (The most important eighteenth-century history of the Royal Society, taking up where Bishop Thomas Sprat left off, i.e. 1667. Birch was Secretary of the Royal Society from 1752 to 1765 and had access to all types of documents important to a historian.)

Burtt, E.A. *The Metaphysical Foundations of Modern Physical Science*. New York, 1952. (Together with Whitehead's study (see below), one of the most penetrating accounts of the fundamental assumptions of empiricism, mechanism and organicism.)

Bush, D. *Science and English Poetry: A Historical Sketch 1590-1950*. New York, 1950. (Bush's third chapter on 'Newtonianism, Rationalism and Sentimentalism' contains perceptive insights, but must be viewed with caution since its author is not over-sympathetic to English literature between Milton and Wordsworth.)

Butterfield, H. *The Origins of Modern Science 1300-1800.* Rev. ed. London, 1957. (A brilliant survey by the distinguished Cambridge historian known also for his 'Whig interpretation of history, medicine and the life sciences'.)

Byrd, M. *Visits to Bedlam: Madness and Literature in the Eighteenth-Century.* Columbia, SC, 1974. (Gathers together the main texts devoted to themes of madness. Much of the author's discussion, however, derives secondarily; little primary research.)

Davie, D. *Science and Literature 1700-1740.* London, 1964. (A useful little work by the English poet-critic now at Stanford University. It is permeated with out-of-the-way insights about literature and science.)

DePorte, M.V. *Nightmares and Hobbyhorses: Swift, Sterne, and Augustan Ideas of Madness.* San Marino, Calif., 1974. (More original than Byrd's *Visits to Bedlam* — especially for its discussion of the medical aspects of madness — but not so comprehensive in gathering the relevant primary texts. Especially good on Swift's works.)

Dewhurst, K. *John Locke (1632-1704) Physician and Philosopher: A Medical Biography.* London, 1963. (The Oxford medical historian who has also written on Sydenham, Locke's teacher and friend, shows how Locke's philosophy of association was enhanced by a scientific education at Oxford.)

Dijksterhuis, E.J. *The Mechanization of the World Picture.* Trans. C. Dikshoorn. London, 1961. (A detailed account by the eminent late Dutch historian of science. Culminating in Newton's mechanical philosophy, the author shows how philosophies of nature took on increasingly mechanistic aspects from the time of the Greeks. A highly specialized study for students seriously interested in the history and philosophy of science.)

Donovan, A.L. *Philosophical Chemistry in the Scottish Enlightenment: The Doctrines and Discoveries of William Cullen and Joseph Black.* Edinburgh, 1975. (A scholarly treatment of the rise of chemistry in eighteenth-century England and Scotland. Also provides a broad panorama of the whole Scottish Enlightenment.)

Foucault, M. *The Birth of the Clinic: An Archaeology of Medical Perception.* Trans. A.M.S. Smith. New York, 1973. (A controversial book, marred by opaque style and frequent factual inaccuracy. Should be used with extreme caution, especially by those unfamiliar with Foucault's methodology and type of subjectivism.)

———— *Madness and Civilization: A History of Insanity in the Age of Reason.* New York, 1965. (Plagued by many of the problems of the previously mentioned book, this work is nevertheless an imaginative account of madness in European civilization from the Middle Ages to

the end of the eighteenth century. No English works cited or referred
to.)

Fraser, R. *The Language of Adam*. New York, 1977. (The final chapters
study the Restoration's search for a universal language and truth. Of
importance to eighteenth-century scientific theories.)

French, R.K. *Robert Whytt, the Soul, and Medicine*. London, 1969.
(Whytt was called in his own day 'the philosopher of medicine', and
this is the only modern biography of his life. Useful for its exposition
of the interrelations of medicine and philosophy in the second half of
the eighteenth century.)

Glass, B., *et al*. (eds) *Forerunners of Darwin: 1754-1859*. Baltimore, 1959.
(Sets the stage for Darwin's theory of the mutability of species put
forward in *The Origin of Species*. A handy anthology of essays on
eighteenth-century biology, embryology and zoology.)

Hill, J. *Hypochondriasis, A Practical Treatise* (1766). Ed. G.S. Rousseau.
Augustan Reprint Society publication no. 135. Los Angeles, 1969.
(The only modern edition of this popular mid-century treatise, plus
an introduction setting it in its Georgian context. Dr Hill was a
medical man and a colourful literary figure. His 'practical treatise'
outlines the main ideas about the fashionable 'English malady'.)

Hunter, R., and MacAlpine, I. *Three Hundred Years of Psychiatry 1535-
1860*. London, 1963. (The most comprehensive list of works in the
history of psychiatry. Proceeds chronologically and contains abundant selections from each author discussed. Nicely illustrated;
reprints many of the title pages of works mentioned. Unfortunately
there is no analysis of the works collected.)

Jacob, M.C. *The English Newtonians*. Ithaca, NY, 1976. (Shows how the
science, religion and politics of the Restoration and early eighteenth
century combined to promote Newtonian science.)

Jones, R.F. *Ancients and Moderns: A Study of the Rise of the Scientific
Movement in Seventeenth-Century England*. 2nd ed. St Louis, 1961.
(The classic study of the Ancient-Modern controversy, containing
copious footnotes documenting its argument. Sets the stage for
understanding the seeming modernity of science in the time of Swift
and Addison.)

Jones, W.P. *The Rhetoric of Science: A Study of Scientific Ideas and
Imagery in Eighteenth-Century English Poetry*. Berkeley, Calif.,
1966. (The book is mistitled and says very little about rhetoric; but it
is a useful study of scientific poems from Pope and Thomson in the
early part of the century to Blake and Wordsworth at the other end.
A useful checklist of scientific poems in English is included.)

King, L.S. *The Medical World of the Eighteenth Century*. Chicago, Ill.,
1958. (Sketches out the highlights without engaging in much
analysis. The author is highly knowledgeable of his subject and
presents it tersely and accurately.)

Knight, D.M. *Natural Science Books in English 1600-1900.* New York, 1972. (A historian of science lucidly explains how natural philosophy evolved throughout the course of the eighteenth century. Illustrated.)

Kuhn, T.S. *The Structure of Scientific Revolutions.* 2nd ed. Chicago, Ill., 1970. (The renowned Princeton philosopher of science originally published this work in 1962. Since then it has been among the most widely discussed hypotheses of the last decade, with clear application to higher criticism of all kinds, not merely historical or scientific. This second edition contains Kuhn's important postscript in which he answers his critics 1962-70.)

Lindeboom, G.A. *Boerhaave and Great Britain: Three Lectures on Boerhaave with Particular Reference to his Relations with Great Britain.* Leiden, 1974. (Although Lindeboom's English style leaves something to be desired, he is the foremost authority on Boerhaave and here chronicles Boerhaave's reception in England.)

Lovejoy, A.O. *Essays in the History of Ideas.* Baltimore, 1948. (These now classic essays by America's most distinguished historian of ideas are now sadly out of print. They show how philosophical and religious ideas perplexed great imaginative writers such as Swift, Pope, Johnson and Coleridge.)

————— *The Great Chain of Being.* Cambridge, Mass., 1936. (The classic work on the subject. Studies the idea of plenitude from Plato and Aristotle to the end of the eighteenth century when the disintegration of the idea was clearly manifested.)

Lyons, H. *The Royal Society 1660-1940: A History of its Administration under its Charters.* Cambridge, 1944. (Useful for facts, tables, charts and statistics pertaining to the Royal Society. Valuable secondary sources.)

McKillop, A.D. *The Background of Thomson's Seasons.* Minneapolis, 1942. (Thomson's most serious student in this study considers the scientific influences on the poem. For certain correctives, see Ralph Cohen's important studies, *The Art of Discrimination* (1964) and *The Unfolding of the Seasons* (1970).)

Mandelbaum, M. *Philosophy, Science and Sense Perception: Historical and Critical Studies.* Baltimore, 1964. (An important American philosopher studies theories of sense perception in their philosophic and scientific contexts c. 1650-1750. Difficult reading but well worth it, especially for the light it sheds on Locke, Hume and other empirical thinkers.)

Manuel, F.E. *The Religion of Isaac Newton.* Oxford, 1974. (Newton considered in his non-scientific aspects. Interesting accounts of Newton's religion, historical works and chronologies of ancient kingdoms.)

Mason, S.F. *A History of the Sciences.* Rev. ed. New York, 1962. (The most useful and compact survey for non-specialists. A clear book, particularly useful for literary students with little or no knowledge of the progress of scientific ideas. Very useful bibliographies for each chapter.)

Meyer, G.D. *The Scientific Lady in England 1650-1760*. Berkeley, Calif., 1955. (Still the standard work on its subject, although recent studies since 1955 make it clear that much research remains to be done on this topic.)

Moore, C.A. *Backgrounds of English Literature 1700-1760*. Minneapolis, 1953. (Even after almost a quarter of a century, Moore's book holds up well for its pioneering research, especially in the long chapter on the 'English malady'. This chapter ought to be read by every serious student of the literature and culture of eighteenth-century England.)

Nicolson, M.H. *Mountain Gloom and Mountain Glory: The Development of the Aesthetics of the Infinite*. Ithaca, NY, 1959. (Taking her cue from a passage by Addison in *The Spectator*, No. 489, Miss Nicolson brilliantly traces the growth of a set of aesthetic ideas regarding sublimity in poetry. She shows how scientific ideas such as those debated in the famous 'Burnet controversy' about crust and the inside of the earth greatly influenced the whole progress of English poetry from Dryden and Pope to Keats and Shelley.)

_____ *Newton Demands the Muse: Newton's Opticks and the Eighteenth Century Poets*. Princeton, NJ, 1946. (This prizewinning book was the first to show Newton's influence on English poets from Pope and Thomson to the Romantics and even beyond them. It opened up in the 1950s a whole new subject for serious study, and first brought Newton, as it were, into the camp of English studies.)

_____ *Science and Imagination*. Ithaca, NY, 1956. (Collects Miss Nicolson's various essays. Of unusual interest to readers of this volume is her essay in collaboration with Nora Mohler on the scientific background of Book III of *Gulliver's Travels*.)

_____ and Rousseau, G.S. *This Long Disease My Life: Alexander Pope and the Sciences*. Princeton, NJ, 1968. (First surveys Pope's intricate medical history — it draws its title from a line in *An Epistle to Dr Arbuthnot* — then studies the scientific context of Pope's poetry, even though Pope is shown by the authors as not being, strictly speaking, a scientific poet. Chapters on astronomy, geology, optics, etc.)

Rather, L.J. *Mind and Body in Eighteenth Century Medicine*. London, 1965. (Confronts the issue of psychosomatic medicine in the eighteenth century through an examination of a few set texts. Of interest to students of sentimental literature and the sensibility movement.)

Rousseau, G.S. (ed.) *Organic Form: The Life of an Idea*. London, 1972. (Brings together important essays by a historian of ideas (G.N. Orsini), a historian of science (P. Ritterbush) and a literary theorist (W.K.Wimsatt) to trace the history and life of the idea. Rousseau provides a detailed bibliography of works treating of organic form from 1823 to the present. A second volume is in progress.)

Schofield, R.E. *Mechanism and Materialism: British Natural Philosophy in the Age of Reason*. Princeton, NJ, 1970. (Surveys the progress of British science from the time of Boyle and Newton to that of Priestley and Black, showing the philosophical and historical relations of mechanism and materialism. Important and scholarly study. Particularly good on science in the 1770s.)

Schwartz, R.B. *Samuel Johnson and the New Science*. Madison, Wisc., 1971. This is the fullest modern treatment of Johnson and science. The author's views are sound and judicious; he shows that Johnson was no enemy of science, and that in many cases — for example, Johnson's prediction of the future uses of electricity — he was a great and enthusiastic friend.)

Stimson, D. *Scientists and Amateurs: A History of the Royal Society*. New York, 1948. (This delightful little book is not really a history of the Royal Society but an epitome of its high moments — moments in which crisis was experienced one way or another. For the period 1700-1800 Stimson shows how applied scientists thought poorly of the virtuosi, gentlemen-amateurs who indulged in things scientific because it seemed the mark of good breeding.)

Toulmin, S., and Goodfield, J. *The Discovery of Time*. London, 1965. (Perhaps the best book on the subject in a general way. Of unusual interest to literary students because it explicates time in non-technical fashion. Not so extensive on the eighteenth century, though, as for other periods.)

Wheatley, H.B. *The Early History of the Royal Society*. London, 1905. (Documents the activities, the fortunes and misfortunes of the Royal Society in the eighteenth century.)

Whitehead, A.N. *Science and the Modern World*. Lowell Lectures. New York, 1925. (Together with Burtt's book, the most important modern statement of the role of science in the modern world. Should be read by all students of English literature.)

Willey, B. *The Eighteenth Century Background: Studies on the Idea of Nature in the Thought of the Period*. London, 1940. (An important discussion of the different ways in which the idea of nature was interpreted in the century from Swift to Burke, Pope to Wordsworth. Like Lovejoy — who had also studied nature in his *Essays in the History of Ideas* — Willey shows how the label meant different things to different readers.)

Wolf, A. *A History of Science, Technology and Philosophy in the 18th Century*. 2nd ed. rev. D. McKie. 2 vols. New York, 1952. (The standard, scholarly work on the subject. Detailed and technical, but still well worth browsing through.)

Articles

Nicolson, M.H., and Rousseau, G.S. 'Berkeley's *Siris* and English Literature 1750-1800'. In *The Augustan Milieu*. Ed. H.K. Miller *et al.*

Oxford, 1970, pp.101-37. (Bishop Berkeley is usually thought of as an idealist philosopher; but he also patented a medicine — tar water — which was as popular in its day as aspirin and made him a large sum of money. A readable account of the discovery of tar water and its reception all over the world.)

Rousseau, G.S. 'Nerves, Spirits and Fibres: Towards the Origins of Sensibility'. In *Studies in the Eighteenth Century III: Proceedings of the David Nichol Smith Conference*. Ed. R.F. Brissenden. Canberra, 1975, pp.137-57. (A pioneering essay correcting R.S. Crane's hypothesis in his 1934 essay, 'Suggestions Towards a Genealogy of the "Man of Feeling"'. Shows that, while benevolence and related ideas of 'doing good' *could* have developed before 1740 and the time of Richardson's novels, a theory to explain the selfconscious personality *could not* have because there was no scientific model for it.)

_____ 'Science and the Discovery of the Imagination in Enlightened England', *Eighteenth Century Studies*, III (1969), pp.108-35. (An original study of how the scientific origins of the Romantic concept of imagination *c.* 1660-1800 created a mechanical notion intolerable to creative writers.)

_____ ' "Sowing the Wind and Reaping the Whirlwind": Aspects of Change in Eighteenth-Century Medicine'. In *Studies in Change and Revolution*. Ed. P.J. Korshin. London, 1972, pp.129-59. (An important general study surveying the rational and empirical strains in eighteenth-century medicine. Discusses the practice as well as the theory of medicine.)

_____ 'Whose Enlightenment? Not Man's: The Case of Michel Foucault', *Eighteenth Century Studies*, VI (1972), pp.238-56. (Surveys all the writings of Michel Foucault, especially *Les Mots et les choses*, and demonstrates how faulty are Foucault's facts *c.* 1700-1800 and how slippery are his style and rhetorical strategies. Rousseau concludes, on a more optimistic note than Foucault, doubting whether man is finally 'dead' and 'finished' and that we ought to dance on his grave with glee.)

Tuveson, E.L. 'Swift and the World-Makers', *Journal of the History of Ideas*, XI (1950), pp.54-74. (Studies Swift's relation to the physico-theologists, especially to Thomas Burnet, author of *A Sacred Theory of the World*. Shows how the Scriblerians were brought into the Burnet controversy.)

_____ 'Space, Deity, and the "Natural Sublime"', *Modern Language Quarterly*, XII (1951), pp.20-38. (Tuveson's first exposition of 'the aesthetics of infinity', a term borrowed by Miss Nicolson and developed at length in *Mountain Gloom and Mountain Glory* (see above). Shows how scientific or quasi-scientific ideas about immensity and space caused a change in eighteenth-century literary sensibility.)

5 The visual arts

PETER WILLIS

The century or so that followed the Great Fire of London in 1666 — culminating in the foundation of the Royal Academy by George III in 1768, with Reynolds as its first president — was one of Britain's finest periods in the visual arts. The theory and practice of painting, architecture, town planning and landscape gardening flourished as men of taste and intellect devoted themselves to furthering the cause of Art. In so doing, as Jonathan Richardson stressed in his *Two Discourses* (1719), they were acknowledging the social importance of connoisseurship and the civilizing influence of the fine arts on 'the reformation of our manners, refinement of our pleasure and increase of our fortunes and reputation'.

Such influences were partly due to the effects of the grand tour, which became a conventional feature in the education of the British gentleman, and took him to France and Italy and, to a lesser extent, to Germany, Austria, Switzerland and the Low Countries. His taste became more cosmopolitan and centred more upon the antique. The resulting passion for connoisseurship enriched many a town house and country seat as engravings, sculpture, sketches, *objets trouvés* and, of course, the paintings of such artists as Claude, Gaspard Dughet and Salvator Rosa were brought back from Rome and elsewhere to add lustre to the collection of many a member of the *cognoscenti*. As the century progressed, the excavations were carried out at Herculaneum, Paestum and Pompeii (1738-56), and were popularized by finely illustrated volumes devoted to the

2 Wren, Church of St Stephen Walbrook, London (1672–9). Photo: National Monuments Record.

1 Wren, Pembroke College Chapel, Cambridge (1663–5). Photo: National Monuments Record.

4 Hawksmoor, North Quadrangle, All Souls College, Oxford (1716–35). Photo: *Country Life*.

3 Wren, St Paul's Cathedral, London (1675–1710). West front. Photo: A. F. Kersting.

5   Vanbrugh and Hawksmoor, Blenheim Palace, Oxfordshire (1705 onwards).
Entrance front.   Photo: Kerry Downes.

6   Gibbs, Church of St Martin in the Fields, London
(1722–6).   Entrance front from National Gallery. Photo:
National Monuments Record.

7 Gibbs, Senate House, Cambridge (1722–30).
Photo: Edwin Smith.

8 Burlington and Kent, Chiswick House, Middlesex (c. 1725 onwards).
Garden front. Photo: Crown Copyright Reserved.

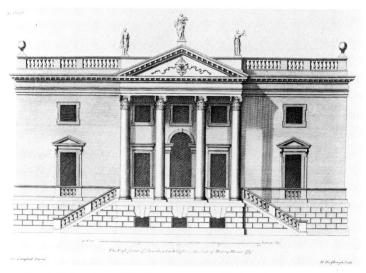

9 Campbell, Stourhead, Wiltshire (1719 onwards). East front. Engraving from Campbell, *Vitruvius Britannicus* III (1725), plate 42. National Library of Scotland, Edinburgh.

10 Kent, Holkham Hall, Norfolk (1734 onwards). Marble hall, with plasterwork by Thomas Clark (*c.* 1754). Photo: National Monuments Record.

11 Robert Adam, Syon House, Middlesex (1762–9).
Entrance hall. Photo: National Monuments Record.

12 Cavendish Square, London, north side. Aquatint by Malton (1800). British
Library, London. Houses at either end by Edward Shepherd (c. 1720), those in
centre built shortly before 1771.

13 Kneller, *Richard Temple, first Viscount Cobham of Stowe* (*c.* 1710). National Portrait Gallery, London.

14 Hogarth, *An Election* (*c.* 1754). Plate 2: 'Canvassing for Votes'. Trustees of Sir John Soane's Museum, London.

15 Reynolds, *Garrick Between Tragedy and Comedy* (1762).
Private collection.

16 Gainsborough, *Mary, Countess Howe*
(*c.* 1763–4). Greater London Council as
Trustees of the Iveagh Bequest, Kenwood.

17 Devis, *Robert Gwillym of Atherton and His Family* (*c.* 1749). Yale Center for British Art, Paul Mellon Collection.

18 Lambert, *Classical Landscape* (1745). Trustees of the Tate Gallery, London.

19　Place, *The Dropping Well, Knaresborough* (1711). British Museum, London.

20　Sandby, *View of Strawberry Hill, Twickenham* (c. 1774). Castle Museum and Art Gallery, Nottingham.

21 Rysbrack, *George II*, marble bust (1738). Windsor Castle. Reproduced by gracious permission of Her Majesty the Queen (Courtauld Institute of Art).

22 Roubiliac, *Handel*, marble statue (1738). Victoria and Albert Museum, London.

24 Hartwell Church, Buckinghamshire. Plasterwork supervised by Henry Keene (1753-5). Photo: National Monuments Record.

23 Thornhill, Painted Hall, Greenwich Hospital (1708-27). Photo: Royal Naval College.

25 William Beilby, glass bowl (Newcastle 1765). Victoria and Albert Museum,
London.

26 Chippendale (attrib.), japanned black and gold dressing commode (c. 1750).
Victoria and Albert Museum, London.

27 Hampton Court, Middlesex. Engraving by Highmore and Tinney (*c.* 1745). British Library, London.

28 Hawksmoor (with Daniel Garrett), mausoleum, Castle Howard (1730s onwards). Photo: National Monuments Record.

29   Kent, *Woodland scene by moonlight*. Drawing. Devonshire Collection, Chatsworth. Reproduced by permission of the Trustees of the Chatsworth Settlement.
Photo: Peter Willis.

30 Rigaud, *View from Gibbs' Building at Stowe, Buckinghamshire*. Drawing (1733–4).
Metropolitan Museum of Art, New York (Harris Brisbane Dick Fund, 1942).

31 Thomas Robins the elder, *Chinese temple at Woodside. Old Windsor, Berkshire.*
Drawing (*c.* 1750). Private collection.

32 Wilson, *Croome Court, Worcestershire* (1758). Birmingham Museum and Art
Gallery.

archaeological finds and to the art of antiquity in general. It became fashionable to explore the sites themselves, and to sketch them, as Robert Adam did. The Society of Dilettanti promoted such studies, and in 1762 the first volume appeared of *The Antiquities of Athens* (2nd volume 1789) by James 'Athenian' Stuart (1713-88) and Nicholas Revett (1720-84). Such concern for the antique found its expression too, in different ways, in painting and furniture as well as in architecture, and in the incomparable work of Wedgwood, whose industrial imagination marks a significant technological stage in the dissemination of taste.

If indeed our period was characterized by the Man of Taste, the quintessential figure must surely be Horace Walpole (1717-97), whose house at Strawberry Hill (Plate 20) became a mecca for the connoisseurs and the curious alike. Walpole's *Anecdotes of Painting in England* (1762-80) provide us with a key document on artistic life in eighteenth-century England, based though it is on the jottings of George Vertue (1684-1756), the antiquary. Likewise Walpole's *The History of the Modern Taste in Gardening* (first published as the last volume of the *Anecdotes*) cannot be ignored in any study of eighteenth-century English landscaping. Much of Walpole's writing illustrates how he succumbed to the lure of antiquarianism — as W.S. Lewis has put it, 'the escape from the vexatious present into what he called "the ages that do not disappoint"'.[1] This led him into a struggle to promote both the gothic and archaeologically correct; but it also made him the most perceptive critic and commentator on the visual arts of his day. Architecture perhaps drew him most strongly of all the arts, and here indeed he lived through an era of dramatic change.

Architecture

In 1660 Inigo Jones had been dead only eight years; 110 years later, a decade after the accession of George III, the neoclassicist Boullée had started work on his 'Essai sur l'art' (not published until 1953) with its influential architectural theories. During the intervening century English architecture had witnessed the dominance of Wren,

---

1 *Horace Walpole*, A.W. Mellon Lectures in the Fine Arts 1960 (Washington, DC, 1961), pp.143-4.

as successor to Jones; the English baroque of Hawksmoor, Vanbrugh and Archer; the individual contribution of James Gibbs; the Palladianism of Lord Burlington and his *protégés* Campbell and Kent; the later Palladianism of Paine and Taylor; and the first phase of the work of the Adam brothers. It was a period rich in both promise and achievement.

It was also a period that saw the gradual emergence of the profession of architect, so that in 1749 George Vertue could remark that 'the branch of ye art of building, in Architecture is much improved', adding that 'many men of that profession [have] made greater fortunes... than any other... branch of Art what ever'.[2] Until Sir Robert Taylor started taking pupils, training was still a hit-and-miss affair, but this produced a profession of rich variety; there were amateur architects such as Lords Burlington and Pembroke, craftsmen architects such as Pratt and Brettingham, and men like William Kent who began as painters. And Sir John Vanbrugh's triumphant progression from soldier and dramatist to architect of Castle Howard is familiar enough.

In this sense, Vanbrugh was in the same mould as Sir Christopher Wren (1632-1723), for he, too, at a stroke turned his hand to the design and construction of buildings. Wren's scientific career had already led him to the Savilian Chair of Astronomy at Oxford before he was thirty. Then, in 1663, his uncle, the aged Bishop of Ely, asked him to design the new chapel of Pembroke College, Cambridge, and the result was a small classical building of considerable elegance (Plate 1). But it was the Fire of London in 1666 which gave Wren the unique opportunity to exercise his talents as an architect— not through his utopian city plan, which was rejected, but through his fifty-two City churches (upon which work began in earnest after the second Rebuilding Act of 1670) with their astonishingly varied steeples and reposeful interiors. In planning, the ingenuity Wren had already displayed in roofing the Sheldonian Theatre at Oxford (1664-9) was now brought to bear in fitting his classical churches into tight, irregular, medieval sites. Perhaps the most majestic of these churches is the domed St Stephen, Walbrook (1672-9), where the detailing and treatment of interior spaces presages St Paul's Cathedral (Plate 2). By the time

2 Walpole Society (ed.), *Vertue Note Books*, III (1934), p.146.

that construction began on St Paul's in 1675, Wren had been appointed Surveyor-General of the King's Works and had resigned his Oxford professorship.

It had been long apparent that Old St Paul's (partly restored by Inigo Jones) was incapable of repair, and, after alternatives had been considered and rejected, Wren's 'Warrant Design' was chosen for the new building — essentially a medieval plan preserved beneath classical dress. The freshness, invention and empiricism of the City churches were here channelled into a restrained form of classicism, with baroque influence prominent in the powerful shape and modelling of the dome, and in the corner towers and west front (Plate 3). Any French feeling we detect about St Paul's may be due to the influence of Mansart and Le Vau, and to the eight or nine months Wren spent in France during 1665-6 when he may have met Bernini. By the time that the cathedral was completed in 1711, Wren had carried out an extensive range of secular as well as ecclesiastical buildings, ranging from the austere Doric barracks at Chelsea Hospital (1682-92) to the grandest of all his works, Greenwich Hospital (1696 onwards), where the painted hall is the finest room of its kind in England (Plate 23). The best known of his commissions at the Office of Works (where his assistant was William Talman) is perhaps his rebuilding of the south and east wings of Hampton Court Palace in 1689-94 (Plate 27).

It was as an assistant to Wren that Nicholas Hawksmoor or Hawskmore (*c.* 1661-1736) began his career. Hawksmoor was essentially a backroom boy, but he obtained various official posts from Wren in his capacity as Surveyor-General, notably at Kensington Palace and Greenwich Hospital. Hawksmoor's highly personal architectural style was vigorous, dramatic and sculptural, and contained an unusual mixture of Roman, Wrenish and gothic elements. His handling of space presaged that of Sir John Soane. In 1711 Hawksmoor was appointed a surveyor under the act for building fifty new churches in London, and the six he designed himself (including St George's, Bloomsbury (1716-31), and Christ Church, Spitalfields (1714-29)) are minor masterpieces. The exuberance exhibited here, or in his neogothic north quadrangle at All Souls, Oxford, of 1716-35 (Plate 4), was at variance with Hawksmoor's character, for personally he was diffident and easily hurt in the rough and tumble of architectural practice. 'Poor

Hawksmoor,' wrote Vanbrugh in 1721. 'What a Barbarous Age, have his fine, ingenious Parts fallen into. What wou'd Monsr: Colbert in France have given for Such a Man?'[3]

Sir John Vanbrugh (1664-1726) was able to speak with authority of Hawksmoor's ability and character, for Vanbrugh — like Wren before him — came to rely heavily upon Hawksmoor's practical know-how in architectural matters. At Castle Howard, where Vanbrugh cut his architectural teeth from 1699 onwards, Hawksmoor was at his elbow from the start, and after Sir John's death demonstrated his abilities in no uncertain terms in his mausoleum there (1729-42), with its Roman *gravitas* derived from Bramante (Plate 28). Meantime, in 1702, Vanbrugh had displaced Talman as Comptroller, and thus became Wren's principal colleague at the Board of Works. Two years later, Vanbrugh was commissioned to design Blenheim Palace, near Woodstock, given by the British nation to the first Duke of Marlborough as a mark of gratitude for his victories over Louis XIV (Plate 5). The vastness of the enterprise suited Vanbrugh's temperament perfectly, and he indulged himself in boldly massed groupings, varied skylines and dramatic recessions and projections — characteristics that led Reynolds to describe Vanbrugh in his thirteenth *Discourse* (1786) as an architect who 'composed like a Painter'. Vanbrugh's desire to give his buildings 'Something of the Castle Air' led him to use medieval massing and composition, as can be seen at King's Weston (1711-14) or Seaton Delaval (*c.*1720-8), where the octagonal corner towers call to mind fortified castles and cities. Vanbrugh also expressed his concern for picturesque effects through the design and siting of garden buildings which, no matter how small, were never less than monumental. Indeed, although Blenheim is the largest of Vanbrugh's houses, others, more modest in size, are more impressive — such as Eastbury in Dorset (*c.*1718 onwards), of which only a fragment remains, or Seaton Delaval, standing stark and proud against the sea in the Northumbrian landscape.

The only British architect to be directly dependent upon the personal and inimitable styles of Vanbrugh and Hawksmoor was Thomas Archer (*c.* 1668-1743). Archer was not, as has been claimed,

3 Bonamy Dobrée and Geoffrey Webb (eds.), *The Complete Works of Sir John Vanbrugh* (London, 1927-8), IV, p.138. Vanbrugh to Brigadier Watkins, 26 August 1721.

a pupil of Vanbrugh, but on occasion his work combines Sir John's ebullience with Hawksmoor's wilful oddity. Archer had studied Continental baroque at first hand, and was influenced strongly by Bernini and Borromini. The best surviving examples of his architecture are the north front at Chatsworth (1704-5), a garden pavilion at Wrest Park in Bedfordshire (1711-12), and three churches — St Philip, Birmingham, now the Cathedral (1710-15, tower 1725), St Paul, Deptford (1713-30), and the London church of St John, Smith Square (1713-28).

Somewhat outside the English baroque stream of Hawksmoor, Vanbrugh and Archer was James Gibbs (1682-1754) who, like Archer, had spent time in Italy, in his case with Carlo Fontana. Gibbs was a Scot, a Catholic and a Tory with Jacobite sympathies. Thanks to the patronage of such friends as the Earl of Mar and Lord Harley he was able to attract a wide range of commissions, and it was partly due to Harley that in 1713 he was appointed as one of the surveyors for building the fifty new London churches. Gibbs's publication of *A Book of Architecture* (1728, 2nd ed. 1739), *Rules for Drawing the Several Parts of Architecture* (1732, 2nd ed. 1738, 3rd ed. 1753) and *Bibliotheca Radcliviana* (1747) did nothing to hinder the dissemination of his style and reputation. His architecture lacks the individuality of Hawksmoor and Vanbrugh, but draws its strength from Italian precedent and from Sir Christopher Wren. His interiors were often sumptuous, it is true, but Gibbs's style overall was accomplished rather than inspired. Even so, it was much copied both in Britain and in her colonies. Gibbs's best surviving building in London is the church of St Martin in the Fields of 1722-6 (Plate 6), a superb development of the Wren manner; outside London, Oxford has the Radcliffe Camera (1737-48), Italian Mannerist in spirit and maybe influenced by Hawksmoor, while Cambridge boasts the Fellows' Building at King's College (1724-49) and the Senate House which, splendid though it is, must be viewed as but a fragment of a larger building programme (Plate 7).

The use by Gibbs of architectural books to promote his ideas was a technique espoused by Lord Burlington and the Palladians. Richard Boyle, third Earl of Burlington (1694-1753), was the exemplar of the eighteenth-century English patron of the arts. Such was his influence that by the 1730s Palladian architecture had become the accepted style for country houses and public buildings: even Hawksmoor's drawings for the mausoleum at Castle Howard were submitted to Burlington for his approval, and given a flight of steps copied from those at Chiswick House. Burlington visited Italy in 1714-15, and again in 1719, when he returned with William Kent in tow, intending to employ him as a history painter. Already the earl had become interested in the revival of Palladian architecture through the appearance in 1715-16 of Leoni's edition of Palladio's *Quattro Libri*, and in 1715 of the first volume of Colin Campbell's *Vitruvius Britannicus*, with its engravings of country houses, churches and civic buildings (mostly by British architects), including Inigo Jones's Banqueting House in Whitehall. Burlington became as enthusiastic about Jones as he was about Palladio, as we can see from the list of publications which he sponsored or initiated: in 1727 there appeared Kent's *Designs of Inigo Jones*, which used mostly the earl's collection of Jones and Webb drawings, and in 1730 *Fabbriche Antiche disegnate da Andrea Palladio Vicentino*, based on Burlington's set of Palladio's drawings of Roman *thermae*. Unpublished drawings in Burlington's collection were used by E. Hoppus in his *Palladio* (1735), by Isaac Ware in his *Designs of Inigo Jones and Others* (1743), and by John Vardy in *Some Designs of Mr Inigo Jones and Mr William Kent* (1774).

Burlington had an obsessive, puritanical urge to preach absolute classical standards — those just and noble rules which, as Pope put it in his *Epistle to Burlington*, were to 'Fill half the land with Imitating Fools'. The earl's own career as an architect seems to have begun about 1717 with the semicircular colonnade at Burlington House, and a bagnio in the garden of his house at Chiswick. As he aged, Burlington's designs became increasingly dry and pedantic, as can be observed from the dormitory at Westminster School (1722-30, rebuilt 1947), Chiswick House itself of about 1725 (Plate 8), Northwick Park in Worcestershire (1730) and the Assembly Rooms in York (1731-2, refronted 1828), which is an exact model of Palladio's Egyptian Hall, based on Vitruvius. Such rectitude did not apply to the gardens surrounding Palladian villas, however, which were both imaginative and progressive.

In 1716 Burlington had engaged James Gibbs to alter his house in Piccadilly, but a year or two later Gibbs was superseded by Colin Campbell (1676-1729) who, with Henry Flitcroft (1697-1769), was to be a faithful ally of the earl; other supporters included Henry Herbert, ninth earl of Pembroke (*c.* 1689-1750), the architect Roger Morris (1695-1749) and the writer and theorist Robert Morris. Under Burlington's aegis, Campbell followed the first volume of *Vitruvius Britannicus* with two more in 1717 and 1725, and in 1729 added to these his edition of *Andrea Palladio's Five Orders of Architecture*. From 1718 to 1719 Campbell was Chief Clerk and Deputy Surveyor of the King's Works, duly emerged as architect to George II when Prince of Wales, and in 1726 became Surveyor to Greenwich Hospital in succession to Vanbrugh. Campbell was a Scot and, as Howard Colvin has speculated, it may be to a Scottish source that we ought to look for the origins of English Palladianism. At any rate, Campbell built enough buildings of real quality to assure him a worthy place among the Palladian architects — including Wanstead House in Essex (1715 onwards), which became the model for the English Palladian country house, and Newby Park in Yorkshire (1718-21), which initiated the idea of the Palladian villa in England. On a similar scale to Newby are Stourhead in Wiltshire (Plate 9), Ebberston Lodge near Scarborough (1718) and Compton Place near Eastbourne (1726-7), both far more satisfying than Mereworth Castle in Kent (1722-5), a version of Palladio's Villa Rotonda at Vicenza. None of these compares in splendour with Houghton Hall in Norfolk, designed in 1721 for Sir Robert Walpole and executed in 1722-35 by Ripley with modifications by Gibbs and interiors by Kent.

Interior design was only one of the activities espoused by William Kent (1685-1748) who, besides being a painter, was also a furniture designer, book illustrator, landscape gardener and architect. Whimsical, impulsive, almost illiterate, he was the complete opposite of his patron, Burlington, and as happy designing in the gothic as in the classical idiom. Kent does not seem to have turned architect until the late 1720s (when he was into his forties), but by 1735 he had been appointed Master Mason and Deputy Surveyor of the Board of Works, largely on account of Burlington's influence. Kent's gothic work includes the addition of wings and other alterations at Esher Place in Surrey (*c.* 1733), a choir screen at Gloucester Cathedral (1741), a pulpit in York Minster (1741), and Merlin's Cave, a thatched folly erected in 1735 for Queen Caroline in Richmond Gardens. He also designed a royal state barge for

Frederick, Prince of Wales (1732), an elegant, not to say exuberant, piece of whimsy. More characteristic of Kent, however, were the classical interiors he produced for the Treasury Buildings (1733-7), for 22 Arlington Street (1741-50) and for 44 Berkeley Square (1742-4), all in London. Kent's best-known commission is, perhaps, his last — the Horse Guards in Whitehall, executed after his death. In architectural terms, however, the Horse Guards is something of a repetition of his masterpiece, the Earl of Leicester's Holkham Hall in Norfolk, designed in collaboration with Lord Burlington, and executed from 1734 onwards by Matthew Brettingham (1699-1769). The origins of many of the stylistic features of Holkham are readily identifiable: externally the 'staccato' quality and use of Venetian windows in decidedly Burlingtonian, while internally the marble apsidal entrance hall (Plate 10), with its columns, coffered ceiling and handsome staircase leading up to the *piano nobile*, is based on a combination of a Roman basilica and the Egyptian Hall of Vitruvius. In the state apartments at Holkham, Kent took his admiration for Roman splendour a stage further in the elaborately carved and pedimented door frames, heavy cornices, damask hangings, and niches for antique marble sculpture. The result is a splendid integration of the decorative arts with few, if any, parallels in Britain.

Palladianism entered a second stage with James Paine (1717-89) and Sir Robert Taylor (1714-88), who were said to divide the practice of the English architectural profession between them during the mid-eighteenth century. Their buildings were highly competent if a trifle uninspired. Taylor at his most original — in, say, the extensions to the Bank of England of 1766-88 — looked ahead to the spatial dexterity of Sir John Soane, but Taylor could never match the combination of good planning, dignified exteriors and fine plasterwork which Paine brought to his country houses. Most of these are in the Midlands and the North of England, and are illustrated in his *Plans, Elevations and Sections of Noblemen and Gentlemen's Houses*, of which the first volume appeared in 1767 and the second in 1783. Gibside Chapel in County Durham (1760-6) is an instance of Paine at his most reposeful and precise; to see him at his most inventive we may turn to Wardour Castle in Wiltshire, which has a magnificent circular staircase set beneath a Roman coffered vault. By 1776, when Wardour was completed,

Paine had been superseded in the public eye by Robert, James and William Adam, and subsequently his reputation and practice declined rapidly.

None the less, the Adams' success was not unchallenged: Sir William Chambers (1723-96) was the greatest official architect of his day, beginning his practice in England in 1755 and by 1782 rising to the post of Surveyor-General and Comptroller of the Board of Works. His writings — particularly those on Oriental subjects and his *Treatise on Civil Architecture* (1759-91) — gave him great influence. He became a fellow of the Royal Society in 1776, and was the first treasurer of the Royal Academy on its foundation two years later. His architectural style is scholarly but eclectic, a fusion of English Palladianism with the neoclassicism of Soufflot and his contemporaries, whom Chambers had known in Paris and with whom he kept in touch. Chambers was fastidious in his ornament and use of the orders, but — despite the gaiety of the pagoda at Kew (1757-62), and the elegance and refinement of some of the interiors of Somerset House, London (1776-96), which rival those of Robert Adam — he cannot escape the criticism of dullness. Chambers was never as fashionable or as spectacular as Adam, but his influence was widespread both as official head of his profession and through his numerous pupils.

Robert Adam came from a Scots family steeped in architecture. His father, William Adam, practised as an architect in a robust, personal style echoing Vanbrugh, Gibbs and the English Palladians (for instance at Hopetoun House, near Edinburgh, begun 1721), and when he died in 1748 he left a widow, four daughters and four sons. Two of the sons — Robert (1728-92) and James (1732-94) — were to make their name as architects. That Robert's name is still a household word is due largely to his brilliance as an interior decorator, for without breaking with established traditions he devised a neoclassical style which was lighter and more elegant than that of the Palladians who preceded or the Greek Revivalists who succeeded him. He increased the repertory of classical decorative motifs — fireplaces, fanlights, ceilings, swags and medallions — and made great play of the spatial sequences between rooms, the use of columned screens and apses, and the meticulous detailing of stucco and plasterwork. His innate inventiveness had been fed by a grand tour which had covered art, architecture and archaeology, and on which he had been tutored by Clérisseau and had met Piranesi. In the earlier years of his practice Adam did almost nothing but contrive new interiors for existing houses, or finish or add to houses built by other architects. At Kedleston (1759 onwards), Osterley (1763-80) and Syon House in Middlesex, where he began work in 1762 (Plate 11), the effects can be seen triumphantly. Adam, as Sir John Summerson has pointed out, was determined to be *original*.[4] This meant that, unlike Chambers, he was fascinated by the gothic, and the neogothic interiors he designed at Alnwick Castle and elsewhere are masterpieces of their kind. Similarly he produced hundreds of pen-and-wash drawings (many of them in the Soane Museum in London) of imaginary castles in romantic landscapes. In the castles he actually built — such as Culzean (1777-92) and Seton (1789-91) — he was able to combine, without embarrassment, classical interiors set within battlemented and turreted outer walls.

In 1773 the first volume appeared of the *Works in Architecture of Robert and James Adam* (2nd vol. 1779, 3rd vol. 1822) which enshrined their style and precepts. Included in it was the scheme for the Thames-side terrace and streets called Adelphi (1768-72), which brought the Adam brothers within an inch of bankruptcy. Elsewhere, however, their contribution to urban planning met with greater success. Several British cities were being laid out with classical terraces, squares and crescents, and landscaped parks between them. In Edinburgh, where James Craig's plan for the New Town was accepted in 1767, Robert Adam contributed Register House (1774-92), the main quadrangle of the University (1789 onwards) and Charlotte Square (1791 onwards). Charlotte Square ranked with the best work of the Woods in Bath, where John Wood the elder (1704-54) had started his revolutionary layout in 1727. His aim — unfortunately only partly executed — was to make Bath once more into a Roman city. He began with Queen Square and the Circus (started 1754), and after his death his son, John Wood the younger (1728-81), took the original concept a stage further with the Royal Crescent (1767-75). It was speculation at its best.

4 See John Summerson, 'Adam — All for Originality', *Observer Magazine* (27 August 1976), pp.22-7.

In London, similarly, merchants, architects and jerry-builders were changing the face of the city, following in the footsteps of Nicholas Barbon (d.1698) who laid out the Red Lion Square district from 1686. The Cavendish-Harley Estate in Marylebone, for instance, was developed from 1717 onwards, and included the spacious Cavendish Square (Plate 12), where Edward Shepherd erected two houses for Lord Harley in the east and west corners. James Gibbs acted as adviser to Harley, and built the Church of St Peter, Vere Street (1721-4), nearby. The surrounding smaller streets, as elsewhere in London, were mostly put up by small-scale speculators who employed no architects, but used pattern books (such as *The Modern Builder's Assistant* of 1742 and 1757), and followed rules-of-thumb when it came to design and construction. Many of these 'rules' were, of course, dependent upon Palladian inspiration, interpreted in terms of brick-and-stucco terraces. The London Building Act of 1774 — which laid down strict regulations of construction and, by implication, design — also encouraged the unity, not to say uniformity, of the street scene. It was such factors, as much as the whims of individual architects, which determined the character of the Georgian town.

Painting and sculpture

British painting between Wren and Adam took a different course from both architecture and sculpture, for there was no classical phase early in the century. Aristocratic patrons were averse to ordering anything but portraits from British painters, and preferred to fill their houses with pictures from abroad. By the accession of George III, however, English painters and water-colourists had made their mark in genre (domestic, theatrical, pastoral and sporting), conversation pieces and landscapes, and their art was recognized throughout Europe.

The two most prominent painters in England during the late years of the seventeenth century were both essentially portraitists: Sir Peter Lely (1618-80) and Sir Godfrey Kneller (1646/9-1723). In 1661 Lely became Principal Painter to Charles II, and from then until his death maintained a large studio turning out portraits reflecting the court's atmosphere of sensual languor. Kneller too was a court artist: he was appointed joint Principal Painter to

William and Mary in 1688, and succeeded to the whole office three years later; he was knighted in 1692, and in 1715 became the first painter in England to be made a baronet. Kneller's mature style had been fully established as early as 1683, and there are hundreds of documented portraits dating from this time. The best of these — in contrast to Lely — have a vitality and down-to-earth quality which show that Kneller had a sharp eye for character. They are painted in a free and vigorous technique which became the normal English style until superseded by the French manner of Allan Ramsay. Kneller is probably best known for the forty-two portraits of the Kit-Cat Club painted between 1702 and 1717 (see above, pp.37-8). This series 'not only surpasses any group of portraits by Lely in historical interest', writes Sir Ellis Waterhouse, 'but includes some masterpieces of direct painting and incisive portraiture, which are the legitimate ancestors of Hogarth and Gainsborough and much of the best British portraiture in the eighteenth century.'[5] Kneller's head of the first Viscount Cobham (Plate 13) is a typical example from the Kit-Cat series.

In 1711 Kneller had become the first Governor of the first Academy of Painting to be set up in London, a precursor of the Royal Academy. Kneller retained a keen interest in it until displaced in 1716 by Sir James Thornhill (1675/6-1734). Thornhill, who was knighted in 1720 and made Sergeant Painter in the same year, became a fellow of the Royal Society in 1723, and achieved a position of eminence reached by no other artist until the advent of Reynolds. Also associated with the Academy were such painters as Michael Dahl and Jonathan Richardson. In 1720 Cheron and Vanderbank founded their academy in St Martin's Lane, which was later re-established in 1735 by William Hogarth. Members of this academy included Joseph Highmore (1692-1780), the portrait painter. Francis Hayman (1708-76) too was making his name with his delightful scenes of social life, such as the famous pictures of Vauxhall Gardens, begun in the mid-1740s. Hogarth (1697-1764) had studied at Vanderbank's academy, which taught him that the highest form of art was history painting as represented by Thornhill's allegories at Greenwich Hospital (Plate 23) and the religious

5 *Painting in Britain 1530-1790*, 3rd ed. (Harmondsworth, 1969), p.93.

histories in the cupola of St Paul's. But Hogarth's own development was to be of a very individual kind.

Hogarth had been apprenticed to a silver-engraver, but began engraving on his own account in about 1720. Soon he started to paint small groups and conversation pieces and by 1729, when he married Thornhill's daughter, he had begun to make a name for himself. Hogarth was an independent spirit, and had become a keen observer of the many facets of London life, anxious to reject Italian and French influence and establish an independent English art. The *Beggar's Opera* (*c*. 1728) marks the transition from his early portraiture to the morality paintings which were to make his name. The first of these was the *Harlot's Progress*, showing the downfall of a country girl at the hands of wicked Londoners, several of whom were recognizable. The original oil paintings were probably executed in 1731-2, but their popularity arose through the engravings published of them in 1732. The pattern was set. The next series was the *Rake's Progress* (published 1735), then *Marriage à la Mode* (published 1745), and finally *An Election*, probably painted in 1754 but not published until 1758. The scene from this entitled 'Canvassing for Votes' (Plate 14) is based on the Oxfordshire contest in the general election of 1754, in which a Tory inn decorated with anti-government slogans is the setting for competing attempts at bribery. Behind, infuriated by high taxation, a Tory mob besieges a Whig tavern. Although such works may owe their celebrity more to the satire and social comment embodied in them than to their painterly or visual qualities, there is no denying that throughout his life Hogarth continued to be a masterly painter of diverse topics. Moreover, he never lost his affection for portraiture, as evinced by *Captain Thomas Coram* (1740) or the *Shrimp Girl* (*c*. 1745). Constantly experimenting with both the form and content of his painting, Hogarth none the less found time and energy to publish *The Analysis of Beauty* (1753) which, as Professor Ronald Paulson points out, was 'the first formalist art treatise in English'.[6]

The spontaneity of Hogarth's portraits, allied to a careful study of the tradition of the old masters, was the springboard for Reynolds's and Gainsborough's elevation of English portraiture to

6 'The Life', in Lawrence Gowing, *Hogarth*, Exhibition Catalogue, Tate Gallery (London, 1971), p.8.

unprecedented heights; George Romney (1734-1802), although he too was famous in his day, artistically was much their inferior. Sir Joshua Reynolds (1723-92) was born into an educated English family, and became a close friend of Dr Johnson, Goldsmith, Burke and Garrick. The key to his art was the deliberate allusion to the old masters and to antique sculpture. By appealing to the educated eye — above and beyond the needs of mere likeness — he was turning the portrait into a history picture. The two years in which Reynolds lived in Rome from 1750 to 1752 were spent in studying the antique, Raphael and Michaelangelo. Here he learnt the intellectual basis of Italian art, something which no other British painter — with the possible exception of Allan Ramsay, the Scottish counterpart of Reynolds and Gainsborough, whose work combined Reynold's learning and Gainsborough's grace — had succeeded in doing before. On his return to London his triumph was rapid, and by 1760 he was able to purchase the lease of a house in Leicester Fields. After his election as first president of the Royal Academy in 1768, Reynolds set about using the Academy as an instrument to forge a British school of history painters to stand beside those of Rome or Bologna. As part of his campaign, he produced his fifteen *Discourses* (1769-90) which expressed his belief that it is possible to learn the rules of art and use the inventions and ideas of one's predecessors to create a new style of one's own. Reynolds exhibited regularly at the Academy, and usually showed a mixture of large portraits treated in a historical manner, history pictures proper, and some curious combinations of the two, such as *Garrick Between Tragedy and Comedy* of 1762 (Plate 15), in which the actor humorously excuses himself to tragedy while being led on the downward path by comedy. The overwhelming majority of Reynolds' vast output (in which he was aided, unlike Gainsborough, by many pupils and assistants) consists of portraits of almost every man or woman of note in the second half of the eighteenth century.

If it may be said that Reynolds pre-eminently wedded portraiture to history, then Gainsborough did so to landscape. Thomas Gainsborough (1727-88) was born in Sudbury, Suffolk, but was sent to London when thirteen years old either as apprentice to Hayman or as assistant to the French draughtsman and engraver Gravelot. One of the principal influences upon him at this stage was seventeenth-century Dutch landscape painting, and indeed all his life Gainsborough regarded landscape as his real vocation. He painted portraits for a living, however, and in 1748 set up in Sudbury, moving to Ipswich in 1752, and to Bath in 1759. While in Suffolk he did small portrait groups as well as landscapes; once in Bath he concentrated on portraits, fashionable and elegant, set against landscape backgrounds, and showing an assurance and sophistication learnt from Van Dyck. His ravishing portrait *Mary, Countess Howe* (Plate 16) can be dated 1763-4 and thus belongs to this period. This picture, writes Dr John Hayes, 'can lay fair claim to be [Gainsborough's] masterpiece. In its simple distinction of pose, the noble bearing and demeanour of the sitter, the accomplished arrangement of the folds of the dress so that one can almost hear the rustle of the silks and satins, and its exquisite delicacy of colour, it is the very quintessence of Gainsborough's transmutation of Van Dyck.'[7] Like Reynolds, Gainsborough was one of the original members of the Royal Academy, and in 1774 he moved to London in order to pit his talent against him. The rivalry was made all the more piquant by the fact that Reynolds was knighted, and head of the King's own Academy, yet all the royal family preferred Gainsborough to paint them. Although Gainsborough's landscapes sold badly on the whole — *The Cottage Door* (1780), now a treasured possession of the Huntington Art Gallery in California, failed to find a purchaser for six years — his portraits were in considerable demand, and he could charge high fees for them. In 1787, the year before his death, he was charging 40 guineas for a head, 80 for a half-length and 160 guineas for a full-length. Only Reynolds was more expensive.

If Gainsborough divides the honours of the elevation of English portraiture with Reynolds, he shares those of English landscape painting with Richard Wilson. But Wilson's achievement must be seen in the light of other artists' explorations of landscape themes earlier in the eighteenth century.

Our first clue is the 'conversation piece', which was well established in England before Gainsborough painted his portrait of *Mr and Mrs Andrews*, set in a midsummer landscape, in 1750. The conversation piece often combined portraiture and landscape, and

7 *Gainsborough: Paintings and Drawings* (London, 1975), pp.211-12.

many painters found it a congenial idiom: we may call to mind Mercier's *Viscount Tyrconnel with His Family* (1725-6), Zoffany's *The Drummond Family* (1765-9) or Stubbs's *Colonel Pocklington and His Sisters* (1769). As intimate and charming as any of these are the conversation pieces of Arthur Devis (1711/12-87). In about 1749 he painted *Robert Gwillym of Atherton and His Family* (Plate 17), in which a country seat occupies the centre of the composition, with the main figures standing in a woodland clearing in the foreground — Gwillym himself, it seems, on the left, his wife and their doll-like children on the right. The members of the family do not, in fact, 'converse', but occupy allotted spaces. Beneath the delightful naïveté of the composition lies the bond which binds the proprietor and his dependants: Gwillym owns all he surveys — park, house, wife and children. If we add to this effect Devis's use of cool, delicate colour, and his high quality of finish, it is not hard to see why he was so popular with the lesser gentry: they admired his paintings, and were prepared to pay for them.

Devis did not indulge in that deeper exploration of the English landscape which was so marked a feature of some of his contemporaries. For instance John Wootton (d. *c.* 1756) often placed his sporting scenes and conversation pieces in landscapes in the style of Claude and Gaspard Poussin — the outcome of a spell in Rome during the early 1720s, sponsored by the Duke of Beaufort. Wootton's pupil George Lambert (1700-65) took a leaf out of his master's book, and in his *Classical Landscape* of 1745 (Plate 18) demonstrates in its composition, subject matter, buildings and treatment of landscape that he learnt much from the same tradition.

Lambert's application of such pictorial principles to the depiction of British scenery was espoused pre-eminently by Richard Wilson (1713/14-82). Born in Montgomeryshire, Wilson was sent to London in 1729 for training as a painter, and was soon found producing portraits in the style of Kneller and Michael Dahl. However, in 1750 he left for Venice, and spent the next six or seven years in Italy. On his return to England he quickly established a high reputation as a landscape painter, and duly joined Reynolds and Gainsborough among the founder members of the Royal Academy. Although Wilson gained renown through such heroic paintings as *The Destruction of the Daughters of Niobe* — completed before

1760, and perhaps influenced by Edmund Burke's *Philosophical Enquiry into the Sublime and the Beautiful* (1757) — it was as the English Claude that Wilson became famous. 'Wilson, at his best', writes Lord Clark, 'understood the two chief lessons of Claude, that the centre of a landscape is an area of light, and that everything must be subordinate to a single mood.'[8] Wilson's paintings of the Welsh countryside often have an austere, not to say grave, beauty, and owe much to both Italian and Dutch precedents: the glow of light he found in the paintings of Cuyp is never far away. His depictions of country seats were in considerable demand, and *Croome Court, Worcestershire* of 1758 (Plate 32) illustrates this fusion between imagination and topographical (and architectural) reality.

Water-colour painting similarly drew nourishment from British topography, and here again Dutch and Italian influence is apparent. The late 1600s and early 1700s produced the landscape drawings of Francis Place (1647-1728), with their dependence upon Hollar: *The Dropping Well, Knaresborough* of 1711 (Plate 19) shows in its treatment of light and shade over masses of rocks and foliage how Place anticipates the work of later artists such as Alexander Cozens. One of the most prominent water-colourists during the mid-eighteenth century was Paul Sandby (1725-1809), whose portrayal of landscapes and buildings displays accuracy and a sensitive eye for detail, as can be seen from his *View of Strawberry Hill, Twickenham* of about 1774 (Plate 20). Rather than pencil and ink, Sandby drew in water-colour with a brush, and often reinforced his effects with the addition of body-colour. Sandby was one of the first water-colourists to appreciate Welsh scenery, and was more concerned to paint nature as he saw it than to ape the picturesque compositions of a Gaspard or a Poussin. Others, however, happily succumbed to the lure of Italy, an attraction which was strengthened by Canaletto's visit to England in 1746. Among them were William Taverner (1703-72), Alexander Cozens (*c.* 1717-86), Francis Towne (1739/40-1816) and William Pars (1742-82). Above all there was John Robert Cozens (1752-97), who returned from abroad to see the British countryside through Italian eyes. Cozens's

8 Kenneth Clark, *Landscape into Art* (London, 1949; paperback ed. 1961), p.70.

feeling for the wildness of nature — expressed in gentle and poetic landscapes, predominantly blue-green or blue-grey — was a major formative influence on the art of Girtin and Turner, and was deeply admired by Constable. Cozens's world was indeed different from that of his near-contemporary, Thomas Rowlandson (1756-1827), whose vigorous drawings and caricatures of popular and low-life subjects are as such unequalled.

The directness of Rowlandson leads us to the most direct of all the arts, sculpture. As post-Restoration architecture in England offered scope for more than tomb sculpture, it was no longer carried out by masons but by men who called themselves 'statuaries'. Apart from Edward Pierce (*fl.* 1656-95), whose best piece is a bust of Wren of 1673, the standard was seldom high. Fortunately, just as Burlington and the Palladians were turning towards imitations of the antique, a group of well-trained sculptors settled in England from abroad, and channelled English sculpture from its provincial backwater into the main European stream.

The three most distinguished of these immigrants were John Michael Rysbrack (1694-1770) and Peter Scheemakers (1691-1781) from Flanders, and Louis-François Roubiliac (?1705-62) from France. All were prolific, making numerous tombs, busts and chimney-pieces. Rysbrack's marble bust of George II, now at Windsor Castle (Plate 21), shows the King crowned with a laurel wreath, and wearing elaborate armour, a field-marshal's scarf, the Star and Garter on his breast, and the jewel of the Garter on a ribbon on his neck. It is a lively portrait, demonstrating Rysbrack's command of fine, decorative detail; equally lively are the portraits by Roubiliac, but in a quite different way. If Rysbrack's were formal baroque, Roubiliac's were informal rococo. Roubiliac combined superb technique and presentation with an unnerving realism: his tombs were decorated with real-life portraits, not dummies, and he made busts of old and ugly men which depicted their frailties with remorseless truth. Roubiliac's most celebrated piece is his statue of Handel, an original blend of realism and allegory (Plate 22). This is, as the late Dr Margaret Whinney remarked, 'a landmark in the history of sculpture ... a perfect blend of homage to the great musician, a leading figure of London's artistic life, and to the eternal power of music.'[9]

9 *English Sculpture 1720-1830* (London, 1971), p.78.

The decorative arts

The decoration of the interiors of buildings brings together all the changes of taste so far discussed: the vicissitudes between classical and gothic, the rise of Palladianism and neoclassicism, and the introduction of new materials and their absorption into fashionable décor. Sculpture, for instance, had its place, though few would be as enthusiastic as William Weddell, who had Robert Adam build him a sculpture gallery at Newby Hall in Yorkshire; painting, on the other hand, could be more readily integrated, either by the hanging of pictures (Burlington's Chiswick villa was originally a picture gallery), or by having the walls themselves decorated.

Wall painting in England was dominated in the early 1700s by Sir James Thornhill (*c*. 1675-1734). Thornhill had appeared at a moment when grand decoration was required, and he was the only English painter capable of competing successfully with the many artists from abroad seeking work in the country. Although he does not appear to have had any direct contact with Verrio or Laguerre, both painters influenced him. Thornhill's decoration is always carefully integrated within an architectural framework, as can be seen in his two most prominent works — the inside of the dome of St Paul's (1714-17), in which incidents from the life of St Paul are depicted in eight grisaille panels picked out in gold, and in Wren's painted hall at Greenwich Hospital (Plate 23), where he was set the problem of treating historical subjects in a grand allegorical setting. This commission was carried out between 1708 and 1727, and consists of a lower hall, upper hall and vestibule. All three rooms are treated with similar themes, the lower hall having a large central oval in which William III and Queen Mary (attended by various mythological and allegorical figures) are shown bestowing peace and liberty on Europe; as subsidiary decoration there are a British man-o'-war and a Spanish galleon, each filled with trophies and surrounded by allegorical figures connected with astronomy. The effect was dazzling, as it was also in the wall and ceiling paintings which Thornhill did at Hampton Court (*c*. 1702 onwards), Blenheim (1716), Wimpole Hall (1724), and elsewhere.

The elaborate interior schema into which such wall painting was set often as not involved the use of decorative plasterwork. As Geoffrey Beard has indicated, the period between the accession of

Charles II and the death of William III was remarkable for the way in which craftsmen threw off the rigours of the Jacobean age. Plasterers and stuccoists were organized by trade guilds, and their techniques can be studied in Joseph Moxon's *Mechanick Exercises* (1678 and later editions). Although plasterwork for the Office of Works was significant in the late 1600s and early 1700s, the most distinguished examples are found in private buildings in which enlightened patrons employed itinerant Italian *stuccatori*. The most famous of these were Giovanni Bagutti (b. 1681) and his partner Giuseppe Artari (d. 1769), whose collaboration seems to have lasted until Bagutti's death shortly after 1730. Although they did important commissions for Vanbrugh, Campbell, Leoni and Francis Smith of Warwick, they were engaged mostly by James Gibbs. Together they worked for him at the Octagon House, Twickenham (1720), St Peter's Church, Vere Street (1723-4), Ditchley in Oxfordshire (1725) and St Martin in the Fields (1724-5), which was described by Gibbs in *A Book of Architecture* (1728) as 'enrich'd with Fret-work by Signori *Artari* and *Bagutti*, the best Fret-workers that ever came into *England*'. This style — which reached its zenith in the work of Thomas Clark (*fl.* 1742-82) at Holkham (Plate 10), shortly after Kent's death — involves delicate decoration of panels, medallions, friezes and chimney-pieces, and represents a complete rejection of the visual cacophony of such late seventeenth-century interiors as Sudbury Hall in Derbyshire (1675-6). Plasterwork became even more delicate and restrained with the advent of neoclassicism and the fashion for Adam interiors. The Adam family themselves used the firm of Joseph Rose and Co. for plasterwork at such houses as Kedleston, Northumberland House and Nostell Priory in Yorkshire (1766-77). It should never be forgotten that in plasterwork, as in the other arts, there was a continuing taste for gothic, as can be seen in the ceiling of Hartwell Church in Buckinghamshire by Henry Keene, carried out around 1753-5 (Plate 24).

It is perhaps to plasterwork, silver, glass, porcelain and furniture that the word 'rococo' seems most apposite in the mid-eighteenth century. English silver benefited between 1700 and 1760 from the intellectual vigour of the Huguenot craftsmen who fled to England after the revocation of the Edict of Nantes by Louis XIV in 1685. The simplicity of the Queen Anne style continued into the reign of George I, but from 1735 or so a more florid style of silverwork emerged, and we find undecorated or lightly decorated coffee urns, teapots and other small vessels, in which the attenuated serpentine or ogee line appears. Similar characteristics appear in glassware, some of it coloured and with fine-cut decorations, in which such provincial towns as Bristol and Newcastle upon Tyne excelled (Plate 25).

Meantime, by the end of the 1750s, there were porcelain factories in production at Chelsea, Bow, Derby, Bristol, Worcester, Longton Hall and Liverpool. Robert Hancock (1729/30-1817), who had trained as an engraver in Birmingham before coming to London, developed the technique of transfer printing, by which works of art were printed on to porcelain; Gainsborough and Reynolds, Watteau, Boucher and Chardin were among the many artists so honoured.

Hancock's name, however, was eclipsed by that of Joseph Wedgwood (1730-95), who patented (1763) and perfected (1769) a glazed, cream-coloured earthenware, and in 1769 opened a new factory at Burslem in Staffordshire, calling it Etruria. He improved marbled ware, invented jasper ware (1773-80) and promoted Greek as against Chinese taste. In 1783 he was elected a fellow of the Royal Society. Wedgwood was notably assisted by his partner Thomas Bentley (1730-80), a Liverpool merchant and a man of classical attainments, and by the sculptor John Flaxman (1755-1826), who modelled elegant designs for him based on Greek vases and Pompeiian fragments. 'The most distinctive contribution of Etruria to European neo-classicism', writes Joseph Burke, 'was the Wedgwood-Bentley portrait gallery of ornamental statues, library busts, medallions, and cameos, for nowhere else were the ideals of the Enlightenment so comprehensively expressed through the commemoration of its heroes.'[10]

As the century progressed, furniture too took on the mantle of neoclassicism. Under the first two Georges, the simplicity that had characterized the furniture of the era of William and Mary and of Queen Anne was increasingly abandoned, as pilasters, broken pediments, elaborate cornices and other classical features were

10 *English Art 1714-1800*, The Oxford History of English Art, Vol. 9 (Oxford, 1976), p.351.

introduced. More exuberant still were the Italianate consoles, scrolls, gilt and marble favoured by William Kent, to be seen in Vardy's *Some Designs of Mr Inigo Jones and Mr William Kent* of 1744. Engravings of furniture — such as those in Batty Langley and Matthew Lock's *A New Drawing Book of Ornament* (1740) and *A New Book of Ornament* (1752) — were crucial in the dissemination of these changes in fashion.

Thomas Chippendale (1718-79) was only twenty-two when the first of these books came out, and he drew extensively on such publications for *The Gentleman and Cabinet-Maker's Director* (1754 and later editions). Chippendale stands out as the finest cabinetmaker in England before Hepplewhite and Sheraton. In this volume Chippendale borrows the style and sometimes the language of the Burlingtonians, but opposes their creed: the three standards he set against Vitruvius, Palladio and Inigo Jones were 'the gothic, Chinese and the modern taste'. His versions of Chinese and gothic furniture were a combination of great freedom and technical brilliance, best expressed in the almost unbelievable delicacy of the frets and lattices he derived from the Chinese, and in the interlacing arch patterns taken from the gothic. He turned his hand to many kinds of furniture — bookcases, commodes, card tables, chairs — and his influence was enormous. His staggeringly beautiful japanned commodes show his Oriental fantasies taken to unprecedented extremes (Plate 26).

During the 1770s Chippendale executed pieces in marquetry, following the neoclassicism of the Adams. Robert Adam personally provided drawings for much furniture, as can be seen from his *Works in Architecture*. For this, in keeping with the rest of his décor, he devised a vocabulary of swags and garlands, urns, decorative medallions and tablets, reflecting the best antique decoration. Among the international group of craftsmen assembled by Adam to execute his elaborate projects were the English cabinetmaker John Linnell (d. 1796), the Italian painters Antonio Zucchi and Michelangelo Pergolesi, and the Swiss painter Angelica Kauffmann (1741-1807). Adam's immediate followers in furniture design, like Chippendale, owed their prominence to publications: George Hepplewhite (d. 1786) to his posthumous *Cabinet Maker and Upholsterer's Guide* (1788), and Thomas Sheraton (1751-1806) to his *Cabinet-Maker and Upholsterer's Drawing-Book* (1791-4).

This transition in furniture design was symptomatic of the changes that affected all the minor arts in England — domestic metalwork, textiles, costume, portrait miniatures, jewellery, musical instruments and bookbinding. Once more, craftsmanship, invention and industrial technique combined to achieve high quality. The setting for all these arts was often the interior of the country seat; the English landscape garden that surrounded it became a fashion which spread throughout Europe.

Gardens and landscapes

So rapidly did the fashion spread for *le jardin anglais, der englische Garten* or *il giardino inglese* that the *World* on 3 April 1755 could only express delight at 'the rapid progress of this happy enthusiasm'. Such enthusiasm was well founded, for the landscape garden was more than just another eighteenth-century indication of widespread *anglomanie*. It offered almost limitless scope. In the layout of his country seat the proprietor of taste could express his understanding and love of poetry and philosophy, painting and architecture; his need for solace in a rural setting; his knowledge of classical mythology; his national pride; his sense of ownership and yearning for social prestige. Above all it afforded a visible demonstration of the fruits of his Continental grand tour, seen particularly in his appreciation of the Italian countryside and the landscape paintings of Claude, Poussin, Gaspard and Salvator Rosa. As economic solvency depended upon taking agriculture and silviculture seriously, British landowners often returned from their grand tour with a collection of plants, as well as the usual rare books, prints, furniture, pictures and sculpture. While abroad they also kept a weather-eye open for improvements in agricultural technique: Jethro Tull, for one, wrought a revolution in methods of cultivation as a result of observing the tillage operations of French vine growers. Farming methods were radically improved, and drainage, fertilization and crop rotation were introduced. Flowers, shrubs and trees were imported from abroad as, following John Evelyn's advice in *Sylva*, owners began to 'adorn their ... demesnes with trees of venerable shade, and profitable timber'. They took inspiration from the Italianate paintings which hung on the walls of their mansions, regarding the open country (as Horace Walpole suggested) as 'but a canvas on which a landscape might be designed'.[11] After all, as the poet and landscape gardener William Shenstone remarked, 'the landskip painter is the gardiner's best designer'.[12]

This fusion of 'use' and 'splendour' (to take our cue from Pope's *Epistle to Burlington*) had obvious appeal. The extension of the practice of enclosure in the early 1700s meant that there were huge estates awaiting exploitation. As deer hunting (which had made extravagant demands on many a pocket) was replaced by fox hunting, so the provision of small coverts in which the fox could breed relatively undisturbed became paramount. The hedges and ditches associated with enclosure, together with rides cut through dense woodland, became part of the idealized landscape for sport. To Pope, and others, planting was as critical as building in the creation of an estate. By the 1730s the country seat had achieved unprecedented popularity, with architects finding it hard to keep pace with their commitments. 'Every Man now,' said *Common Sense* in 1739, 'be his fortune what it will, is to be *doing something at his Place*, as the fashionable Phrase is; and you hardly meet with any Body, who, after the first Compliments, does not inform you, that he is *in Mortar* and *moving of Earth*; the modest terms for Building and Gardening.' Eager tourists, guides in hand, travelled around looking and comparing. The widespread building boom was reflected too in the proliferation of topographical poems, and in the numerous engravings, paintings and water-colours that advertised the glories of the British country house.

The gardens that accompanied the palace or house of the latter half of the seventeenth century were essentially formal, such as those at Hampton Court (Plate 27). Under the aegis of Henry Wise (1653-1738) and George London (d. 1714) the royal gardens reflected their stylistic and personal debt to the court of Louis XIV. There was a debt to the Netherlands too, owing to the influence of William and Mary, and the result was a mixture of clipped evergreens, formal waterscape, fountains, topiary and elaborate parterres. Following the lead of Timothy Nourse in *Campania Foelix* (1700), such writers as Stephen Switzer (1682-1745) began to

---

11 Quoted from Isabel W. U. Chase, *Horace Walpole: Gardenist* (Princeton, NJ, 1943), p. 37.

12 'Unconnected Thoughts on Gardening', in *The Works in Verse and Prose of William Shenstone, Esq.* (London, 1764), II, p. 129.

propound a landscape which was different both in style and in origin from what had gone before. Switzer's *The Nobleman, Gentleman, and Gardener's Recreation* of 1715, expanded into his three-volume *Ichnographia Rustica* of 1718 (2nd ed. 1742), called on classical and Oriental sources to support the claim that a new view of nature was required. Switzer's books, and James's translation (1712) of Dézallier d'Argenville's *Theory and Practice of Gardening* of 1709, gave practical support to the celebrated clarion calls of Pope and Addison in their articles in the *Tatler* and *Spectator* of 1711 and 1712.

Landowners themselves, often men of taste and discernment, must have played a crucial part in the establishment of the English landscape garden; after all, many of them were *au fait* with forestry and planting techniques, and undoubtedly controlled the professional men whom they employed. On the other hand, there was a group of architects and designers whom we can specifically suggest contributed substantially to these changes — notably Sir John Vanbrugh, Charles Bridgeman (d. 1738) and William Kent. They were involved in the creation of some crucial landscapes — for the Marlboroughs at Blenheim, for Burlington at Chiswick, for Cobham at Stowe and for the Pelhams at Esher Place (where, said Horace Walpole, Kent was 'Kentissime'). Here, and elsewhere, the 'genius of the place' was improved with an appropriate repertoire of ha-has, sinuous walks and streams, classical and gothic temples and follies, and other evocative structures. Castell's *Villas of the Ancients Illustrated* (1728) invoked the authority of the younger Pliny (no less) to show that there was classical precedent for the villa set in an informal landscape; visitors to Italy knew that the temples in sacred groves took on mystic meaning. The Temple of the Sibyl at Tivoli was a powerful image: Hawksmoor's mausoleum at Castle Howard (completed by Daniel Garrett) remains one of the most evocative and solemn of its British counterparts (Plate 28), with a seriousness which makes Kent's landscape sketches seem frivolous. Kent is at his best in his exploration of wood and water (Plate 29), when he is free to absorb and reinterpret a concept of nature which owes nothing to direct classical allusion.

The key layout which links these early gardens to the work of Capability Brown is Stowe in Buckinghamshire, the seat of Richard Temple, first Viscount Cobham (Plate 13), where the rich array of temples surely was intended as a visual pun on the family motto of *Templa quam delecta*. But it was not only its garden ornaments that made Stowe so significant. Here, as can be seen from Jacques Rigaud's drawings of 1733-4 (Plate 30), Vanbrugh, Gibbs, Bridgeman and Kent created a layout of variety and visual richness. More than that. For, especially in the Elysian Fields and Grecian Valley, it is full of intellectual and political irony and allusion. The Temple of Ancient Virtue, the Temple of British Worthies, the Temple of Modern Virtue and other features all take on deeper significance as their meaning is explored. Pope was a frequent visitor to Stowe on his summer rambles, and doubtless advised Cobham on its design.

As the century progressed, other gardens associated with the inspiration of one man emerged — Philip Southcote's Woburn Farm in Surrey (from 1735), Charles Hamilton's Painshill (from 1738) and Henry Hoare's Stourhead (from *c.* 1743). In the Midlands there was a trinity of key landscapes lying close together — Hagley, owned by George Lyttelton, Lord Stamford's Enville, and the poet William Shenstone's The Leasowes, which Walpole called 'a perfect picture of his mind, simple, elegant, and amiable'. The delights of some of the more whimsical mid-century gardens — with their sinuous paths, exotic temples and flower-entwined trellises — are captured in the paintings of Thomas Robins the elder (d. 1770), seen in his view of Woodside in Berkshire (Plate 31).

Bridgeman died in 1738, and shortly afterwards Lancelot 'Capability' Brown (1716-83) became head gardener at Stowe. Brown's work was more radical than that of his predecessors in its emphasis on the materials of the site — the lines, shapes and contours of its ground, waters and trees. He neglected buildings, statues, mottoes and inscriptions, and swept the lawns straight up to the very walls of the house, eliminating terraces and other remains of the 'specific garden'. Richard Wilson's painting of Croome Court (Plate 32) reflects the tranquillity and simplicity of Brown's work both there and elsewhere, such as Warwick Castle (*c.* 1750), Bowood (1761), Ashburnham (1767) and Dodington Park (1764). The weakness of Brown's landscapes proved to be, ironically, their studied elimination of designed elements. Reynolds presumably was tilting at Brown in his thirteenth *Discourse* (1786) when he wrote: 'Gardening, as far as Gardening is an Art, or entitled to that appellation, is a deviation from nature; for if the true taste consists, as many hold, in banishing every appearance of Art, or any traces of the footsteps of man, it would then be no longer a Garden.' As for Chambers, he found that Brown's designs 'differ very little from common fields, so closely is common nature copied in most of them'.

Chambers himself was not without critics, of course, and many regarded his exploration of *chinoiserie* as nothing more than spurious Orientalism. Horace Walpole considered Chambers's *Dissertation on Oriental Gardening* with disdain. It is 'more extravagant than the worst Chinese paper,' he wrote, 'and is written in wild revenge against Brown; the only surprising consequence is, that it is laughed at, and it is not likely to be adopted.' William Mason, to Walpole's evident delight, responded with *An Heroic Epistle to Sir William Chambers* which took the architect soundly to task for his absurdities. Frenchmen were only too pleased to see in Chambers's writings, and in his layout of the grounds of Kew, sound evidence (as Le Rouge put it) that 'tout le monde sait que les Jardins Anglais ne sont qu'une imitation de ceux de la Chine'. Fuelled by the theoretical and topographical writings of William Gilpin, and Burke's *Philosophical Enquiry*, all was now set for the controversies of Knight, Price and Repton which began in the 1790s and ran into the nineteenth century.

The century that spans the period between the Fire of London and the foundation of the Royal Academy was a dynamic and significant one for the visual arts in England. Horace Walpole, who lived through many of the years we have considered, and was familiar with the rest, loved and promoted the fine arts with boundless enthusiasm. He had a few words about the recording of such achievements. 'It is pleasing to expatiate on the just praise of one's country,' he wrote in the Introduction to his *Anecdotes of Painting in England*, 'and they who cannot perform great things themselves, may yet have satisfaction in doing justice to those who can.'

Select bibliography

This list does *not* include eighteenth-century works referred to in the text.

General

Allen, B. S. *Tides in English Taste (1619-1800): A Background for the Study of Literature.* 2 vols. Cambridge, Mass., 1937; repr. New York, 1958.

Burgess, A., and Haskell, F. *The Age of the Grand Tour*. London, 1967.

Burke, J. *English Art 1714-1800*. The Oxford History of English Art, Vol. 9. Oxford, 1976.

Foss, M. *The Age of Patronage: The Arts in Society 1660-1750*. London, 1971.

Hook, J. *The Baroque Age in England*. London, 1976.

Lipking, L. *The Ordering of the Arts in Eighteenth-Century England*. Princeton, NJ, 1970.

Saxl, F., and Wittkower, R. *British Art and the Mediterranean*. London, 1948; repr. 1969.

Turberville, A.S. (ed.) *Johnson's England: An Account of the Life and Manners of His Age*. 2 vols. 2nd ed. Oxford, 1952; repr. 1965.

Whinney, M., and Millar, O. *English Art 1625-1714*. The Oxford History of English Art, Vol. 8. Oxford, 1958.

Whitley, W.T. *Artists and Their Friends in England 1700-99*. 2 vols. London and Boston, Mass., 1928; repr. New York, 1968.

Architecture and town planning

Campbell, C., et al. *Vitruvius Britannicus, or The British Architect*. 6 vols. London, 1715-71. repr. 3 vols. New York, 1967-70. With *Guide to 'Vitruvius Britannicus'*, by Paul Breman and Denise Addis. New York, 1972.

Chalklin, C.W. *The Provincial Towns of Georgian England: A Study of the Building Process 1740-1820*. London, 1974.

Clark, K. *The Gothic Revival: An Essay in the History of Taste*. New ed. London, 1974.

Colvin, H.M. *A Biographical Dictionary of British Architects 1600-1840*. London, 1978.

Crook, J. M. *The Greek Revival: Neo-classical Attitudes in British Architecture 1760-1870*. London, 1972.

Cruickshank, D., and Wyld, P. *London: The Art of Georgian Building*. London and New York, 1975.

Downes, K. *Christopher Wren*. London, 1971.

———— *English Baroque Architecture*. London, 1966.

———— *Hawksmoor*. London, 1959.

———— *Vanbrugh*. London, 1977.

Fleming, J. *Robert Adam and His Circle in Edinburgh and Rome*. London, 1962.

Fleming, J., Honour, H., and Pevsner, N. *The Penguin Dictionary of Architecture*. rev. ed. London, 1975.

Hussey, C. *English Country Houses: Early Georgian 1715-60*. 2nd ed. London, 1965.

———— *The Picturesque: Studies in a Point of View*. London and New York, 1927; repr. London, 1967.

Jenkins, F.I. *Architect and Patron: A Survey of Professional Relations and*

Practice in England from the Sixteenth Century to the Present Day. London, 1961.

Jourdain, M. *The Work of William Kent.* London, 1948.

Kaufmann, E. *Architecture in the Age of Reason: Baroque and Post-Baroque in England, Italy, and France.* Cambridge, Mass., 1955; repr. New York, 1968.

Lees-Milne, J. *Earls of Creation: Five Great Patrons of Eighteenth-Century Art.* London, 1962.

_____ *English Country Houses: Baroque 1685-1715.* London, 1970.

Macaulay, J. *The Gothic Revival 1745-1845.* Glasgow and London, 1975.

Olsen, D.J. *Town Planning in London: The Eighteenth and Nineteenth Centuries.* New Haven, Conn., and London, 1964.

Sitwell, S. *British Architects and Craftsmen: A Survey of Taste, Design and Style during Three Centuries 1600-1830.* New ed. London, 1973.

Summerson, J.N. *Architecture in Britain 1530-1830.* 5th ed. Harmondsworth, 1969.

_____ *The Classical Language of Architecture.* London, 1964.

_____ *Georgian London.* 3rd ed. London, 1978.

Wittkower, R. *Palladio and English Palladianism.* London, 1974.

Painting and sculpture

Croft-Murray, E. *Decorative Painting in England 1537-1837.* 2 vols. London, 1962, 1970.

Gunnis, R. *Dictionary of British Sculptors 1660-1851.* 2nd ed. London, 1968.

Hardie, M. *Watercolour Painting in Britain. I: The Eighteenth Century.* 2nd ed. London, 1967; repr. 1969.

Hayes, J. *Gainsborough: Paintings and Drawings.* London, 1975.

_____ *Rowlandson: Watercolours and Drawings.* London, 1972.

Herrmann, L. *British Landscape Painting of the Eighteenth Century.* London, 1973.

Irwin, D. *English Neo-classical Art: Studies in Inspiration and Taste.* London, 1966.

Irwin, D. and F. *Scottish Painters at Home and Abroad 1700-1900.* London, 1975.

Paulson, R. *Emblem and Expression: Meaning in English Art of the Eighteenth Century.* London, 1975.

_____ *Hogarth: His Life, Art, and Times.* 2 vols. Hew Haven, Conn., and London, 1971.

Physick, J. *Designs for English Sculpture 1680-1860.* London, 1969.

Taylor, B. (ed.) *Painting in England 1700-1850.* The Collection of Mr and Mrs Paul Mellon. 2 vols. Richmond, Va., 1963.

Waterhouse, E. *Painting in Britain 1530-1790.* 3rd ed. Harmondsworth, 1969.

_____ *Reynolds.* London, 1973.

Whinney, M. *English Sculpture 1720-1830*. London, 1971.
————— *Sculpture in Britain 1530-1830*. Harmondsworth, 1964.

The decorative arts
Beard, G. *Decorative Plasterwork in Great Britain*. London, 1975.
————— *Georgian Craftsmen and Their Work*. London, 1966.
————— *The Work of Robert Adam*. Edinburgh, 1978.
Connoisseur Period Guides: The Early Georgian Period 1714-60. London, 1957; repr. 1963.
Connoisseur Period Guides: The Late Georgian Period 1760-1810. London, 1956.
Fitz-Gerald, D. (ed.) *Georgian Furniture*. London, 1969.
Fleming, J., and Honour, H. *The Penguin Dictionary of Decorative Arts*. London, 1977.
Fowler, J., and Cornforth, J. *English Decoration in the Eighteenth Century*. 2nd ed. London, 1978.
Hammelmann, H.A., and Boase, T.S.R. *Book Illustrators in Eighteenth-Century England*. New Haven, Conn., and London, 1975.
Honour, H. *Chinoiserie: The Vision of Cathay*. London, 1961.
Impey, O. *Chinoiserie: Western Interpretation of Oriental Styles*. Oxford, 1977.
Osborne, H. (ed.) *The Oxford Companion to the Decorative Arts*. Oxford, 1975.
Ward-Jackson, P. *English Furniture Designs of the Eighteenth Century*. London, 1958.
Wintersgill, D. *The Guardian Book of Antiques 1700-1830*. London and Glasgow, 1975.

Landscape gardening
Hadfield, M. *A History of British Gardening*. 2nd ed. London, 1969.
Hunt, J.D. *The Figure in the Landscape: Poetry, Painting, and Gardening During the Eighteenth Century*. Baltimore and London, 1977.
Hunt, J.D., and Willis, P. (eds) *The Genius of the Place: The English Landscape Garden 1620-1820*. London, 1975.
Hussey, C. *English Gardens and Landscapes 1700-50*. London, 1967.
Jones, B. *Follies and Grottoes*. 2nd ed. London, 1974.
Malins, E. *English Landscaping and Literature 1660-1840*. London, 1966.
Manwaring, E.W. *Italian Landscapes in Eighteenth-Century England: A Study Chiefly of the Influence of Claude Lorrain and Salvator Rosa on English Taste 1700-1800*. New York, 1925; repr. London, 1965.
Moir, E. *The Discovery of Britain: The English Tourists 1540-1840*. London, 1964.
Stroud, D. *Capability Brown*. 3rd ed. London, 1975.
Willis, P. *Charles Bridgeman and the English Landscape Garden*. London, 1977.

_____ (ed.) *Furor Hortensis: Essays on the History of the English Landscape Garden in Memory of H.F. Clark*. Edinburgh, 1974.

Woodbridge, K. *Landscape and Antiquity: Aspects of English Culture at Stourhead 1718-1838*. Oxford, 1970.

Note

Grateful thanks are due to Mr Geoffrey Beard, Miss Jane Heller, Mr John Ingamells, Mr A.F. Kersling, Mr Hendrik Louw and Mrs Olive Smith for their help in the preparation of this section.

Index

a) *Persons*

Adair, James, 184, 196
Adam, Robert, 209-10, 217-19, 227-8, 230
Addison, Joseph, 2, 6, 10-12, 15, 18-19, 23, 28, 35, 37, 38, 46, 50, 65-6, 72, 98, 122-3, 133, 157, 193, 233
Akenside, Mark, 62, 163, 187, 194
Anne, Queen of England, 2, 5, 16, 37-8, 43, 81-92, 94-5, 97, 99, 101, 104, 126, 201, 229
Arbuthnot, John, 64, 155, 171, 177
Archer, Thomas, 210, 212-13
Arkwright, Richard, 26, 35
Atterbury, Francis, 95, 102
Austen, Jane, 22, 29, 69, 151

Bacon, Francis, 121, 160, 201
Banks, Joseph, 157-8
Barber, John, 39, 48
Battie, William, 182-5
Beattie, James, 150-1, 201
Berkeley, George, 23, 63, 73, 128, 131-6, 139, 150-1, 192, 199, 200
Bernini, Giovanni, 211, 213
Blackstone, William, 34, 49, 108

Blair, Robert, 61, 187, 194
Blake, William, 4, 165, 199, 201
Boerhaave, Hermann, 173-4, 176, 191
Bolingbroke, Henry St John, Viscount, 6, 22, 43, 48, 65, 73, 87, 89, 94-5, 101-3, 108, 118
Boswell, James, 2, 21-3, 41, 44, 47, 51, 58, 64, 67, 71, 75, 153
Boulton, Matthew, 26, 169
Boyle, Robert, 129, 159, 161, 189, 192, 201
Brettingham, Matthew, 210, 216
Bridgman, Charles, 233-4
Brown, Lancelot 'Capability', 233-4
Burke, Edmund, 2, 18, 22-3, 47, 63, 111, 114, 116, 191-2, 196-201, 222, 225, 235
Burlington, Richard Boyle, Earl of, 4, 50, 210, 213-16, 226-7, 233
Burney, Charles, 47, 72
Burney, Fanny, 29, 32, 68
Burns, Robert, 2, 18, 51, 59, 60, 196
Bute, John Stuart, Earl of, 107-12
Butler, Joseph, 134-6, 139, 151

b) *Subjects*